# Intercultural Sourcebook: Cross-Cultural Training Methods

## VOL. 1

**Sandra M. Fowler**

Editor

**Monica G. Mumford**

Associate Editor

# Intercultural Sourcebook: Cross-Cultural Training Methods

## VOL. 1

**Sandra M. Fowler**

Editor

**Monica G. Mumford**

Associate Editor

INTERCULTURAL PRESS
*A Nicholas Brealey Publishing Company*

BOSTON · LONDON

First published by Intercultural Press, a Nicholas Brealey Publishing Company, in 1995. For information, contact:

Intercultural Press
a division of
Nicholas Brealey Publishing
100 City Hall Plaza, Ste. 501
Boston, MA 02108 USA
Tel: 617-523-3801
Fax: 617-523-3708
www.interculturalpress.com

Nicholas Brealey Publishing
3-5 Spafield Street
Clerkenwell
London, EC1R 4QB, UK
Tel: +44-207-239-0360
Fax: +44-207-239-0370
www.nbrealey-books.com

ISBN-13: 978-1-877864-29-2
ISBN-10: 1-877864-29-3

Cover concept by Greg Frizzell
Cover design by Lois Leonard Stock

Printed in the United States of America
10   09   08   07   06    7   8   9   10  11

**Library of Congress Cataloging-in-Publication Data**

Intercultural sourcebook : cross-cultural training methods / Sandra M.
   Fowler,  editor; Monica G. Mumford, associate editor.
      p.   cm.
   Includes bibliographical references.
   ISBN 1-877864-29-3 (v. 1)
   1. Multicultural education.   2. Employees—training of.   3. Cross-
cultural orientation.   I. Fowler, Sandra M. (Sandra Mumford)   II. Mumford,
Monica G.

LC1099.I596   1995
370.19'6--dc20                                                        94-48401
                                                                        CIP

# Table of Contents

# Acknowledgments

There is no way to predict how a book will be received. We believe all books are created with the hope that each person who reads them finds something special to take away and use. We are no exception, and harbor the hope that the *Intercultural Sourcebook* becomes a treasured resource and guide.

For many people already in the intercultural field, this book contains the work of old friends. For newcomers to the intercultural field, we hope you find new friends within the covers of the *Sourcebook*.

We believe that volumes of this magnitude are created by the many; not the few. We extend our gratitude to the authors for their effort and patience. Our gratitude also goes to the staff at the Intercultural Press. We are especially indebted to them for coping with the mountains of manuscripts, discs, correspondence, faxes, and all the multiple pieces brought into existence by the *Sourcebook*.

There are several individuals who earned specific recognition. Diane Zeller shepherded the *Sourcebook* through the early stages of SIETAR International's decision to update the book. George Renwick kept reminding us how good it would feel to hold these volumes in our hands. Fanchon Silberstein offered inspiration and a quiet place. Craig Storti and Al Wight reviewed some of the most challenging chapters.

Without the guidance and editing craft of Peggy Pusch, these volumes could not have been published. The *Sourcebook* benefited immensely from her line-by-line editing and her insistence on the clarity of each thought.

Finally, for his support and unlimited faith that we would see this project through to the end, Ray Fowler receives our applause and bouquets of roses.

Sandra M. Fowler
Monica G. Mumford
Washington, D.C.
January 1995

# Preface

It was fifteen years ago, in 1979, that the first edition of the *Intercultural Sourcebook* was published. It was a slight volume, though for the field it was a major event. For the first time, persons concerned with intercultural education and training were able to survey the range of training methods available and get a full sense of the breadth of the field. They could also for the first time draw materials for their work from a single source and obtain systematic guidance in developing their own. Perhaps most significant, the book furthered the search for methods more precisely suited to the special and complex needs of cross-cultural training. There were two particularly important dimensions to this search. First, the focus of the training as it affected the trainee had to be more clearly defined. A distinction had to be made between culture and personality, with the former identified as the proper domain of cross-cultural training—and the latter left to qualified psycho-therapists. Second, a more effective means of integrating cognitive and experiential learning had to be found. The indeterminate "feelings" left over from sensitivity training—and/or the body of abstract information acquired in the classroom ("university") model of training—were both inadequate to the development of needed cross-cultural skills.

Over the years the integration of culture, cognition, and experience in cross-cultural training has been achieved and is reflected in virtually every page of this new edition of *Intercultural Sourcebook*. That achievement demonstrates, among other things, that the field is alive and well. It will be immediately apparent that this second edition is much larger than the first, appearing as it will in two volumes. The author list reads like a *Who's Who* in the field. Most important, it has a weight and meatiness and a sophistication of analysis and richness of example which we hope will give guidance for at least another fifteen years.

In the course of preparing the original edition of *Intercultural Sourcebook* for publication, I was blessed by the able assistance of Paul Ventura, George Renwick, Toby Frank, and Ned Seelye—and SIETAR, which sponsored and funded its publication. Credit for the second edition of *Intercultural Sourcebook* belongs to Sandra Fowler and Monica Mumford. Without the dogged work and perceptive insights of these two skilled editors, there would not have been a second edition.

David S. Hoopes
Intercultural Press

# Introduction

## Sandra M. Fowler and Monica G. Mumford

Many people skip introductions and head for the real page numbers, not the roman numerals. But who better to guide you into a book than the people who have lived with the material during the years of preparation for publication? Taking that responsibility seriously, we offer an overview of the *Intercultural Sourcebook*—its history, what it contains, and what it does not.

## Background

In 1979, David Hoopes ended the introduction of the first edition of the *Intercultural Sourcebook* by saying: "There is still a long way to go. The methods need further refinement. They have not been sufficiently evaluated. Cross-cultural training still remains unsystematized. But these will come. The important thing is that all the evidence indicates that we are now on the right track." Much of this forecast has come true. Cross-cultural training methods have been refined, and the training has become more systematized. Although evaluation may not have received all the attention it deserved, the goals of intercultural training are still valid, and we are still on the right track.

The decision to update the *Sourcebook* was an easy one. It was the only book dedicated specifically to the wide variety of training methods available to the growing numbers of cross-cultural trainers, educators, consultants, program managers, and others interested in knowing more about the topic. Although some methods have not changed appreciably, others have metamorphosed over the years. Video, a method in frequent use today, was not included in the original *Sourcebook* but will appear in Volume 2. Case studies, role plays, and critical incidents seem much as they were a decade and a half ago.

The names of the methods may not have changed but the manner of using them, the content, contexts, trainers, and audiences have gained in sophistication. Indeed when the first edition was written, the purpose of intercultural training was almost exclusively to train people to live and work overseas. Currently, much cross-cultural training targets the at-home intercultural experience. Known as diversity training in the United States, it has become quite popular for organizations to engage trainers to develop programs aimed at facilitating communication skills to meet the challenges of a multicultural workforce or campus. While the methods and examples described in the *Intercultural Sourcebook* can be readily adapted to meet the needs of diversity training, they were chosen primarily to aid the cross-cultural trainer who works in the international arena.

Origins of the first edition of the *Intercultural Sourcebook* are anchored in the International Society for Intercultural Education, Training, and Research (SIETAR International) state-of-the-art project conducted by George Renwick in 1978. Cross-cultural training materials gathered during that study were published in 1979 as the original *Intercultural Sourcebook*. The focus then as now is how— not what or who or when—to use methods that lend themselves to cross-cultural training.

In the introduction to the first edition of the *Sourcebook*, David Hoopes discussed the development of cross-cultural training. The model Hoopes used to illustrate the evolution of cross-cultural training approaches is reproduced below.

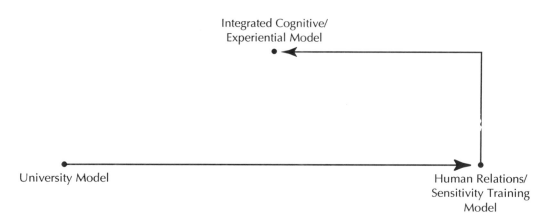

Hoopes traced the origins of the controversy surrounding the university model versus the personal growth model. The university model "left the trainees largely unprepared for the realities of functioning in a radically different sociocultural environment. Perhaps even more significant was the dawning recognition that becoming effective overseas involved a heavy measure of self-understanding and awareness." In the 1960s when human relations or sensitivity training peaked, these training techniques pervaded education of all kinds. "It soon became apparent that while the communication and self-awareness skills which resulted from human relations training were of some relevance and value overseas, there were major deficiencies in the methodology." Training directors were stung by sensitivity training and "beat a hasty retreat.... Increasingly trainers experimented with methods which, while tapping into trainee feelings and bringing unconscious cultural attitudes and values to the surface, stopped short of penetrating deeply into emotions and personality structures. At the same time, more attention was paid to the theoretical framework of intercultural communication and cross-cultural human relations so that cognition and experience were joined effectively in the training process" (Hoopes and Ventura 1979, 4-5).

It is important to know that this debate was part of the history of the field, but these issues are not so hotly discussed any more. The debate was resolved just as Hoopes predicted it would be. Trainers have found ways to integrate effectively cognitive, affective, and behavioral learning to the benefit of participants in intercultural training programs.

# Intercultural Training

## Goals

There are almost as many different goals for intercultural training as there are training programs. The overarching goal of most programs is to make participants more effective in overseas, cross-cultural, or multicultural situations. According to Pusch (1993), nearly all the intercultural research identifies three general behavioral skills or abilities that are critical to being effective overseas:

1. the ability to manage psychological stress
2. the ability to communicate effectively
3. the ability to establish interpersonal relationships

Intercultural trainers need to break each of these general goals into component parts. For example, trainers can work toward the first goal—the ability to manage psychological stress—through sessions on culture shock, adjustment, self-esteem, tolerance for ambiguity, and the like. The second goal—the ability to communicate effectively—addresses such functional elements as language training, cognitive flexibility, dual perspectives, and awareness of our own culture and communicative styles. The third goal—the ability to establish interpersonal relationships—can be fostered with sessions on such topics as cross-cultural empathy and culturally sensitive ways to develop friendships and working relationships.

Specific examples of the training methods that can be used to achieve these and other goals are found in the *Intercultural Sourcebook*. Only you can decide which method is most appropriate for your participants. It is recommended (see Levy in this volume) that a needs assessment be conducted to provide the data required to support your decisions.

## Methods

We prefer the term "method" to the term "technique." Method is a more general word describing a procedure or process for achieving an end. It implies an orderly arrangement, a systematized way of doing something. A methodology is a body of methods and rules that embody the principles or procedures of inquiry in a particular field. A technique is the way in which one handles technical details—the procedures for accomplishing a complex task or process. Using that scheme, the *Sourcebook* itself comprises the methodology of the intercultural field. The systematized procedures used to achieve goals such as intercultural effectiveness and cross-cultural competence are the intercultural training methods. Intercultural techniques are less easy to define. They may be as specific as the step-by-step directions for implementing a method or as general as the way in which a trainer handles a training process.

Methods per se are neutral. In themselves, methods are not pleasant or threatening or sentimental or idealistic—but content can be and trainers can be. We know that one of the most important things any trainer can do is to present a realistic picture of cross-cultural challenges, difficulties, and rewards. An unrealistic portrait of what a trainee can expect in dealing with an intercultural experience is a prescription for disillusionment, failure, and, in the worst case, disaster.

Methods are also not ethical or unethical. Using someone else's material without proper attribution is unethical. Using a method that does not fit the audience or the content is a mistake in judgment but not unethical. Ethical responsibility for professionals is equally as important as using the right method at the right time with the right group.

The methods described in this book can be used in many different cultures and many different ways. Some of the methods were developed in the United States. All of the methods are used quite widely in the Western world. However, there are as many ways of using the methods as there are cultures in the world. The focus on methods may be typically American, but methods are an essential part of any trainer's tool kit—that collection of knowledge, expertise, and skills that every trainer has to offer the world. Reading or referring to this book and others can increase knowledge of training methods, but to increase training skills, practice and experimentation are needed.

Some of the training methods in *Intercultural Sourcebook* have long been in general use. For example, role plays, critical incidents, case studies, and simulation games are used to meet the needs of a wide variety of training situations. Content, and sometimes technique, make generic training methods cross-cultural. On the other hand, the culture assimilators and the contrast-culture method were designed specifically for cross-cultural learning. It is conceivable that the culture assimilator format might be used for some professional development, such as law or psychology. But the underlying theory of cultural attribution and the content of the incidents make this method inherently cross-cultural. Since the stimulus material is presented as a kind of critical incident, some people consider assimilators to be a form of the critical incident method. We would argue that although the assimilator incidents may look like generic critical incidents, they are constructed according to predetermined, empirical parameters, making this an unmistakable method in its own right. Similarly, the contrast-culture method is viewed by some as a role play or a simulation or a role-play simulation. The very fact that it is difficult—if not impossible—to decide what part of the contrast-culture method is simulation and which part is role play suggests that it is a distinct form of training. The substance of this well-researched method is so embedded in the dynamics of intercultural interaction that it is difficult to imagine it being used for any other type of training.

# Overview of *Intercultural Sourcebook*

The *Intercultural Sourcebook* comes from personal experience with the methods. Reading it is like having a conversation with the people who developed and have successfully used the materials.

Decisions regarding what to keep, what was new and needed to be added, what was no longer being used and should be deleted were not easily reached. Deciding what anyone really needs to know about cross-cultural training seemed both daunting and presumptuous. We began by reviewing the directions cross-cultural training has taken over the years since the first edition. We did not set out to create a two-volume work, but as we explored trends in intercultural training, there was convincing evidence that two volumes were needed to do justice to the developments in the profession and the needs of trainers. Volume 2 is forthcoming from Intercultural Press.

This volume of the *Intercultural Sourcebook* contains six categories of training methods. Twenty-four individuals with extensive intercultural training and design experience contributed the chapters. The authors were selected because they developed the methods or are known for their expertise with the method, or are especially representative of trainers who use the method. The authors provide many perspectives. They are natives of several countries although most represent Western cultures.

The authors serve clients typical of those encountered by intercultural trainers. Some work with college students, some at the pre-college level. Others work with employees of the government, industry, or nonprofit organizations. They also work with people from their home culture and with those from a variety of foreign cultures.

## Organization of the Material

Each section of the *Intercultural Sourcebook* focuses on a specific method and begins with an overview chapter on the method, followed by several chapters containing examples. Authors of the overview chapters were asked to describe the method in some detail, provide important considerations for using it, and indicate specific domestic and international situations in which it might be used. They were also to list the benefits of using the method and to describe some outcomes trainers could expect. Further, they were to compare, when possible, their method to other methods and, finally, they were asked to provide a listing of the most important resources for learning more about the method.

Authors of the chapters containing examples were asked to provide an introduction to the example, its history, and the step-by-step procedure for using it. They were also to describe contexts in which the example has been used, to discuss any problems or pitfalls to watch for in using it, and to provide a list of relevant resources.

The *Intercultural Sourcebook* chapters cover some important ground in addition to providing technical training details. The origins of some cross-cultural training methods have been lost with time, and the book freshens our memories of how such methods as the cultural assimilator and the contrast-culture technique were developed. Awareness of the empirical research that supports these methods enables us to understand them better and can give us greater confidence using them.

## Structure of the *Intercultural Sourcebook*

To the extent possible, the *Intercultural Sourcebook* was constructed by systematically arranging the methods to build from one method to the next. Reviewing the issues involved in intercultural training design seemed a good place to begin. Following that, the first three sections focus on interactional methods, while the next three deal with what are commonly referred to as cognitive methods.

**Design** considerations are addressed by Jack Levy. Levy defines important terms, presents several models, describes a training classification system, examines the content of intercultural training, and walks us through the design process.

**Role Plays** are introduced in the second section by Jim McCaffery, who provides the overview for this interactional method. McCaffery points out the trouble resulting from the misuse of role plays and three common mistakes trainers make. He shares his long experience with role plays by providing detailed steps for delivering a good role-play session that avoids the pitfalls.

There are two examples of specific role plays to complete our coverage of this important intercultural training method. John Pettit and Graeme Frelick tell us how to prepare and conduct a role play that has been used in many multicultural settings. Shirley Fletcher describes a role play between an American tourist and a Caribbean tour guide and taxi driver that demonstrates differing culture-based attitudes toward time and a number of tourist-host problems.

The contrast-culture method uniquely combines role play with simulation. Edward Stewart recounts the history of the contrast-culture method, including the development of the character of Mr. Khan to play the contrasting cultural role. He points out that this method gives trainees the opportunity to practice interacting with someone who embodies contrasting cultural characteristics and the insights they can gain from such an experience. Cajetan DeMello relates the unusual insights derived from his many years playing Mr. Khan. Paul Kimmel describes his approach to working with Mr. Khan, how he prepares the group, conducts the role play, and debriefs it.

**Simulation Games** add action and a more complex structure to role-play-like situations. Dorothy Sisk defines simulation games and describes the method. Garry Shirts reviews the history of his classic simulation game, *BaFá BaFá*. Barbara Steinwachs shares her excitement over *Barnga* and describes its many applications. Judee Blohm describes *Markhall,* a cross-cultural management simulation game. Dianne Hofner Saphiere gives us *Ecotonos* as a final example of a simulation game of great versatility.

The **Critical Incidents** section is the point at which we shift focus from interactional to cognitive training methods. The first, critical incidents, are thoroughly described by Albert Wight. Bill Dant tells us how participants can draw on their intercultural experiences to write their own critical incidents. Milton Bennett links critical incidents to a specific topic—cross-cultural conflict resolution—to demonstrate how they can be used in intercultural training.

The **Culture Assimilator** is an empirically based refinement of the critical incident method. Rosita Albert's overview provides thorough grounding in its development. Richard Brislin explains the usefulness of a culture-general assimilator, and Harry Triandis describes a culture-specific assimilator.

**Case Studies** are more than just critical incidents grown large. Lee Lacey and Janie Trowbridge describe the case-study method. The example, Pregnancy at St. Theresa's by Joe DiStefano, illustrates how engaging and complex a case study can be. Janet Bennett's example uses the complicated issues surrounding Salman Rushdie's *Satanic Verses,* demonstrating how diverse materials can add realism to a case study.

The **Effectiveness Connection,** by Robert Hayles, serves as an epilogue to this volume. In it Hayles makes the link between training and outcomes and underlines its importance.

### How to Use the *Intercultural Sourcebook* Material

Start out by studying the Table of Contents and skimming the book from cover to cover to become familiar with what it contains. Then you can sit down and read it through carefully, if that's your style, or you can consult it selectively when you need a new idea or when you want to see if your thinking about some training issue is on the right track.

When you become familiar with the structure of the *Intercultural Sourcebook,* you will be able to use it with a great deal of flexibility. You will find the variety of examples, the number of audiences addressed, and the mix of training methods allow you to structure a training program to meet your specific needs. Draw on your cultural knowledge and sensitivities to adapt the methods described. In their descriptions, the authors set specific goals and target certain groups, but the material can be used at many levels and for many purposes. Modifying the methods and the examples to fit your group is part of the creative process.

### Some Things You Will Not Find in the *Intercultural Sourcebook*

Focusing on methods, as we intended, resulted in the exclusion of some things trainers have to take into consideration in developing training programs. Needs assessment and evaluation were two of them. But information about those subjects can be found elsewhere. Also links, connectors, and bridges from one segment of a training program to another have not been described. Subtle refinements of training are best achieved by observing a proficient, seasoned trainer. In training, as in other parts of life, the best teacher is experience.

## Some Final Thoughts

Experiential learning is a hallmark of intercultural training. We think all the methods in the *Intercultural Sourcebook* are experiential. Participants' experience (past and present), their perceptions of the training activity, and their reactions to it determine what and how much they learn. This is in contrast to more traditional training in which the trainer or expert's decisions, interpretation, and presentation are of utmost importance.

This collection marks a stage of development in the history of intercultural training. Putting the methods in one place allows us to view the range and scope of the field. Reading it years hence, people will be able to see where intercultural training was as we prepared for the twenty-first century. It is our hope that the *Intercultural Sourcebook* becomes an identifying feature of the intercultural training landscape.

# References

Hoopes, David S., and Paul Ventura, eds. *Intercultural Sourcebook: Cross-Cultural Training Methodologies.* Washington, DC: Society for Intercultural Education, Training, and Research (SIETAR International), 1979. (Out of print.)

Pusch, Margaret D. *The Chameleon Capability.* Paper presented at the Council for International Education Exchange (CIEE) Annual Conference: Washington, DC: November, 1993.

# Intercultural Training Design

## Jack Levy

The design of intercultural training (ICT) differs somewhat from other experience-based instruction. Through its focus on the concept of culture and its view that the training itself is a cross-cultural event, ICT possesses unique characteristics. This chapter begins with some definitions, then discusses several design considerations, and ends with an examination of a number of common designs and other training issues.

## Definitions

I define intercultural training as a cohesive series of events or activities designed to develop cultural self-awareness, culturally appropriate behavioral responses or skills, and a positive orientation toward other cultures. I use it synonymously with the term "cross-cultural training" and frequently refer to it simply as "experiential training." To achieve these outcomes, trainers use experiential, workshop-type designs. In this chapter the term "program" is used to mean an event lasting longer than one day with a curriculum comprised of a number of sessions. The terms "trainer" and "designer" define the person or persons who develop and implement the ICT event.

The goals and processes of experiential training can be stated in a number of different ways. I have adopted the approach suggested by Dugan Laird (1985):

**Pre-Training Period:**

1. Learners acquire experience in normal day-to-day activities.
2. The designer provides an experience which will tap learners' values and beliefs.

**In-Training Period:**

1. Learners are provided new experiences with which to compare and match their previous experience and learning.
2. Learners distill new values and new learnings from those experiences.
3. Learners try out new behaviors in the training environment.

**Post-Training Period:**

Learners have acquired the ability to examine and learn from their experiences on a continuing basis.

Experiential training with experienced adults has a special advantage, as the learners themselves are often the richest resource in the training program. Consequently, techniques which make use of their experiences are emphasized: group discussion, simulations, laboratory and field experiences, problem-solving projects and the like (Knowles 1984, 10). It is these types of activities which I envision throughout this chapter.

I must emphasize, however, that experiential training is not simply a series of techniques, but must reflect cohesion and purpose. As Kolb and Lewis state:

> ...there is an art involved as well—the art of managing the experiential learning process. Sometimes experiential learning is misunderstood—considered only as games and exercises, "bull sessions," or the "blind leading the blind." When experiential learning techniques are used as contributors to the creation of a learning environment that maximizes learners' skills in learning from their own experience, the full potential of these techniques can be realized (1986, 100).

## Design Considerations

The following ICT design considerations are discussed in this section: the importance of culture, needs assessment and objectives, trainer background, cultural awareness approaches, skill building, and risk level.

### Importance of Culture

While ICT shares some attributes with human relations, conflict resolution, and other types of experiential training, spotlighting "culture" as a core influence on behavior makes it unique. As Ferguson states, ICT recognizes that the "individual is a prisoner of his[/her] culture, but need not be its victim" (1987, 12). ICT should present culture as a potentially liberating, holistic concept. It should allow the individual to learn about self by learning about others, and vice versa. By locating culture at the center of behavior, ICT highlights it as a defining human characteristic.

Designing ICT is similar to designing training events in other fields in that one must do many things at once: identify training needs, classify objectives, respond to trainee idiosyncrasies, deal with logistics and the physical and social context within which the training is taking place, and select methodologies and structure the program.

ICT derives its uniqueness, however, in its basic focus on and approach to culture. How does the designer intend to apply the concept of culture? How does the trainee want it applied? What is the most beneficial approach for the trainees? for the organization? These questions must be applied to all facets of the design.

## Needs Assessment and Objectives

Writing clear objectives is a canon of training design. They are supposed to be what remains after the needs assessment separates the real from the ideal. But be alert to ambiguous outcomes in your needs assessment, since "culture is a word for which everyone has a definition" (Ferguson, 14). These definitions may be quite imprecise. Such phrases as "we need some race-relations training" or "we've got cultural problems here" are often heard in the diagnostic phase. As the designer, you must clarify needs and problems as well as encourage participants and clients (though the latter may not be participating in the training) to take ownership of the program. This can be furthered by getting as many opinions from as many clients and participants as possible, meeting with a variety of people regarding perceived problems, and sharing drafts of the ICT training agenda.

## Trainer Self-Assessment

It is relatively easy for you to press for behavioral descriptions of events during the needs assessment. It is more difficult to be aware of your own concept of culture. What cultural framework lies behind your behaviors? How will your cultural filter affect the interpretation of trainee needs? In my opinion, the designer's cultural disposition is more critical to the outcome in ICT than in any other type of training. It is impossible to compensate or allow for your cultural background and baggage if they remain unexplored. Cultural assumptions, beliefs, values, and the like tend to be subtle and subconscious, but they are not inaccessible to rigorous self-examination. So self-scrutiny is a necessary starting place when designing an ICT program.

## Trainer Background

This leads to the consideration of trainer background. A classic issue in intellectual discourse is the degree to which a commentator on some subject needs direct, hands-on experience with, or expertise in, that subject. Must the music critic be a musician? No doubt direct experience is beneficial. But is it required?

This question also pertains to ICT. Many people feel that cross-cultural experience is an absolutely essential prerequisite to conducting cross-cultural training. Others feel that highly sensitive individuals can—based on cognitive knowledge of the subject—design and conduct reasonably effective intercultural training, especially if they use cross-culturally experienced cotrainers.

But if the "subject" is behavioral and involves coming to terms with the out-of-awareness influence of cultural conditioning and/or if you are seeking to develop cultural self-awareness, tolerance, and culturally appropriate behavioral responses in the trainees, then it would seem logical, indeed imperative, that you yourself possess these skills and attributes. Although a sensitive designer could conceivably learn along with participants, the best way to connect with them is to have "been there." You should have had some kind of in-depth experience in another culture and have committed (and learned from) personal cross-cultural faux pas and be able to bring this learning to the table.

The training will benefit from the trainers' ability to find parallels between their cross-cultural experiences and those the participants expect to encounter. Experience can also facilitate the selection or structuring of activities, since the cross-culturally experienced trainer is more likely to be aware of the kinds of training activities that will lead participants to the insights they need.

The identity of the trainers should reflect participant needs. For example, a group concerned with race relations should be led by a multicultural training team; training which focuses on sexual harassment issues should be led by male and female trainers. While this trainer complementarity is not as crucial as trainer background, it has significant symbolic value. Having cotrainers who have lived through cross-cultural experiences enriches the learning potential.

## Cultural-Awareness Approaches

There are two basic approaches to developing cultural awareness in training participants. One might be called "inside-out" and the other "outside-in." In the former, participants are led from cultural self-awareness to other-culture awareness; in the latter, from other-culture awareness to self-awareness. In the inside-out strategy, the training may concentrate on the participants' own cultural identity and the culture groups to which they belong—national, gender, and/or ethnic, for example. Once they have established an understanding of culture and its influence on their group, they can examine its effect on their personal behavior, which desirably results in an increase in cultural self-awareness. From there the group can explore the nature of their relationships with other culture groups, come to grips with culturally loaded problems which exist between them, and develop skills in intercultural communication and problem solving. The process can be reversed, of course, resulting in the outside-in design.

In this context, we may consider intercultural training itself as a cross-cultural event in which, to start with, participants represent different subcultures, or at least a range of individual perspectives and views. You can capitalize on these according to whatever path you take in fostering cultural awareness.

A caution is in order. Trainers sometimes view cultural awareness by itself as an appropriate objective for a session, especially if they are faced with limited time (one or two hours) and a small number of trainees (fewer than five) they have never met. Achieving a cultural-awareness objective might involve a low-risk activity such as a demonstration, lecture, or video. Unfortunately, such sessions are practically worthless in terms of changing behavior. Emphasis should be placed instead on building skills.

## Skill Building

Even if you have only a few hours, you should try to work on at least one cross-cultural communication skill from the hundreds that have been identified as important in cross-cultural interaction. Choose a skill based on the needs of the participants and involve them in a learning experience. For example, have participants learn to describe a situation in nonjudgmental terms. This is a generic cross-cultural skill which can be introduced in almost any ICT session. In your design make sure participants know what to do with such a skill and how it would be useful. Then clarify the process, perhaps through a lecturette. Now participants are ready to recall situations from their own experience and practice describing them in an unbiased manner.

Keep in mind as you design your training sessions that the objective of culturally appropriate behavioral responses or skills is dependent upon an understanding both of the cultural situation one is responding to and of one's typical responses to this type of situation in one's own culture. Your design needs to help participants achieve that understanding. This emphasis on skill building naturally forces you to focus on skill identification during the needs assessment. Even if such a diagnosis cannot be conducted, generic skills can be introduced.

## Risk Level

The path to skill development is through knowledge, experimentation, feedback, and analysis. Generally, materials and activities should proceed from the lowest to the highest level of risk. Occasionally, especially among Americans in the United States, you first have to get the participants' attention, so sometimes a little shock treatment is in order. However, the majority of your designs will reserve the highest risk activities until the end. Your design should take into account the need to build trust to make this progression from low to high risk possible.

You might, for example, have participants do an analysis of someone involved in a cross-cultural encounter through a demonstration or a video identifying the cross-cultural skills needed or exemplified. They could then practice the identified skills (through role play or simulation) in dyads or triads. If there is sufficient time and the trust level is high, they might present themselves for others' analysis—through a fishbowl, videotaped simulation, or large-group role play. In this manner the ICT session becomes a true laboratory for skill development.

This laboratory approach has several advantages. In effect, the trainer is bringing a mirror to the group. In seeing how they are seen, participants can begin to understand the consequences of their behavior. ICT sessions provide trainees with an invitation to change. One way to emphasize the need for change is to demonstrate the consequences of *not* changing. This is one reason why the *Barnga* simulation (see Steinwachs, this volume) is extremely powerful when videotaped. Participants can experience the consequences of not checking assumptions or misinterpreting nonverbal signals.

As a designer, you want to work continually toward creating a safe training environment in which participants will be able to develop their cross-cultural abilities. This notion of a safe environment can be expressed in a variety of ways but its outcome is constant: participants feel free to experiment with their behavior, receive feedback, and analyze its effectiveness. They will not change because you tell them they have to. They will change only when their own insights provide the motivation.

Designing curriculum with the right intensity of emotion and appropriate level of risk is an art. It is a skill developed out of many cross-cultural and training experiences. There are no perfect needs assessments, hence no perfect designs. You must make an endless series of best guesses on the level of intensity you allow to build in the group, the level of risk participants are able to manage, and the kinds of training activities that will produce the outcomes you want. While all trainers have a ready supply of favorite activities, the challenge is to create a design that employs them in the right place at the right time and in the right way.

# Training-Program Models

There are a number of design models from which to choose. With the exception of the experiential model, which is discusssed separately and focuses on individual training sessions rather than on the training program as a whole, all seem to follow a basic design and delivery process: needs assessment, goals/objectives, content selection/sequencing, development of materials and activities, implementation, and evaluation.

## Critical-Events Model

Nadler (1982) states that this model is more useful for training than for education or development. This means that the critical-events model works best for learning programs related to the job the individual now has, rather than one which she/he may assume in the future. The "events" indicated in the title refer to the various stages in the model, which appear in Figure 1. This model is noted for its insistence that the designer continually check his/her work with others (Nadler calls this "evaluation and feedback") throughout the process. This requirement led Nadler to characterize it as an "open" model, one in which the design process can be halted when an unexpected outside factor (such as a long-forgotten policy or practice) suddenly appears.

## Training and Development Systems Approach

William Tracey's training and development system (1984) presents a more technical, linear view of design than the critical-events model. As shown in Figure 2, this model is a closed-loop system which begins with goals and functions and continues through to evaluation of the end products before returning again to goals and functions. Tracey sees it as a "constantly repeating cycle of evaluation, feedback and improvement" (1984, 41). He believes that it is useful for a broad range of training, education, and development activities.

**Figure 1**

# The Critical-Events Model

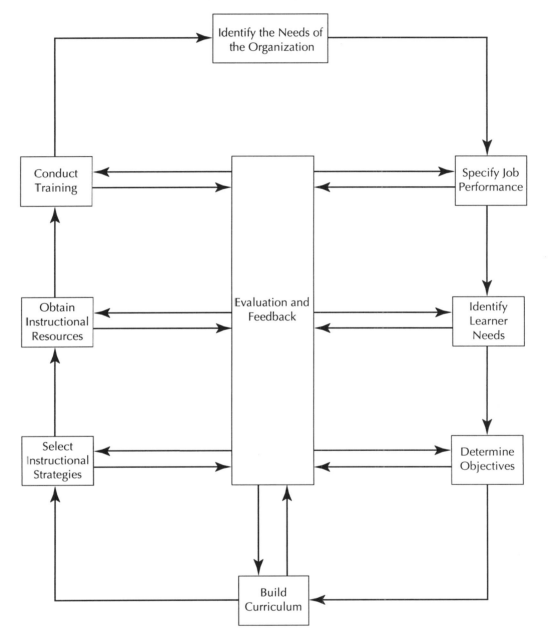

**Figure 2**

# Training and Development Systems Approach

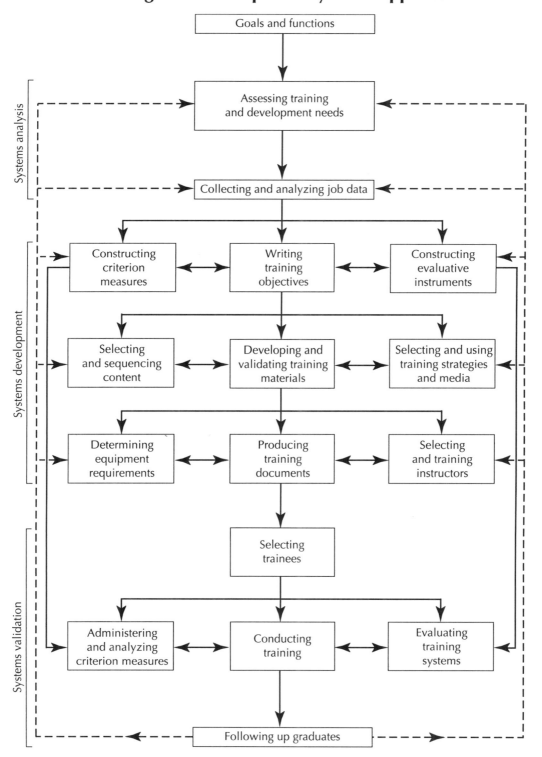

## Instructional Systems Design

The primary purpose of this model is to produce print- or computer-based instructional materials, though it can be used for general training purposes. It evolved from behaviorism and the instructional-objectives movement, and its earliest examples were programmed instruction and learning activity packages. While the stages presented in Figure 3 (Dick and Carey 1990, 2-3) do not differ a great deal from those of Nadler and Tracey, the approach is known for its reliance on educational psychology and cognitive science. After a needs assessment, instructional goals are categorized according to their domains of learning: psychomotor skill, intellectual skill, verbal information, and attitudes. Each goal is then painstakingly broken down into behaviors or steps which the learner must accomplish to be successful. Each of these behaviors becomes the focus of a microdesign (Dick and Carey 1990, 33-38). Instructional-Systems Design became popular in the late 1970s and 1980s with the rise of educational technology and the publication of works by Leslie Briggs (1977), Robert Mager (1984), and Robert Gagne (1985; et al., 1988).

## Experiential Culture-General Training Design

While many authors have written about experiential training (Silberman 1990, Eitington 1989, Lewis 1986, McCaffery 1986, Marks and Davis 1975, among others), I have generally adopted the model outlined by Gormley and McCaffery (1984). They refer to the design of individual activities, though I have also found them useful in designing larger sequences.

1. INTRODUCTION, CLIMATE SETTING (Icebreaker, Opener)

    Stimulates interest, curiosity, induces participants to begin thinking about the subject at hand. Provides rationale for why subject is important to participants and how it will be useful to them. Links this training session to previous ones and places it into the overall design of the program.

2. GOAL CLARIFICATION

    Presents to the participant statements which describe the intent, aim, or purpose of the training activity.

    Provides opportunity for participants to seek clarity on goals, add additional issues, or raise concerns.

3. EXPERIENCE

    An activity which participants engage in that will provide opportunity for them to "experience" a situation relevant to the goals of the training program/session. The experience becomes a data-producing event which participants analyze as they complete the experiential-learning cycle. Common experiences are role plays, case studies, critical incidents, and the like.

**Figure 3**

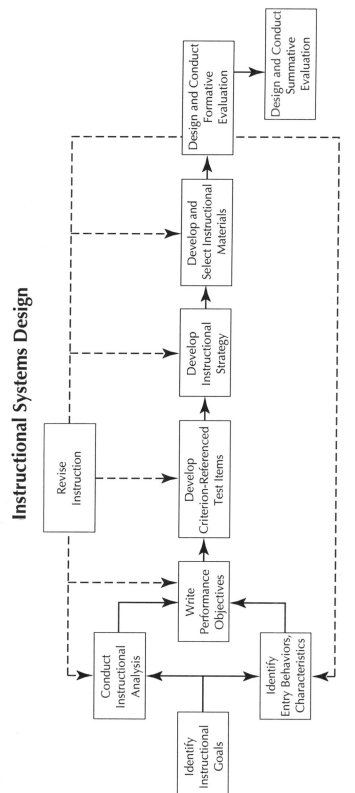

Instructional Systems Design

4. PROCESSING

> Participants share individual experiences and reactions to the experience. The experience is analyzed and reflected upon thoughtfully by the group; the trainer guides and manages this process.

5. GENERALIZING

> Participants seek to identify generalizations or summary statements which can be inferred from the experience.

6. APPLICATION

> Using insights and conclusions gained from previous steps, participants identify means and ways to incorporate new learnings into daily life. This step answers the questions "Now what?" and "How can I use what I have learned?"

7. CLOSURE

> Brief summary of events of training session. Refers back to goals and seeks to determine if they have been met. Wraps up training session and gives sense of completion. Links session to next stage of training program.

After an extremely comprehensive analysis of different attempts to classify intercultural training, Gudykunst and Hammer (1983, 118-54) offer their own classification system. It proceeds according to two dimensions: experiential versus didactic and culture-general versus culture-specific. The experiential dimension has been discussed throughout this chapter. The didactic approach, sometimes referred to as the "university model," largely employs lectures and discussions to impart information about foreign cultures. While it is generally agreed that culture-specific training is limited to preparing people for contact with a particular culture or culture group, there is some disagreement on the definition of culture-general training. Some designers believe that it should develop cultural awareness and foster a general sensitivity to other cultures. Others feel that it should expose the participant to a range of specific cross-cultural experiences which can be generalized to any group on earth. A third position views culture-general training as increasing the trainee's understanding and/or appreciation of culture's influence on behavior. Intercultural training which combines all three views is not uncommon.

The two dimensions yield designs in four quadrants: experiential culture-general, experiential culture-specific, didactic culture-general, and didactic culture-specific. The ideas presented in this chapter represent the first quadrant. Gudykunst and Hammer believe that experiential culture-general training designs are the most commonly used and widely discussed in the literature. The following techniques are included in this category:

1. Modifications of traditional human relations training to include, in my opinion, the increasingly popular subject of conflict resolution/management.

2. Intercultural communication workshop.

3. Culture-general role plays or simulations such as the *Contrast American* and *BaFá BaFá* (Gudykunst and Hammer, 126-33).

The content of ICT can be, and generally is, divided into three familiar domains: knowledge, skills, and attitudes. However, while you are working on your design you need to remember that people typically do not learn in discrete categories. There is always some mixing or blending even though one might remain dominant. For example, when people are learning about cultural differences, they are adding to their store of knowledge, but they are also enhancing attitudes such as tolerance and adding to their behavioral repertoire by learning ways of dealing with cultural differences.

### Knowledge

The knowledge domain includes definitions, concepts, and information. A goal of some ICT events is for participants to learn the meaning of such terms as culture, identity groups, race, and ethnicity. Concepts such as prejudice, stereotyping, and cultural conditioning are also usually covered. ICT sessions often include information in the form of research results or compiled data on, for instance, demographic trends in the workforce. Culture-specific training might use maps, slides, or video presentations.

While the knowledge can be presented didactically, it is most often learned experientially. This is frequently done through activities designed to also develop skills or change attitudes. An example might be the simulation game *BaFá BaFá*, which teaches about cultural conditioning (knowledge) while providing an opportunity to experiment with cultural entry skills and promoting tolerance for ambiguity (attitude).

### Skills

As mentioned, there are hundreds of cross-cultural skills which can be included in the goals of ICT. Commentary on cross-cultural competencies can be found in Dinges (1983) or Levy (1983). Also see above for my discussion of skill building. Two sample skills:

❖ Ability to recognize that the way a person sees things is a selective process and is often culturally influenced

❖ Ability to withhold judgmental responses to a new situation until more information about it is available

### Attitudes

The difficulty in changing attitudes, that is, moving participants toward greater levels of tolerance, receptiveness to change, respect, and so forth, through ICT is well-known. For this reason most training designers will not select attitude change as the primary goal. Unless you are conducting a long-term ICT program, or participants will be working on a cross-cultural project, you will find attitude change difficult to achieve.

One exception to the difficulty of working on attitudes refers back to my definition of intercultural training at the beginning of this chapter as a cohesive series of events or activities which seek to develop (among other things) a positive orientation or attitude toward other cultures. A positive realistic attitude is one of the best predictors of success in cross-cultural situations. Consequently, you need to consciously design opportunities for trainees to frame their expectations positively and realistically.

# The Design Process

The process of designing training reflects the personalities of the individuals who do it. I cannot tell you exactly what you should do when you sit down at your desk to prepare a design, because it depends on how detailed, how global, how compulsive, or how structured you are. You have to discover the process that is right for you. Some trainers have actually been known to train by winging it—not preparing at all. That is not recommended. Most trainers spend hours working on design. Some figure one hour of design for each hour of training; others find a four to one ratio (four hours of design to one hour of training) is closer to reality.

### Beginning

Some people begin to design by starting at the end. They find that developing the generalizing questions to be asked at the end of training (such as "what did you learn?") and imagining the preferred answer helps them set the objectives. Others find that the needs assessment generates desired outcomes, and they use those to write the ICT objectives. Outcomes which call for developing knowledge naturally require different objectives and techniques from those for skill building or attitude change. Trainers need a broad repertoire of methods in order to match strategies appropriately to learner needs and desired outcomes. It is in making the decision on outcomes that you actually identify a target level of emotional intensity for the session. Generally, the more the design focuses on skills and attitudes, the more interactive it will be. As participant interaction increases so does the potential for meaningful discussion, reflection, learning, and feeling.

In working on your design, especially in the early stages, you will have to juggle factors such as the physical environment, number of trainees, and the amount of time, materials, equipment, and other resources which are available. Carefully consider these elements when selecting methods.

### Middle

Once you have a sense of how you will start, you can plan the rest of the training according to your goals. Select methods that achieve the goals, not the other way around. The balance of this book is devoted to describing methods commonly used in intercultural training. While all trainers have favorites, there are clearly no "best" ICT methods. Most trainers realize that what is best depends on how the learners, the trainer, the outcomes desired, and the setting interact with each other.

It bears repeating that an analysis of learner needs provides the foundation for the ICT design. You may have collected data on preferred learning styles as well as identifying knowledge and skill deficiencies. This is particularly important when you are training in a culture other than your own. Through interviews, surveys, and evaluation of other training events, you can determine if the trainees prefer structured, cooperative, or independent activities. People tend to like what they have been exposed to. A person who has never been through experiential training, for example, cannot be expected to prefer this learning style.

### Ending

Even after you have designed your entire training program, it is not complete unless you attend to the question of how participants will apply what they have learned. The best knowledge, understanding, and skills are useless if they are not tied to everyday realities. It is important, therefore, to focus periodically, and especially at the end of the program, on applications. You can simply ask something like, "How will you apply what we did today when you return to the office?" or have participants develop an action plan for their first few weeks overseas or reflect on and discuss how they can use the training.

One thing on which most trainers agree is that you rarely start designing at the beginning and work in a straight line to the end. You move around in the design—changing, adding, deleting, modifying—much as you might do with wet paint on a canvas. Clearly, designing intercultural training is a creative process.

# References

Briggs, Leslie, ed. *Instructional Design: Principles and Applications.* Englewood Cliffs, NJ: Educational Technology Publications, 1977.

Copeland Griggs Productions. *Valuing Diversity. Part I: Managing Differences. Teacher's and Trainer's Guide.* San Francisco: Copeland Griggs Productions, 1990.

Dick, Walter, and L. Carey. *The Systematic Design of Instruction.* Glenview, IL: Scott, Foresman, 1990.

Dinges, Norman. "Intercultural Competence." In *Handbook of Intercultural Training,* vol. 1. Edited by Dan Landis and Richard Brislin. Elmsford, NY: Pergamon (1983): 176-202.

Eitington, Julius. *The Winning Trainer.* 2d ed. Houston: Gulf, 1989.

Ferguson, Henry. *Manual for Multicultural Education.* 2d ed. Yarmouth, ME: Intercultural Press, 1987.

Gagne, Robert. *The Conditions of Learning.* 4th ed. New York: Holt, Rinehart and Winston, 1985.

Gagne, Robert, Leslie Briggs, and W. Wager. *Principles of Instructional Design.* 3d ed. New York: Holt, Rinehart and Winston, 1988.

Gormley, Wilma, and James McCaffery. "Design Components of an Experiential Training Session." Unpublished. Alexandria, VA: Training Resources Group, 1984.

Gudykunst, William, and Mitchell Hammer. "Basic Training Design: Approaches to Intercultural Training." In *Handbook of Intercultural Training,* vol. 1. Edited by Dan Landis and Richard Brislin. Elmsford, NY: Pergamon (1983): 118-54.

Hopkins, Robbins. Interview, April 1992.

Knowles, Malcolm S., and Associates. *Andragogy in Action* 10, San Francisco: Jossey-Bass, 1984.

Kolb, David, and L. Lewis. "Facilitating Experiential Learning: Observations and Reflections." In *Experiential and Simulation Techniques for Teaching Adults: New Directions for Adult and Continuing Education,* no. 30. Edited by Linda Lewis. San Francisco: Jossey-Bass (1986): 99-107.

Laird, Dugan. *Approaches to Training and Development.* 2d ed. Reading, MA: Addison-Wesley (1985): 130-31.

Levy, Jack. "Developing Intercultural Competence in Bilingual Teacher Training Programs." In *Handbook of Intercultural Training,* vol. 3. Edited by Dan Landis and Richard Brislin. Elmsford, NY: Pergamon (1983): 55-80.

————. "Designing Workshops for Race Relations/Cultural Diversity." Unpublished workshop handbook. Fairfax, VA: George Mason University, 1991.

Lewis, Linda, ed. *Experiential and Simulation Techniques for Teaching Adults.* San Francisco: Jossey-Bass, 1986.

Mager, Robert. *Preparing Instructional Objectives.* 2d ed. Belmont, CA: Pitman Learning, 1984.

Marks, Stephen, and W. Davis. "The Experiential Learning Model and Its Application to Large Groups." In *The 1975 Annual Handbook for Group Facilitators,* edited by John Jones and J. W. Pfeiffer. San Diego: University Associates, 1975.

McCaffery, James. "Independent Effectiveness: A Reconsideration of Cross-Cultural Orientation and Training." *International Journal of Intercultural Relations* 10, no. 2 (1986): 159-78.

Nadler, Leonard. *Designing Training Programs.* Reading, MA: Addison-Wesley, 1982.

Silberman, Mel. *Active Training.* Lexington, MA: Lexington Books/D.C. Heath, and San Diego: University Associates, 1990.

Tracey, William. *Designing Training and Development Systems.* New York: AMACOM, 1984.

# The Role Play: A Powerful but Difficult Training Tool

## James A. McCaffery

While the role play is a particularly powerful training technique, people are sometimes reluctant to participate. A personal example illustrates one reason for such hesitation.

During a training of trainers course we tried to get participants to volunteer for a role play, but no one volunteered. We asked several different ways, but still there was no response. This surprised us, especially because the participants were trainers. Finally we said, "Hey, what is going on here? Why is no one volunteering?" The response came immediately. "Purple buttermilk—we don't want any more purple buttermilk." Although this was said somewhat tongue in cheek, there were several enthusiastic nods of agreement from the group.

Slightly confused, we asked, "Purple buttermilk, what do you mean?" They explained that apparently some time ago, someone had been leading an in-service training session for them and had done a role-play session with them that was entitled "Purple Buttermilk." They described the session in great detail and said that several of them had felt "sandbagged" (made to look foolish by being told the role play was intended for one thing when it was really intended for another purpose that was not explicitly shared with everyone). Even though this in-service session had taken place several years ago, the memory of this event was still so strong for most of the people in the group that they simply would not volunteer to participate in another role play. They definitely did not want to be fooled again.

### The Role Play: An Uncertain Training Legacy

Unfortunately, when it comes to role plays, anecdotes like the one above are not all that uncommon. Of all the training methods available, role plays may be the most misunderstood and misused. Their use has created so much trauma that people say "We don't do role plays around here" in much the same tone as they might say "We don't do windows." Why?

# Considerations for Using This Method

### Three Common Mistakes Trainers Make When Using Role Plays

1. **Role plays are used for the wrong purposes.** Using role plays to surprise or sandbag people will destroy trust in the trainer; using role plays as a vehicle for negative modeling ("You see, here is what Harry did wrong") or to allow the trainer to make teaching points from a live situation makes participants feel like guinea pigs or dummies. These are simply incorrect purposes for a role play.

2. **Role plays are poorly designed.** It is important to note that once the purpose is wrong, no amount of good design will save the role play. If it is used for the wrong purpose, it will end up wrong. However, even if the purpose is valid, there can be several design problems, including:
   - ❖ paying inadequate attention to the delivery steps (the trainer must think through each step);
   - ❖ writing roles poorly;
   - ❖ not establishing a tie between role plays and a clear and appropriate training purpose/rationale; and
   - ❖ making the exercise too much like a game and thereby trivializing the activity.

3. **Role plays are incorrectly delivered.** Delivering a role play is an intricate process, involving a series of small steps, all of which have a place. When a trainer leaves out key steps in the delivery, it can mean trouble. For example, not debriefing the role players can cause them to feel that they have taken a risk but have not had a chance to explain things from their perspective. This can prove very frustrating to them.

All of these trainer mistakes create problems in role-play sessions. And, even though there may be only two people actively engaged in the role play, everyone else in the session sees what happens, notices if the trainer uses this method incorrectly, and says, "Not me, I am not going to get involved in *that.*" And the memory lingers on for years.

### Using Role Plays in International Settings

The same problems show up when role plays are used in international settings and will be exaggerated because of cultural and linguistic differences. Some problems are especially important. For example, it is especially hard to communicate the rationale and purpose of a training session using a role play if the method is new to an international audience. Handling a debriefing becomes especially important in regions or countries where "face" is critical—the trainer must look to the positive and phrase things differently. A role play can be most risky for a participant group that is not used to experiential training, since the role play is really a prime example of an experiential method.

On the other hand, I have used this technique in countless international settings with success. If the purpose is appropriate and the role play carefully designed, it works extremely well—in some cultures even better than in North America because of the existence of oral traditions and storytelling.

# Description of the Role-Play Method

### What Is a Role Play?

The basic role play is a training activity where two participants (or more, though larger numbers are not common) take on characteristics of people other than themselves in order to attain a clearly defined objective. These "other people"—or roles—are usually fictitious, although they must be completely believable in the eyes of the training population for the role play to work. Participants who are not actively involved in the role play function as observers and look for certain things related to the overall objectives as the role play unfolds. Although a role-play session may run up to an hour, which includes preparation and debriefing, the actual role play runs from five to seven minutes.

Of course, there are many variations of this type, as we will see later on. For now, I will concentrate on the basic type of role play, as described above.

# Purpose of the Role-Play Method

The most appropriate use of role plays is to build skills. Therefore, role plays should be used in training programs that are aimed at building interpersonal skills, such as a management-training course that includes sessions on delegating, negotiating, managing conflict, giving and receiving feedback, and so on.

You can use role plays to teach these same skills in multicultural settings. There are many ways in which cross-cultural training (and language training) can include role plays. These training programs might focus on topics like meeting people from another culture for the first time, trying to influence someone who is culturally different, carrying out international negotiations, saying no to someone in an unfamiliar cultural situation, and so on. There are skills involved in each of these areas, skills that can be modeled and that participants can observe and practice through role plays.

In addition to skill development, other purposes exist for using role plays; for example, attempting to create attitudinal change (asking a manager to play the role of a secretary) or generating a sense of empathy for a person from another culture. In this latter case, objectives are normally met through role reversal (inviting a Thai to play the role of a Canadian, for example).

Although the role play may have other purposes, it is important to emphasize that the major and most appropriate purpose is still skill building. This purpose also has the most face validity. If there is a training program to teach people from one country ways to negotiate effectively with people from another country, then giving those participants a chance to practice after they have learned a theory or model is quite clearly appropriate. And this practice is, basically, a role play. In fact, to avoid practice would mean that the session would not be particularly effective. Participants can intellectualize a lot about international negotiations, but they will only begin to improve when they actually *practice* the skills it takes to be competent.

### Components of a Well-Designed Role Play

We should be referring to the role play as a "role-play session." You should never conduct a role play by itself or conduct one just to do it. It should be done as part of a larger session that has a beginning, some clear training goals, established and well-developed training procedures, and an ending.

A role-play session is based on a goal, normally builds around a specific situation, is well-defined, clearly described, and very familiar to the participant group. There are also two written roles, usually a typed half page or less. In some cases participants may not be familiar with the behavior being modeled in the role play. For instance, in predeparture training for people going to live and work in another culture, many of the participants have had little if any experience with the other culture. The role play becomes practice for a future experience that can be predicted and for which there can be preparation.

In order to be well-written, the role play must

❖ be clear and concise;

❖ be open-ended (that is, not have a predetermined end, in which case it becomes a different training method);

❖ have some element of dynamic tension; and

❖ be interesting to participants, perhaps even use language from their everyday work or social settings.

# Procedure

### Steps to Delivering a Role-Play Session

1. **Share goals and rationale, and ensure understanding.** After sharing the goals and rationale, ask for questions. Try to make sure everyone understands the purpose of the role-play session. This step is especially important for international groups, at least for the first role-play delivery. You must completely clarify the linkage between the purpose of the role play and the reason that the group is engaged in the training. If the purpose is not clear, a certain number of the participants will spend what could be productive time wondering why they are participating in a role play. People may also fail to see the benefit of participating.

2. **Share, review a theory or model; describe a skill or approach.** Sometimes a role-play session is reinforced by an actual model, in person or on videotape. At other times, the model may be a description of a certain skill or approach to an interpersonal situation.

If a model or theory has been discussed earlier in the workshop or session, this step is optional. However, you may still need to review the relevant part on which the role play is based.

3. **Share the background of the situation.** Share the situation, characters (roles), and details of the role play with participants. If the role play is written well, its details should closely match the present or future situation of the participant group. For example, if the session covers management techniques that can be used in multicultural settings, then an appropriate description might be as follows:

> In this situation, there is a manager from one country and a worker from another country. The manager is responsible for giving performance feedback. Keeping in mind the model we discussed for giving cross-cultural performance feedback, we would like to provide the opportunity for one of you to be the manager....

4. **Hand out the protagonist role.** The protagonist role is the one the participants will identify with or be practicing (in the above example, the manager's role is the protagonist). You may need to provide a quick review of the whole situation before beginning. The role should reinforce the goals and allow participants to practice skills. This step is very important, as it allows everyone to get comfortable with the situation, and it shows you are being open with participants, not hiding information or sandbagging.

5. **Give participants time to prepare for the task.** Give individuals or pairs time to prepare for dealing with others in the role play. They will need time to think about how they will actually employ the skills that the course is highlighting, what language they will use, and exactly how they will perform the role play. This is a critical step, since it gives people time to think in a directed way about the task.

> You will now all have time to prepare for this performance-based feedback conference—to decide what you will do and say, how you will say it, and perhaps what you will not say, keeping in mind the cultural characteristics of the other person.

6. **Recruit volunteers to play the roles.** First describe the "other" role, providing clear background information. Ask for volunteers for both roles. Generally, it is easy to get volunteers at this stage because everyone has had time to prepare for the protagonist role, and the other role is usually easy to play. Give the other role player a written description of his or her role (usually a half page or less). As you do this, explain to the rest of the group:

> I am giving some more information to (Nancy) in order for her to be as realistic as possible in the role—and that is what we are aiming for here—realism—since that will give us the best practice.

7. **Outline what the observers must do.** Assigning a clearly defined task to the role-play observers ensures that they remain an integral part of the training activity. Their task should be clear, very specific, and relate to both the goals of the session and to the role play itself. For example, if the session goal is about using techniques for giving feedback in multicultural settings, the observation task might be as follows:

> Please observe the actions you see (the protagonist) taking to provide clear, descriptive feedback to (the "other"). Also, observe the impact the actions have (on the "other").

> Please note that, in this case, the observation task is worded in such a way that the actions observed may be either positive or negative—it does not predetermine an outcome; it lets the observer draw conclusions based on what happens.

8. **Coach the role players.** In addition to a description of the role, provide any further information that the players must have to feel comfortable in carrying out their task. It is especially important to encourage the participant playing the "other" role not to overact, but to be as real in the situation as possible. Generally you do not coach role players in front of the group, since that would make it difficult for the players to concentrate.

9. **Set the scene.** Physically arrange chairs and, if necessary, other props in front of the group so that an environment is created that reflects the spirit of the role-play situation. Remind the overall group which person is playing which role.

10. **Start the role play.**

11. **Stop the role play.** Stop the role play at the appropriate time, which is usually between five and seven minutes after its start. A lot can happen in that time. This is the most intuitive decision you make during the role play. Ask yourself if enough has happened to give the group a basis for a thorough discussion on the subject. It is very important to ask the role-play participants to remain seated where they are during the debriefing period.

12. **Facilitate a debriefing.** Begin the debriefing with either the observers or the role players. I favor beginning with the observers for two reasons. First, the observers have been relatively passive during the actual role play, and this gives them a chance to participate. Second, it gives the role players a chance to catch their breath and reflect on the role play. As you begin the debriefing, it is important to state that you will begin with the observers and then continue with the role players. Debriefing questions for the observers should derive from the task given to them at the beginning of the role play. Typical questions for observers might include the following:

  ❖ what did you see happening?
  ❖ how did X accomplish his/her goals?
  ❖ what did X do?
  ❖ what was the result of X's actions?

It is important for you to keep the discussion descriptive and performance-based in order to reduce defensiveness. It is also important for the trainer to help participants focus on behaviors and observations, and to avoid the "well, what I would have done" comments at this stage. The richness of the role play comes from people really observing carefully what happens and discussing it thoughtfully after the role play ends. You play a key role in making sure that this happens.

13. **Debrief role players.** Once the debriefing of the observers is complete, move to the role players and ask them questions like the following:
   - ❖ what were you trying to accomplish?
   - ❖ what particular skills were you trying to emphasize?
   - ❖ what did you find most difficult to accomplish?
   - ❖ how did it feel to be in that position?

14. **De-role role players.** During Steps 12 and 13 above, you should be referring to the two role players by their fictitious names, and they should remain in their role-play seats in front of the group. To de-role these players, you can say something like the following:

   > Well, I think the discussion is just about finished; is there anything either of you would like to add? [allow for additions from the role players].

   Then, mentioning the role players by their actual names, say something like:

   > Please resume your regular chairs, you are no longer [names in the role play].

   De-roling is very important—it lets people leave the role behind them, and it helps to create a safety net by emphasizing to the group that these people were, in fact, playing roles (it was not really me up there).

15. **Discuss other approaches.** During this stage (which may vary in length depending on time and the goals), remind people that everyone planned an approach to the situation, and ask people to share an approach that was different from the one just observed. This is also a good time to run another edition of the role play, that is, ask if someone else would like to try a different approach.

16. **Help participants draw conclusions and apply their learning.** It is important to ask participants to draw conclusions and apply what they learned to their real-world situations rather than for you to try to do this for them.

Each of the steps in conducting a role play is important. Generally, if a step is omitted, it has consequences similar to the lasting impressions of "Purple Buttermilk." For any participant group, these steps must be transparent. The trainer must be utterly open about almost all information, letting participants know what is happening and not hiding anything. If there is any information about one of the roles that must be limited to one role player to make the situation more realistic, then you need to disclose that fact to the whole group. *(Role player X will get some further information from me in order for the role play to be more realistic—after all, we don't always know everything in a real situation.)* The reason for keeping things transparent is to increase a sense of safety and to reduce even the appearance of trainer manipulation.

## Variations

One very powerful, highly recommended role-play variation involves dividing the whole group into trios and asking each trio to do the role play with two people as actors and the third person as the observer. Do three rounds so everyone gets a chance to try out his or her approach. This form of skill practice should be done after you have completed one or more basic role plays, as described above.

## Relationship to Other Methods

Role plays can also evolve out of cross-cultural case studies or critical incidents. Often, the content of these other training methods also involves human interaction, and participants are asked to devise strategies for dealing with specific situations. At some point, rather than just talking about the situation, conduct a spontaneous role play. This type of role play should only be done with an experienced group that is comfortable with role plays.

The role play is also related to a simulation. In fact, one way to view some simulations is to see them as giant role plays, where everybody is assigned a role of some sort, and where there may be other rules and norms that help to guide and direct behavior.

## Outcomes and Benefits: Why Use Role Plays?

There are many benefits to conducting role plays. Some of the most important include:

❖ participants get a clear sense of identifiable skills in interpersonal situations, how they work, and the impact of things done effectively and ineffectively;

❖ the trainer can exert more control over what is seen as effective and ineffective by the participant group;

❖ participants have an opportunity to feel what it is like to try out new or enhanced skills in real situations;

❖ participants also get a chance to feel what it is like to be in another role; and

❖ role plays represent a training method that, if done correctly, will generate much interest.

In international settings, the role play is especially powerful, since intercultural effectiveness depends so much on interpersonal sensitivity and skills—and the prime training reason for using a role play is to increase both interpersonal sensitivity and skills.

## Summary

The role play is a powerful, experiential-training technique. Its primary use is to build or refine interpersonal skills in work or social situations. All good training is nonmanipulative, and special care has to be taken when conducting role plays to make the steps transparent and reduce any sense of manipulation. There are many steps involved in delivering the role play correctly, and it takes much planning beforehand to complete them effectively.

Role plays delivered correctly work very well for international participant groups. The following steps are particularly important when dealing with multi-cultural groups: you must

1. carefully and clearly spell out the purpose and rationale so that the reason for doing the role play closely matches the reason why the group is attending the training;

2. ensure that the emphasis of the debriefing is descriptive (describes behavior and its impact) and not judgmental ("That was bad work"); and

3. give people a lot of positive feedback for participating.

Of course, these actions—a clear purpose, careful debriefing, and positive feedback—would enhance the performance of any training session regardless of the cultural mix, but they are especially important for multicultural groups.

# Preparing and Conducting the Muni and Abdi Intercultural Role Play

## John Pettit and Graeme Frelick

Rarely do trainers have an opportunity to work with a group that has a diverse range of cultures. Twenty to thirty non-Western participants regularly attend the Training of Trainers (TOT) workshop organized by the Office of International Cooperation and Development of the United States Department of Agriculture (USDA). On the first day we are always struck by the diversity among this group of people: Nigerians wear the brilliant colors of their national dress; Indonesians come in carefully tailored batik shirts; and Ethiopians arrive in shimmering white shamas.

Many who attend the course are instructors, extension workers, directors of training institutes, and managers of government programs in adult education, agriculture, and forestry. They want to develop their training skills and their ability to manage programs in their home organizations. The course uses a participant-centered training approach which actively engages the participants. The trainers and the participants share in the responsibility for learning. As the trainers, we are charged with creating and implementing a thoughtful, systematic training design based on adult learning principles. The design also provides the conditions for a good learning environment. The participants are responsible for contributing to the learning environment through active participation.

Underlying this approach is an experiential-training philosophy. In brief, participants learn the different training methods by actually using training tools such as role plays, case studies, and other techniques. They share their responses to the experience, generalize key learnings, and apply them to course activities and back-home situations. The trainers assist this process and provide appropriate theoretical input. Within this setting, the role play is an important technique for them to know, and it is taught in a way that involves participants in their learning.

# History

In 1981 Wilma Gormley and James McCaffery of Training Resources Group were challenged to develop a culturally suitable role play for just such a diverse group of participants. They had to be concerned about such things as choosing appropriate names for the role-play characters and a context that reflected the working relationships between supervisors and subordinates in the participants' respective countries. The role play also needed to provide a model for the participants, who were expected to write and deliver their own role plays. The model had to be a simple one so that participants would feel encouraged in their first role-play writing experience. The result was the Muni and Abdi role play.

In addition, it was necessary to derive multiple learnings from the activity. Consequently the developers created Abdi and Muni, employees of a government training organization, who address a training problem during the role play, a situation with which all of the course participants could identify. The role play was also designed to strengthen the participants' ability to explain experiential-training methodology to those who do not know it well or have doubts about it. Since experiential-learning philosophy is an underpinning of the TOT, it is important to reinforce this skill. Furthermore, the role play—as an active skill-building learning technique—shows participants how this method improves instruction. Finally, the processing of the role play provides participants with an opportunity to practice giving descriptive feedback, a key communication skill for trainers.

# Procedure

In all the training of trainers workshops that incorporated this role play, two trainers worked as a team. When we refer to "the trainer," it may therefore be one or the other, depending on how they divide the steps between them. The procedure for delivering this role play comprises ten steps:

1. **Describe the purpose.** Explain that the purpose for the role play is to give participants a chance to develop and practice a strategy for encouraging people to use experiential methodology in their training sessions.

2. **Describe the situation.** Even though written roles may be used, explain that Muni is the director of the ministry's Educational Training Center who is encouraging his five trainers to use a more experiential model in their training; he is planning to meet with Abdi, one of these trainers, who is still not using this model. Then explain that Abdi is a popular trainer who finds the methods he has been using to be successful and has concerns about the new approach.

3. **Determine the players.** Either ask for volunteers to play the two roles or select the players, depending on the group, while explaining that each player will receive a background sheet and will have time to prepare for the role.

4. **Brief the players.** One trainer gives about five minutes of preparation time to each player, preferably outside the training room, distributing to each the role description sheet (see page 33) and telling each of them to make up information that may not be covered in the role instructions. Instruct the players to be

firm, not agreeing too rapidly with the other's point of view and to play their roles without overacting or trying to stump the other player.

5. **Assign tasks to observers.** Since there are usually two trainers—while one trainer briefs the players, the other asks the rest of the participants to be observers. Their specific task is to observe Muni's strategy in trying to convince Abdi to use the experiential model.

6. **Arrange the physical setup.** Set up two chairs at the front of the training room at a 45-degree angle, so that the players can see each other, and so the observers can see the players.

7. **Set the stage.** One of the trainers, standing behind the two chairs, explains that the two players are in Muni's office and that Muni is about to meet with Abdi to discuss his training approach. Remind everyone of the real names of the role players.

8. **Begin the role play.** Ask Muni and Abdi to begin. As the role play unfolds, take note of things the players say in order to highlight important points in the discussion with the observers later on.

9. **Stop the role play.** Usually the role play will come to a natural end after five minutes. If it appears that it is going to last longer, intervene and stop the role play. In either case, thank the players and encourage the other participants to applaud while asking the players to stay in their seats. This step is the first one in the de-roling process, during which the players gradually move out of their roles and regain their own identity. This de-roling process is critical so that points of contention that arose during the role play do not create tension between the players after the role play is over. It also allows you to move the attention of participants away from the players by asking people to think of other ways they might have approached the situation.

10. **Process and de-role.** Ask participants a series of questions in a sequence designed to increase their ability to give descriptive feedback, to give players more opportunities to de-role, and to challenge everyone to think of other strategies.

Ask the following questions:

a. the group: what was the strategy of Muni? how did it work?

b. the group: what was the strategy of Abdi? how did it work?

c. Muni: what was your strategy and how did it work?

d. Abdi: what was your strategy and how did it work?

e. the group: what other strategies might Muni have used and what difficulties could one expect to encounter with these other strategies?

Exploring the difficulties that may be encountered is important because it helps participants appreciate that each strategy has potential pitfalls. It also helps the players because it avoids giving the impression that they may have "failed."

Usually you should ask the role players to return to their own seats after Step d. Thank them, using their real names and applauding one last time. Their de-roling should be complete. When they rejoin the group at this point, they can respond to the final question  as a member of the group, not as a former "Muni" or "Abdi."

The reason for having the group describe what they observed before giving the role players the opportunity to speak is to give them time to reflect on the role play as others describe their strategies. They are usually less defensive and more articulate when given this reflection time.

The initial questions force participants to describe each player's strategy in nonevaluative terms. Participants tend to evaluate the players' performances immediately, which can make players feel bad and reduce the quality of the description. Trainers therefore need to insist that participants be descriptive. It not only helps the players feel better, but it provides a basis for questions about alternative approaches. Overall, participants improve their skills at giving descriptive feedback during the discussion period. Previous to this session, it would be helpful to have participants learn and practice the rules for giving and receiving feedback. Then the processing of this role play would provide an opportunity to reinforce their feedback skills.

When all ten steps are completed, the trainers move on to the next activity, or to the next step in their design, which may be to ask questions aimed at drawing generalizations or expanding learnings from the session or at developing ideas for applying what they learned back in their work situations.

## Contexts in Which the Role Play Has Been Used

The Muni and Abdi role play has been used with over 200 participants from twenty-five developing countries in the USDA TOT, which has been conducted by Training Resources Group every summer over a six-week period since 1981. There are fifteen to twenty-three participants in each course, including trainers, training managers, project managers, university professors, researchers, extension workers, nutritionists—all with content expertise in agriculture.

This role play has also been used in ten TOTs conducted in various developing countries for over 140 participants from a variety of backgrounds and professions:

a. family planning workers, including doctors, nurses, and public health agents in Mali, Rwanda, Burkina Faso, and Thailand, between 1986 and 1988.

b. health educators in Malawi in 1985.

c. trainers with backgrounds in urban finance and management, including city managers, budget officers, social workers, legal advisors, and urban management trainers in Côte d'Ivoire and Senegal, in 1987 and 1988.

## Considerations for Use

The problems in preparing and delivering this role play are similar to those encountered in any role play. For example, when the design gives too little or too much detail, the impact of a role play is reduced. Keep some of these other points in mind when using the Muni and Abdi and similar role plays.

## Preparation

When writing role plays, avoid the tendency to write scripts—in our experience, many course designers are so intent on getting their message across, they put too much description into the role play.

A role-play situation with a too obvious solution is not going to be very challenging for people—make sure the participants see the point of contention from different perspectives and thus play out different approaches to the problem.

Use a situation with a clear point of contention—if the players do not see the issue clearly, their rendition of the role may not lead to the learning goal of the session.

One of the key aspects of role play is that the players get to practice a skill and the observers to see a skill demonstrated—it is not effective to use role plays to convey content knowledge about a subject. If the content of the role play is inappropriate or unfamiliar, people will have trouble being natural and comfortable in the roles they are asked to play; in the same vein, observers may have trouble making a clear analysis of or judgment about the results.

Avoid complicated language or situations—clear, concise, easily understandable material will make it easier for the players to remember their parts.

# Conclusion

In closing, it is important to remember some very simple guidelines for using this and other role plays.

## Delivery

Describe the situation. Keep it brief and clear. Our experience in the TOT is that people can err on both sides—saying too little or saying too much. Perhaps the best advice we can offer is to write an introduction that engages the participants but allows them room for discovery and to practice with a colleague who will provide helpful feedback.

Be sure to involve the observers by asking them to look for key points throughout the role play.

Have clear instructions or background information for the players. Allow them enough time to read and understand and, perhaps, briefly practice the roles.

## Processing

Role plays need effective processing. To skip this part or not do it well will very seriously diminish the impact of the role play.

Avoid close-ended questions because they tend to limit discussion.

Stick to the sequence and type of questions outlined earlier. It is a safe and sure way to guarantee that the processing will be effective.

Maintain a sense of "play" when doing role plays. It should be fun to act in them and to discuss what occurred even though the learning is substantial and serious.

# References

Gormley, W., and J. McCaffery. *Guidelines for Processing Role Plays.* Alexandria, VA: Training Resources Group, 1982.

Pfeiffer, J. William, and John E. Jones. "Role Playing." *Annual Handbook for Group Facilitation.* San Diego: University Associates Manual, 1979.

# Demonstration Role Play

The following role descriptions are for use in the demonstration role play. They are good examples of how a role should be written for training sessions. For use in training, they would be on separate sheets of paper.

**Role Description 1**

# Muni

As the director of the ministry's Educational Training Center, you have been encouraging your five trainers to use a more experiential model in their training. Three of the trainers are very excited about the new methods and are using them in their training sessions. The other two are not in disagreement with the new methods, but you have noticed that they still use the lecture method as their only way of instructing.

Because you are anxious for all of your staff to be using the same experiential methods, you have decided to have a meeting with one of the two—Abdi—this morning. You are also concerned since you have already conducted several training sessions with Abdi and the others on how they can use this new approach. But Abdi is still not using it.

**Role Description 2**

# Abdi

You have been a trainer in the ministry's Educational Training Center for several years. Your courses have always been popular, and your performance appraisals have been excellent. During the last several months (after returning from a training course in the U.S.) your director, Muni, has been requesting you to use a more participatory, interactive approach in your courses. He has worked with you and the other trainers on how this can be done. And you have tried. You are open to the new methods, and you have used them, but they simply are not working! First, it is very time-consuming, and you are falling behind in covering the necessary content. Secondly, the students consider the new methods games. They clearly prefer the lecture method.

Muni has asked you to come to his office to discuss how you are doing with this new methodology. You are glad to have this opportunity to tell him your concerns.

# A Role Play to Enhance Cross-Cultural Understanding in the Caribbean Tourist Industry

## Shirley A. Fletcher

Experiential learning is a very effective methodology in training programs designed to assist personnel in the Caribbean tourist industry increase cross-cultural understanding. Since written cross-cultural training materials for the Caribbean are hard to find, it is necessary to develop your own. This role play can serve as a model not only for developing materials for use in the Caribbean but for role plays for other groups.

## History

In 1985, I designed a ten-day program for training tour guides in the Caribbean for the Organization of American States. During the needs assessment, no one indicated that attitudes and behaviors in relation to time created problems in tourist-host interaction. During the training, however, when we discussed differences in cultural characteristics between Americans and Caribbean people, participants had great difficulty understanding that Americans perceive time as precise, linear, and limited.

My response to this problem was to engage in a spontaneous, unstructured role play with a participant in the role of a tour guide who arrived late. I played the role of the American tourist. This really captured their attention. Processing the role play facilitated a shift from treating attitudes toward time as a frivolous issue to one that merited consideration.

As Pierre Casse (1980) notes in *Training for the Cross-Cultural Mind,* "it seems that the best way to make people sensitive about this need of understanding oneself as well as others from a cross-cultural perspective is not to talk about it, but to experience it either through case studies, simulations, or controlled real-life situations" (95).

This role play was further developed as a structured learning experience in March 1989, when it was tested in Washington, D.C., where a group of Caribbean people played the roles of tour guides and taxi drivers. Based on the results of that trial, the role play was modified and used as part of the government-sponsored BAHAMAHOST training program for tour guides and taxi drivers in Nassau in April, 1989. Well received by participants and by the BAHAMAHOST staff, the Ministry of Tourism has asked that the role play be included in their ongoing BAHAMAHOST training package. Entitled "Conflict between the Taxi Driver and the Tourist," it will also be used by the training staff of the Jamaica Tourist Board in Jamaica.

# Description

First, I will present the goals and objectives, then describe the situation, and finally provide a step-by-step procedure for conducting the role play.

## Goals

❖ To increase professionalism among taxi drivers and tour guides and thereby improve the tourism product.

❖ To improve cross-cultural understanding.

## Objectives

❖ To accept that people from different cultures may see the same situation differently.

❖ To identify some assumptions that people from different cultures make about one another in times of conflict.

❖ To identify differences in cultural characteristics between Caribbean people and Americans.

❖ To identify specific steps that may be taken to avoid or minimize cross-cultural conflicts with tourists.

## Background of the Situation

George has been a taxi driver in the tourist industry for two years, and he is a member of the Taxi Association. Roger, the tourist, is a white American on his first visit to the Caribbean.

George picked up Roger at the airport and drove him to his hotel. Because Roger was impressed with George's knowledge of the island and with his courteous service, he asked George to take him on a tour of the island the following day. It was agreed that Roger would pay $80 for the tour and that George would pick him up at his hotel at 10:00 the next morning. Roger paid his fare (from the airport to the hotel), tipped George generously, and said that he was looking forward to the tour.

The next morning Roger was on the steps of his hotel at five minutes to 10:00 waiting for George. When George had not appeared by 10:15, Roger assumed that there had been a misunderstanding. Not wishing to waste a day, he jumped on a tour bus that was leaving the hotel at that moment.

## The Situation at Present

Roger has just returned to his hotel after an enjoyable but tiring day. He is surprised to find George waiting for him. It is obvious from George's facial expression and general demeanor that he is very upset. Roger is somewhat puzzled by this and thinks, "After all, George agreed to provide me with a service and broke our agreement. If anyone should be upset, it should be me!"

Three separate briefing sheets contain the following information.

# Briefing Sheet 1

**Role of George the taxi driver.** George enjoys his job as a taxi driver because it allows him to meet people from all over the world and to share his vast knowledge of the history and geography of his country. A very dignified man, he takes pride in his work and his appearance, and he passionately loves his country.

He is the sole supporter of his wife and six children and of his mother and grandmother. He is very proud of the fact that he has always been able to provide for his family.

Over the past few years the cost of living has been rising steadily, and George has been finding it difficult to make ends meet. It is particularly important to him, therefore, when a tourist requests a day tour, because he can make really good money.

He set out from home in good time to get to the hotel at 10:00 A.M. to pick up Roger, but his car broke down. By the time he had repaired it and arrived at the hotel, it was almost 10:20 A.M. When he asked at the front desk for Roger, the receptionist told him that Roger got tired of waiting and had gone on the tour bus.

George was shocked and extremely angry. He felt that Roger had treated him with contempt.

**Important consideration for this role.** You feel that you have lost a day's income through no fault of your own. You made a contract with Roger and he has broken it. Since the tour did not come off, you will be willing to settle for a reasonable percentage of the agreed-upon $80. You are angry, but in the interests of tourism, you will try to keep your temper under control. However, you will not allow any foreigner to come into your country and take advantage of you! You will speak up in your self-interest, but you will stay calm, dignified, and courteous.

# Briefing Sheet 2

**Role of Roger the tourist.** Roger is an American tourist on his first visit to the Caribbean. He was excited by the TV ads and needed little encouragement to purchase a trip to paradise!  In fact, this is just his second trip outside of the United States. The first time was his tour of duty with the U.S. Army in Germany.

He was feeling somewhat anxious when he arrived, but had been reassured by George's friendliness and his expertise as a driver on incredibly narrow roads. He was also comforted by the fact that George was a fountain of information. By the time he got to his hotel, he had made up his mind that George should be his guide to the island. He looked forward with great pleasure to the rest of his trip.

Roger was really surprised and disappointed the next morning when George did not show up. He prides himself on being punctual and hates to be kept waiting. Nevertheless, since George was his only link to the island, he waited for him for fifteen minutes before giving up and joining a group of his fellow Americans on the tour bus.

**Important considerations for this role.** George broke his contract with you. He had agreed to pick you up at 10:00 and he should have been there at 10:00. Not being an unreasonable fellow, you waited for fifteen minutes. In vain! As far as you are concerned, you owe George nothing. You cannot imagine why George wants to see you. You are tired and anxious to get to your room, but out of courtesy you decide to listen to what George has to say.

# Briefing Sheet 3

**Role of observers.** As an observer, you play a very important role in this training event. We would like you to make note of any aspect of the discussion between Roger and George that concerns or interests you.

We would also like you to pay particular attention to the following: what emotions do you observe in George and Roger at different stages of the role play?

What assumptions did Roger, the tourist, seem to make about George, the taxi driver? What did Roger really think of George?

What assumptions did George seem to make about Roger? What did George really think of Roger?

# Procedure

## Getting Started

❖ Present and clarify the goals and objectives of the training session.

❖ Define the term cross-cultural as one which refers to "interaction, communication, and other processes which involve people or entities from two or more different cultures."

❖ Use a climate-setting exercise that raises some of the basic concepts in intercultural communication and cross-cultural interaction.

## Introducing the Role Play

❖ Ask for two volunteers or select two players and give them their briefing sheets: the role of the taxi driver and the role of the tourist; ask them to leave the room and prepare, separately, to play their roles. Your cotrainer may assist in clarifying these roles. If you are working alone tell them they have approximately ten minutes to prepare, while you rejoin the group in the training room.

❖ Distribute information on the background of the situation and the situation at present to each participant.

❖ Ask questions to ensure that participants are clear about the situation and the characters.

❖ Distribute the briefing sheet for observers and draw their attention to the questions, which will help them to focus on specific aspects of the role play.

❖ Return to the role players outside. Ask questions individually to ensure clarity on the roles to be played; ask each player, separately, to share with you what he/she might say during the role play to explain his/her position on the issue, and clarify further if necessary.

❖ Tell George the taxi driver that he will begin the role play. Ask him what he might say to start, as a means of further clarification.

❖ Return to the training room and ask the taxi driver and the tourist to sit or stand facing the group.

## Conducting the Role Play

❖ Remind the observers of the importance of their role and that the observations they share will be critical to the learning process.

❖ Ask the taxi driver to begin.

❖ Get out of the way and observe/listen carefully as the role play develops.

❖ Intervene by stopping the role play if either player seems stuck/unable to respond or if either is going off track. Explain how they may continue the dialogue or start again from the beginning if this seems appropriate for the learning of the group.

❖ Intervene *only* if absolutely necessary.

❖ End the role play when you feel that enough material has been generated. Try not to be abrupt, but stop action appropriately when the role play has arrived at a natural end point.

## Processing the Role Play

❖ Ask the players for their overall reactions to the role play.

❖ Ask Roger to describe his feelings. (Capture on newsprint.)

❖ Ask George to describe his feelings. (Capture on newsprint.)

❖ Ask the observers to share their perceptions of Roger's and George's feelings—add these emotions to your lists on newsprint.

❖ De-role the players. Use their real names and thank them for playing the roles. Ask them to join the other participants. The processing of the role play continues with the following questions: what assumptions did Roger the tourist make about George? What did Roger really think of George? (Capture responses on newsprint.)

❖ What assumptions did George the taxi driver make about Roger the tourist? What did George really think of Roger?

❖ What are you learning about differences between American tourists and Caribbean people? What are you learning about interactions between American tourists and people who work in the tourist industry? (Capture learnings on newsprint.)

❖ What will you do to avoid situations like this or to minimize conflict if it occurs?

## Closure: Drawing Conclusions

❖ Present a prepared list of cultural differences between Americans and Caribbean people. Be sure to include: (1) desirable pace of life, (2) judging/evaluating others, and (3) definition/value of time.

❖ Point out that Caribbean people make assumptions about tourists based on their own cultural characteristics and values.

❖ Point out that American tourists make assumptions about the behavior of Caribbean people based on their own cultural characteristics and values.

❖ Refer to the exercise used earlier to point out that different cultures may see/interpret the same situation very differently, and it is therefore easy for cross-cultural conflict to occur.

❖ Summarize by pointing out that understanding cultural differences helps bridge the gap between hosts and tourists and facilitates professionalism.

# Cultural Context of This Role Play

The historical background against which tourist-host interaction occurs in the Caribbean is important for understanding the significance of this role play designed to be used in training taxi drivers in the tourist industry in the English-speaking Caribbean.

The majority of workers in the tourist industry in the Caribbean are black. The majority of tourists for whom they provide a variety of services are white and predominantly North American and European. Thus tourism in the Caribbean is a confrontation of cultures as well as a confrontation of race. Given the history of slavery and colonialism in the region, it is not surprising that this confrontation sometimes results in conflict.

Some people believe there are five primary characteristics that influence tourist-host interactions in many regions, including the Caribbean. These are derived from the ideas of Horace Sutton. Trainers can use the characteristics as theoretical input before or after the role play has been processed. The first two characteristics relate to the sense of time: the transitory nature of the personal relationships between tourists and hosts, and an orientation to immediate gratification. Regarding the first characteristic, knowing that personal encounters are not likely to develop into long-term relationships affects interpersonal dynamics. The second characteristic, the orientation of both parties to immediate gratification, also exerts an influence on the character of the interactions. The third characteristic is the asymmetrical quality of the contact. The host clearly has the knowledge of the culture and skills to get around in it that the tourist lacks. On the other hand, the tourist has money and status that the tour guide does not have. In this situation, power tends to flow toward the host or tour guide. Money and status, which ordinarily would give the tourists power, do not balance their dependency on the tour guide. They must place themselves in the tour guide's hands, thus giving power to someone else. Fourth, the novelty and lack of familiarity for visitors creates an ephemeral or transitory situation in which they may not behave as they would in their home culture. Finally, in any host-tourist interaction there will be a cultural distance separating both parties. Any one or a combination of these factors can lead to or fuel conflict.

When conflicts occur in tourist-host interaction, behaviors that are culturally appropriate for both parties may easily be misinterpreted by either party. The Caribbean host may perceive disrespect or contempt based on racial prejudice or superior social status, while the tourist may perceive dishonesty or lack of professionalism based on stereotypical views of people in the region.

Additional theoretical input may include "two patterns of behavior," inspired by C. Argyris and developed by J. Ingalls (1976). If you use this, try to help participants understand that Pattern B is more effective in managing cross-cultural interactions.

# Two Patterns of Behavior

### Pattern A

1. Cognitive consistency: always trying to make sense out of everything (order, structure, logic).
2. Judging: making comparisons, evaluations, passing value judgments.
3. Attributing: giving motives to others as reasons for their behavior.

### Pattern B

1. Openness and tolerance toward ambiguity: openness to experience, flexibility, capability to adjust to various situations.
2. Descriptive: describing rather than judging.
3. Asking: enhancing the capacity to check out assumptions by asking people directly why they did what they did.

## Considerations for Use

In order to facilitate this role play effectively, you need to pay attention to the following factors:

**Knowledge of the culture and history of the participants and the culture with which they are interacting.** This is necessary to clarify the objectives and to interpret and build on the data generated in the processing. Such knowledge will also be important in helping participants identify their learning and figuring out how to minimize cross-cultural conflicts.

**Use of the climate setter.** Do not be tempted to skip this, because it not only establishes the tone and atmosphere needed for this training, but it legitimizes different perspectives. Without this preparation, participants tend to gloss over or deny their real feelings and attitudes toward time and, instead, will say what they perceive you, the trainer, want to hear: that the tourist was right and the driver was wrong.

**Briefing the players.** It is critical that the actors and the observers understand their roles. Briefing sheets or handouts are helpful, but in addition you need to take the time to ensure clarity before the role play begins.

**Brief the training staff.** This is a difficult role play for one trainer to manage. Ideally, briefing the actors and the observers should take place simultaneously or participants are likely to become restive or bored. The momentum and stimulation provided by the climate setter need to be maintained. Additionally, a great deal of data will need to be captured on the newsprint during the processing of the role play. For these reasons two trainers are recommended for effective facilitation.

**Be current.** For example, cost and length of tours must reflect what is currently available in the destination where the training is done or the participants will not see the situation described in the role play as credible.

**Gender.** If one of the actors in the role play is female, this adds another layer of complexity to the training. You will need to pay attention to the impact of gender relationships in the culture of the participants and treat the issue of gender appropriately in processing the role play.

**Time.** Allow a minimum of two hours to conduct this role play. For that time period the maximum group size should be fifteen.

**Assumptions about the simplicity of the topic being explored.** It is necessary to stay alert to the complex issues that may be triggered by conflict related to punctuality. These may include, for example, stereotypes of the host held by the tourist and perception of prejudice and racist behavior on the part of the tourist by the host.

# References

Casse, Pierre. *Training for the Cross-Cultural Mind.* Washington, DC: SIETAR, 1980.

Ingalls, J. *Human Energy.* Reading, MA: Addison-Wesley, 1976.

Pusch, Margaret D., ed. *Multicultural Education: A Cross-Cultural Training Approach.* Yarmouth, ME: Intercultural Press, 1979.

# Resources

There are few published training materials that have been designed for use in the Caribbean. As a trainer working in the region, I design my own materials based on the needs of the client, the participants, and the nature of the particular situation in which I am working. Over the years I have developed and/or used the following materials:

*Cultural Patrimony and the Tourism Product: Towards a Mutually Beneficial Relationship* (Final Report). Organization of American States/Caribbean Tourism Research Centre Regional Seminar, 1983.

Fletcher, Shirley A. *Enhancing the Positive Socio-Cultural Impact of Tourism: Public Attitudes and Awareness Programme,* vol. 2. Organization of American States, 1984.

———. *Reference Manual for the Design, Organization and Implementation of a Tour Guide Training Seminar.* Organization of American States, 1986.

Parris, D. Elliott. *Enhancing the Positive Socio-Cultural Impact of Tourism in the Caribbean,* vol. 1. Organization of American States, 1984.

# Contrast-Culture Training

## Edward C. Stewart

Since the early days of 1965, when the contrast-culture model was developed and then implemented as a method, the notion of culture and a cultural perspective has gained widespread acceptance. However, even today businesspeople only reluctantly accept that culture influences business methods and outcomes, preferring instead to fall back on the belief that everybody has the same basic needs and will respond similarly in a given situation. The contrast-culture method accepts cultural differences. Indeed it celebrates them and uses them to train individuals to interact effectively with people from diverse cultures.

## History

Between 1962 and 1966, I participated in a research project in the field of cross-cultural communication, developed and carried out by the Human Resources Research Office (HumRRO) of George Washington University.[1] The objective of the research was to develop a strategy for training Americans to live and work in foreign countries.

In the first phase of the project, we collected empirical information on the performance of American military personnel sent to Laos in the 1950s. Their mission was to provide community, medical, and communication services and to give military advice in a country torn by strife. The White Star teams, as they were called, were military because it was considered too dangerous to send civilians or volunteers into a country divided by insurgency.

---

[1] The project divides into three convenient phases. The first phase was the research on the experience of army personnel in Laos. Research was conducted by Alfred J. Kraemer, Edward C. Stewart, and Frank Osanka. The second phase was the development of the contrast-culture approach. Research staff was Edward C. Stewart and Jack Danielian. Special notice should be taken of the contribution of Cajetan DeMello and of Turgut Akter, the two actors. John Pryle was the able assistant. Martin Sternin, as staff, and Sheldon Smith, as assistant, participated in the work. Arthur Niehoff, anthropologist, provided supporting critique throughout this second phase. The third phase consisted of preparation of the final draft of the report with Robert J. Foster assisting with editing.

Two major conclusions of the field study eventually led to the formulation of the contrast-culture concept: (1) the White Stars made judgments about and attributed intentions to Laotians that were incorrect because the White Stars' perceptions and inferences were based on American cultural assumptions and (2) the interpersonal dimensions of cross-cultural communication, which are significant, had been neglected in training.

In devising a training strategy, we examined existing training resources—area studies, briefings, orientations to daily life, and university courses on international relations—without finding any programs which prepared Americans for the cultural and interpersonal dynamics of life and work in another society. Inspired by the needs brought to light in the White Star experience, the social scientists involved in the project launched a program of continuing research. They reviewed the literature, cooperated with anthropologists, and conducted extensive interviews with people who had lived and worked outside the United States. Although the White Stars were military, the nature of their activity permitted us to generalize from their experience and apply that learning to the training of Americans in other sectors such as development, business, and education. The critical factors were that the Americans lived and worked inside a foreign society, their activities involved interpersonal cooperation, and their decisions affected the members of the host society. Studying the White Stars convinced us that it was necessary to assess any American success or failure within the context of both American and Laotian cultures. Finally, we concluded that the critical issue in cross-cultural performance was *intercultural interpersonal interaction,* and these three "eyes" became a metaphor for the training content. We had to look at it through the three eyes, starting with an analysis of American culture.

## The Training Model

### The First "Eye"—Intercultural Dimensions

Since we planned to design the training for Americans, we adopted a dominant, middle-class, white variation of American culture as the most representative for the kind of trainees with whom we expected to be working. I came to speak of it as "reference culture," believing that the model constructed could be developed as an appropriate training method for people in any culture.[2] If trainees were non-Americans, the same procedures could be used with the exception that the culture of the trainees would replace American culture as the reference. For example, if trainees were from Japan, Japanese would be the reference culture. One's own culture, and thus a reference culture, is understood from the inside out as procedures for how to get things done. Experience of it tends to be

---

[2]I have adopted the convention of using *model* to refer to the conceptual organization of cultural elements, cultural interactions, and contrast culture. When a model is taken off the shelf and adapted for application, such as using interview techniques to bring out the meaning of contrast culture, I refer to it as *method.* The words "strategy," "procedure," and "technique" are used to introduce variety. I do not imply technical meanings.

unconscious and typically conveys the feeling that it is natural and normal, while that of other cultures is strange, exotic, or unnatural. Understanding cultures from the inside out, in the form of recipes, is known as *emic* knowledge.

In contrast to reference culture, perception of the other culture is more conscious. We tend to see members of other cultures behaving according to patterns and principles which impose regularity and conformity. This kind of knowledge from the outside has been called *etic* knowledge. Understanding the other culture is particularly difficult because the unconscious aspects of reference culture influence how we perceive members of other cultures. The silent assumptions of reference culture are central to the perception of others in what is known as *ethnocentrism:* perception of others through the eyes (that is, the "I") of one's own culture. Specific views and perceptions are distorted into *stereotypes* which defend the integrity and serve the needs of reference culture. The dynamic relation between the reference and the other culture is the key issue in cross-cultural training.

The challenge for the trainer is how to separate reference from other cultures so that the trainee can gain an objective view of how his or her own culture contributes to or inhibits performance in the other culture. But training for reference culture can be awkward. In the case of American culture, it is not always easy for the trainer to start out by telling trainees that they are now going to get some training on American culture so they can do well when they reach Japan, Brazil, Egypt, or Germany—or wherever the destination may be. American individualism does not mix well with the notion that a shared system of values and patterns of thinking (known as culture) directly influences how individual people act. Although there is more acceptance now than there was in 1966 that culture influences behavior, it is still a sticky proposition to convince John Smith that he acts the way he does because he is American.

## Dimensional Analysis of Culture

An effort was made to develop universal dimensions which can be used to describe all cultures. Variations within American culture, or any culture for that matter, would occupy a certain range on these broad dimensions. The pattern for each culture would be different, but at the same time there would be considerable overlap.

**Values.** The content of culture was categorized under four value dimensions: form of activity, form of social relations, perception of the world, and perception of the self. As an example of a value dimension, one can think of identity of the self as individualism (American), or as a role identity (Indian), or in some social form of a group (Japanese). In regard to this value, American culture is at the individualism extreme.

**Patterns of thinking.** The relations among values and other elements of thought—perception, language, emotion—can be summarized as patterns of thinking. One major difference among cultures is movement from abstract to concrete thought (deduction) and the opposite movement from concrete to abstract (induction). For example, the French pattern tends to be abstract and deductive, while American thinking is closer to induction. But Chinese correlational logic is even more concrete than American thinking. We can place American culture somewhere in the middle of this dimension from patterns of thinking. Patterns of thinking (style) and values (content) provide the substance of culture and comprise what we now call deep culture.

**Contrast culture.** We often lack information about others, but we can always learn about our trainees—in this case Americans—and their reference culture. Taking advantage of this fact, we adopted the strategy of developing the other culture based on a contrast to reference culture.

We examined each of the universal dimensions (such as deduction/induction) used to analyze American reference culture and determined the end positions that defined the dimensions. Next we located American culture in the most appropriate position on a continuum for each dimension. We then labeled the positions which differed the most from American reference culture, "contrast culture."

In many cases, American culture is at the extreme end of the dimension. For example, Americans are perhaps more individualistic and more action prone than members of any other well-known culture. Along other dimensions or continua, however, Americans are somewhere in the middle. The Germans, for example, are cognitively more theoretical than Americans, but the Japanese are much less so. American culture's position in a network of cultural differences turns out to be complex. In order to describe more precisely the relations between Americans and other cultures, we decided to develop two contrast cultures which were loosely labeled "concrete" and "abstract." Concrete thinking stresses perceptual forms, while abstract thought relies more on linguistic and conceptual symbols. Japanese and German vocabulary provide a convenient example.

The Japanese use the word *nezumi-iro* to refer to gray. *Nezumi* means "mouse" and *iro* is "color." The Japanese word "mouse-color" retains a perceptual root, while the German *Grau* conveys an abstract meaning of color detached from any shade of perception. This single example could be multiplied indefinitely to show that Japanese expressions of thinking rely significantly on the use of metaphors, images, proverbs, and folk stories. In comparison, German expressions of thinking stress abstract concepts and logical construction based on the grammar and lexicon of the German language. Even though the differences are a matter of degree, they serve to identify the extreme patterns of concrete and of abstract contrast cultures.

Since the researchers wanted trainees to actually experience cultural differences, the construction of the two contrast cultures made it possible to avoid discussing culture in the abstract. The rules for constructing contrast cultures specify that only contrast-cultural differences having empirical roots in some well-known culture should be used and, second, that the criterion for selecting the differences will always be the trainees' reference culture. Keeping in mind that our research was based on a specific reference culture, we called contrast cultures, "contrast-American cultures."

## The Second "Eye": Interpersonal Method

Interpersonal behavior is, in essence, communication, giving rise in the context of cross-cultural training to a focus on intercultural communication. Remember, we have established that reference culture affects the perception and judgments of sojourners in their intercultural communication. This presents a technical challenge in training: how to bring out the assumptions of reference culture so that trainees consciously grasp them and can be trained to perceive both their own and the other culture objectively, progressing beyond ethnocentrism and stereotypes.

**The problem.** The problem with reference culture, and it is probably universal in varying degrees, is that assumptions, ethnocentrism, and stereotypes lie outside awareness. On the other hand, one consciously encounters another culture, which means that the other culture can be treated directly in training.

American reference culture has a quality which is not universal. Typically, Americans tend to see similarities in the other culture, while both Japanese and French, for example, are more attuned to differences. Consequently, Americans may overlook small cultural differences, dismissing them as personal idiosyncrasies, mistakes, or variations of the same basic pattern as their own. The reason that Americans ignore or pass over slight differences seems to derive from their belief that human nature is rooted in basic needs which impose cultural uniformity on everyone, but, perhaps, with individual variation. The predisposition toward similarity implies that a good training strategy for American reference culture should emphasize and even exaggerate differences.

## Training Response: Role Playing

The distortion of perception and judgment inflicted by reference culture persuaded us to use a training model which is both interpersonal and interactional. We selected role playing for the American. The choice of method raised two theoretical issues which deserve brief mention.

Thus far, I have restricted the discussion of culture to values and patterns of thinking, but this view is too narrow. In reality, human behavior is governed not only by cognitive factors but also by relations to others and by social and material circumstances of the environment. These additional influences on behavior were summarized as *roles* and *events*, and the two became central operational concepts in developing the experiential part of training programs.

In conducting training exercises, we asked trainees to play the role of "Smith." They were given a scenario which presented a cross-cultural event. The role defined Smith's task and purpose while the event specified the situation in which the interaction would take place. The scenario contextualized role and situation, serving to guide Smith's interaction during role playing.

Trainees develop cultural awareness and understanding of their own culture only when the role playing provides a comparison with another culture. The next problem in training was how to represent the other culture.

## Training Solution: Simulation

Implementing the contrast culture was carried out by a trained actor, who was called Mr. Khan. In a training session, Mr. Khan received the same scene given to Mr. Smith. (The Army trainees were always male.) Rather than role-play himself, Mr. Khan had been trained to represent contrast culture. For this reason, his part in the exercise was called simulation in distinction to the role playing of Mr. Smith, who played himself.

The training of Mr. Khan to simulate contrast culture passed through two stages. First, Mr. Khan repeatedly simulated the contrast culture using scenes written specifically for purposes of training. American subjects role-played American reference culture and Mr. Khan learned to govern his behavior by the actions of Mr. Smith. Whatever Smith said or did, Khan responded with the contrast. Elaborate rules were written using the previously described dimensional analysis of American culture to guide Mr. Khan in selecting the correct contrast response to the stimulus of Mr. Smith's actions.

This approach inevitably led to an oppositional stance on the part of Mr. Khan, which was not the intention of the training. The purpose was and still is to promote a keenly sensitive social interface between Khan and Smith, so that all of Smith's actions release a calculated contrast response in Khan. This calculated response is the training dynamic which exposes and elucidates the reference culture by contrast.

Once the principle of responsiveness was firmly established in Khan's repertoire, his training moved into the second stage, in which his behavior attained its own integrity as it developed along the lines of contrast culture. For example, if Smith learned to act in a contrast manner, Khan would not contrast this new behavior by shifting his response to American reference culture; Khan continued to respond and retain the integrity of the contrast American.

## The Third "Eye": Interaction

To succeed in training for interpersonal interaction, the exercises should be realistic and engage the wholehearted interest of the trainees. In the early days of our research, we were uncertain about meeting the criterion of realism in the simulation of contrast culture but our doubts turned out to be unjustified; the method has been well received and Mr. Khan has left an enduring impression. I believe that there are at least four reasons for this success.

First, an analysis of contrast cultures revealed that no single well-known culture existed which provided the perfect contrast to American reference culture, but several cultures came close. The actor who played Mr. Khan-concrete was selected from an Asian culture in the Far East, while the actor who played Mr. Khan-abstract came from a Middle Eastern culture. *In both cases, the actors' original cultures approximated their respective contrast cultures,* which undoubtedly contributed to the success the two actors enjoyed in playing the contrast roles.

Second, once the two Mr. Khans were selected, they were carefully trained in specific role-playing scenes to display contrast culture even if their natural cultural dispositions were different from what the part required. During the process of training, the core of their own cultures was extended to support the range of behavior and emotional expression required in the simulation.

Third, we decided to work only with actors. There were several reasons for this decision, the most important one being that the role of Mr. Khan required a person who held his emotions and perceptions under control. The role also demanded a person who could take an impression or a feeling and express it convincingly in words, gestures, or acts, conveying its meaning to others. This quality that we needed in Mr. Khan is the skill of the gifted actor. Paradoxically, working with actors in the beginning introduced obstacles, since actors are accustomed to scripts. In training situations, requests for scripts always received the same answer: "Your life is your script."

Fourth, the material used to compose the scenes (based on occurrences in the field), was realistic. In playing the role of Mr. Smith, experienced trainees sometimes relived explicit past experiences. Mr. Smith often was given the role of advisor and, at times, the role of subordinate to Mr. Khan. In some business scenes, Mr. Smith became the supervisor from the home office who traveled to Mr. Khan's place of business to review and resolve business problems. With these scenes, both Smith and Khan assumed familiar roles, which gave direction and substance to the interaction.

## The Training Method

In the early days of implementing the contrast-culture method, the trainers consistently observed the intractability of most Americans to accept culture as an important influence on behavior. The difficulty experienced by the trainees in perceiving contrast-culture dynamics led to the development of special procedures in staging the training sessions.

Since the behavior of Mr. Khan is carefully programmed in the simulation, it is possible to identify the dynamic of Khan's behavior and to describe accurately the motives driving it. At times, it has been a stunning experience to hear Mr. Smith evoke elaborate American assumptions, values, and procedures to explain contrast behavior.

The opening part of the training session was an introduction to the topic of culture. The content and style of the presentation have varied tremendously from trainer to trainer and over time but the objective remains the same: to convey to the audience the practical reality of culture as an unconscious influence on their behavior in the practical patterns of daily life. Unless this idea is assimilated and put to work in the training exercises the sessions may be interesting, exotic, and even educational, but, for most trainees, experiential learning does not occur.

We took two steps after the introduction to help this assimilation occur. The first was always to use Mr. Khan-concrete to begin the exercises, since he was lower key, softer in manner, and less abrasive than Mr. Khan-abstract. The purpose of this sequence was to ease the trainees into the cultural climate of the simulation. The researchers believed that trainees would find it easier to establish empathy with Mr. Khan-concrete than with Mr. Khan-abstract.

In the second exercise, Mr Khan-abstract worked with a different Mr. Smith so that both contrast cultures and two variations of American reference culture were presented to the trainees at the outset. The sequence of two exercises, using two Mr. Khans and two Mr. Smiths, effectively conveyed the idea of cultural variations and neutralized the possibility that trainees would develop narrow-gauge stereotypes of members of either the contrast culture or the American culture.

The second step taken to create experiential learning, and by far the more important one, was to develop debriefing and interviewing techniques. At the end of each exercise, Mr. Khan was asked to leave the room while the trainer interviewed Mr. Smith. All trainers were encouraged to participate in the debriefing with questions and comments. The purpose of the interview was to permit Mr. Smith to report his feelings and impressions of the event and to identify his own American cultural pattern and, second, to comment on his understanding of Mr. Khan's culture. After finishing with Smith, the trainer brought in Mr. Khan for his interview. The trainees, as with Smith, were encouraged to ask questions in the pursuit of a deepening understanding of Mr. Khan's culture. In addition, in speaking with Mr. Khan, the trainees were motivated to sharpen their skills in how to collect cultural information from a contrast American.

The results we obtained with the interviewing techniques were outstanding. American trainees in the role of Mr. Smith came out of their role easily and commented on their performance as Mr. Smith. When Mr. Khan's turn for interviewing arrived, the American trainees assumed that he had been playing a role and that he would explain it. But Mr. Khan remained Mr. Khan; he neither discarded the role nor abandoned the customs of contrast culture. He continued to speak from the inside, refusing to get outside himself to explain how he had acted during the simulation. The frequent silence in the group, the jolt of surprise, and the emotional tone in the air indicated experiential learning was occurring. After my years of experience with this method, I believe that the interviewing and the participation by all trainees in the debriefing is the most important segment of the entire procedure.

## Potential Problem

The use of the two contrast Americans in the same exercises ended early. The last time that both Mr. Khans were on the same program, at the Business Council for International Understanding (BCIU) in Washington, D.C., may have been 1974. Using only one contrast American allows trainees to view the world in the dichotomy of "we," of reference culture, versus "they" of contrast culture. This dichotomy is the cognitive base for stereotypes and ethnocentrism; therefore, training based on such a polarity runs the risk of more firmly establishing existing stereotypes, while increasing their level of sophistication. At least three points of reference are necessary for the trainee to develop a relativistic point of view.

Trainers can use various procedures to help trainees develop realistic views of culture and, simultaneously, abandon stereotypes:

❖ Use behavior elicited in the training exercises, from both Smith and Khan, as the basis for interpreting reference and contrast cultures. This is far more instructive than presenting academic interpretations of culture.

❖ Explore the variations of cultural behavior displayed by different Smiths, emphasizing that this is evidence that culture is the organization rather than an imposition of uniformity.

❖ Process each scene to demonstrate the true cultural sources of individual behavior. Each scene used in the training exercise presents a specific event, a purpose, and a role for participants which contextualizes behavior, eliciting different variations of values and patterns of thinking from a cultural repertoire available in any culture.

❖ Ask trainees to play the part of Mr. Khan to gain an intuitive understanding of their own flexibility of behavior. Acceptance of variations in the behavior of individuals, including that of the trainee, as well as contrasting the behavior of individual members of the group, neutralizes the effect of cultural stereotypes.

## Contexts and Applications

The major target for contrast-culture training is reference culture, one of the cultures involved in any cross-cultural interaction. In addition, trainees learn a frame of reference for a second culture which approximates but does not specify another culture. This design was satisfactory for many programs in the 1960s. For example, a government agency and a leading corporation in the United States each wished to develop an in-house pool of managers who were aware of the important cultural issues that arise in international operations. No one culture was designated as the object of interest. In both situations, the contrast-culture concept as we have described it served as the appropriate training method.

Beginning in the 1970s and increasing in the 1980s, the demand for training that prepared Americans to go to a specific country grew. In these instances the contrast-culture concept was used in conjunction with role playing by natives of the host country. Two examples describe this kind of design.

In the first case, three groups of businessmen were trained to go to Iran in a training program that began on Sunday evening and ended on Friday afternoon. The experiential-learning portion of the program was designed around the contrast-culture concept. From Monday morning through Thursday, the trainees were asked to participate in role-playing exercises. The scenes for the first two role plays were with Mr. Khan-concrete, to develop awareness of American culture and provide a contrast that approximated the trainees' destination. These were followed by role plays that involved trainees with Iranian role players in situations similar to those that would be encountered during the assignment in Iran.

Another example of a culture-specific training design focused on a specific subject, such as "public relations." In a typical one-day program, two or three countries are designated for training, for example, Japan and France. In one case, scenes were written to represent the technical problems of public relations in each country. The training program began with Mr. Khan-concrete and then continued with a Japanese and then a French national as role players following the pattern discussed above, focusing specifically on the cultural implications in the subject area. For these kinds of programs, it is necessary to train nationals of the selected countries for the roles they are expected to play within the professional area they must represent.

These applications demonstrate some of the range for the contrast-culture model. The scenes present details of Mr. Smith's mission in-country, which convinces the trainees that they are dealing with practical issues. With Mr. Khan, they gain intercultural awareness of their own culture and that of the other, which then they can refine into skills for application in specific cultures.

## Benefits and Outcomes from Using This Method

The critical dynamic of the contrast-culture method of training is the simulation in which trainees are confronted with their own cultural assumptions and strategies during interactions. The experience probes reference-culture values and cultivates understanding of cultural interaction with members of other cultures. Trainees gain subjective insight into how their own culture is perceived by others and how its assumptions and strategies contribute to or detract from cross-cultural interaction. Trainees learn to distinguish between sensitivity toward and cultural understanding of the other culture. Finally, trainees have the opportunity to improve cultural performance with members of the other culture by cultivating cross-cultural skills when they practice interacting with culture-specific role players.

## Conclusion

I believe that culture is an organization of diversity and not of uniformity. Cultural diversity can be an impediment to communication and an obstruction to cooperation, or it can be a path toward greater creativity. The training method, contrast-culture American, accepts cultural differences as human resources and urges every Mr. Smith and Mr. Khan to use them judiciously for the benefit of all of us.

In the applications of the theory and method since 1967, the basic idea of culture, contrast culture, and even of training is sometimes realized and sometimes not. I am not sure that the implications of contrast culture and the method are well understood. Whenever I hear trainers speak of sensitivity, cultural adaptation, and even of behavioral change, I quake at the thought that American ideology is on the march, promoting cultural uniformity and stereotypes rather than an exploration of cultural differences and their implications for improving cross-cultural performance. The feeling of uneasiness is a premonition of the changing of the guard: the ethic of sensitivity replacing the ethic of good works.

# Resources

Kraemer, Alfred J., and Edward C. Stewart. *Cross-Cultural Problems of U.S. Army Personnel in Laos and Their Implications for Area Training.* (Research memorandum). Alexandria, VA: HumRRO (1964).

Stewart, Edward C. "The Simulation of Cultural Differences." *Journal of Communication* 16, no. 4 (1966).

Stewart, Edward C., and Milton J. Bennett. rev. ed. *American Cultural Patterns: A Cross-Cultural Perspective.* Yarmouth, ME: Intercultural Press, 1991.

Stewart, Edward C., Jack Danielian, and Robert J. Foster. "Simulating Intercultural Communication Through Role-Playing." (Technical Report 69-7). Alexandria, VA: HumRRO (May 1969).

# Acting the Culture Contrast

## Cajetan DeMello

I n the first *Intercultural Sourcebook*, this chapter appeared under the title "Acting the Contrast-American," which was indeed an appropriate title to describe the training we were doing more than two decades ago, since the training was for American military advisors being assigned overseas. This training method continues to be referred to as the contrast-American technique, but the broader and more appropriate title is "contrast culture." The base or reference culture in which the training occurs could be anywhere in the world. The contrast-American character is a specific example of the contrast-culture role. Much of the material that appeared in the earlier *Sourcebook* is included here to preserve the exceptionally creative ideas of the originators of this method. I have added developments in acting the culture contrast that evolved in the ensuing years due to the realities of the user marketplace. I also discuss differences between acting the contrast American and the culture contrast.

## History

The Human Resources Research Office (HumRRO) needed an actor to create a role in a role-playing situation for a research project in cross-cultural communication. The role was that of a foreign national, a counterpart of the U.S. Military Advisor stationed abroad. There was to be no written script. The role playing was to be spontaneous and unrehearsed, and the character consistent and realistic enough to be believable. I accepted these challenges. An actor ought to be willing to explore new vistas of artistic endeavors (DeMello 1975).

My participation as an actor involved working principally with research scientist Dr. Edward C. Stewart, who created the concept of the contrast American—a foreign counterpart of the U.S. national abroad. Dr. Stewart was responsible for planning and developing the research program; Dr. Jack Danielian, research associate, developed role-playing situations (scenes) and testing instruments to assess the training implications of the simulation. When Dr. Stewart left HumRRO in 1967, Dr. Alfred J. Kraemer took over the research and brought it to a conclusion. The phase of the research discussed here took place under Dr. Stewart's direction.

The role-playing technique consisted of simulating an encounter between an American and his or her counterpart, the contrast American. The HumRRO researchers defined simulation as a sociopsychological representation of a natural phenomenon in which time is condensed and in which cultural parameters (such as motivation, individualism, and competition) may be simplified or abstracted but their relationship remains unmodified. The simulation was used for instruction and training to enhance cultural self-awareness and cross-cultural communication.

## The Actor's Challenge

In order to understand and embody the character of the foreign counterpart and subsequently to role-play culture-based simulated encounters, I employed the Stanislavski (1963) method of acting using his psycho-technique system to assimilate and role-play the culture-contrast character. It would be good to keep in mind that as I refer to contrast American, it could be contrast Japanese, or contrast German, or any culture in which the training is taking place. However, in my case, in the beginning it was always contrast American.

For an actor to role-play the contrast American was a real challenge, since there was no dramatic character already created. The contrast American is an abstract character, a creature of the research scientist, created as a theoretical abstraction to provide a cultural contrast, serving as a mirror image, if you will, to reflect American values in a cross-cultural encounter. The contrast American, derived from various cultures, does not exist as a total being anywhere as such, but only in parts here and there.

An actor needs a concrete definition of the character to role-play the contrast American effectively. Being merely speculative is not at all helpful. It is valuable to understand the theoretical concept of contrast American, but an actor also needs specific ideas and images of the state of being and the nature of the character. An actor will have particular difficulty if only given the instruction to engage in a controlled dialogue which will elicit responses pregnant with American assumptions, values, and behaviors. The actor can and does make up things as the conversation progresses, but must have some kind of framework in which to function.

The contrast-American character shares many of the cultural traits associated with traditional societies. If any cultures comes close to that of contrast American, it is the culture of the people of India. There are also patterns of behavior and characteristics which can be identified as belonging to the cultures of Latin American and African nations. In addition, contrast-American behavior could be seen to depict traits belonging to the cultures of the Arab and the Asian worlds. Cognitive characteristics are also portrayed. Cognition is used here very broadly to refer to the processes of perceiving, recognizing, conceiving, judging, and reasoning (Kraemer 1973). Nonetheless, in every situation the contrast American exemplified social and cultural mannerisms, values, assumptions, ideas, beliefs, and modes of thought quite different and, in many cases, opposite from those of the American. The contrast American is an evolving character, "becoming" as the role is played. Given few fundamental descriptors of family, social position, profession, and so forth, the actual character takes on form and shape in each and every role-playing situation.

The actor portraying the contrast American, Mr. Khan, is deliberately constrained by being required to perform in accordance with the nature of the research. During the HumRRO project, I was directed and trained by the researchers to bring out culture-worthy materials of maximum value for educational and training purposes. In fact, as an actor, I had to refrain from my own attitudes and views except when they coincided with the contrast-American's way of life.

It is important to bear in mind that the cultural norms and mores of the contrast American are not arbitrarily contrived. The contrast-American style is valid. The politics, the economics, the religious beliefs, the value system, and other traditions attributed to the contrast American are based on authoritative research and authenticated by fieldwork. Not all of these activities, whether manifest or subtle, come into play in every role-playing situation, nor should every opportunity be seized by an actor to present an opposite view. Much depends upon the talent of the actor-role player, who is expected to engage in a realistic dialogue and establish spontaneous rapport with the subject role player. Nevertheless, the cultural contrasts are there.

The actor must concentrate on various things in addition to the creative process. Since we are dealing with role playing in a simulated situation and not playing a dramatis persona in a theatrical production with a script, the scenes were written with the objectives for training ingrained in them. For example, one scene explores the notion of publicity. The trainee is told that he or she has determined that publicity should do much to neutralize suspicions and swing public opinion behind the community development programs. The creative objective for this scene requires the actor to lead the trainee in a conversation by drawing forth ideas about the desire and need for publicity. Thus, the creative objectives are the same as the research-based training objectives.

Very early during the period of preparation, it became clear to me that to be most effective as a role player, I would, to the extent possible, have to experience things in life consciously as a contrast American. I should be so thoroughly steeped in the character that it should be possible for me to step in and out of the role at will. Therefore, for a substantial part of the day, I began to live as a contrast-American character—mentally, psychologically, and experientially, in order to become knowledgeable about the American way of life by contrast. From daily conversation with my American friends, colleagues, and other people, I familiarized myself with the style of their language. A scene in a movie, a passage in a novel, television programs and commercials, newspaper advertisements and other items, articles in magazines, all would fire a spark of learning, great imaginings, and create a reservoir of knowledge for me. And I would long to be engaged in a genuine conversation with my Captain Smith friend (the trainee role player), feeling supremely confident to deal with whatever the occasion demanded. In this manner the contrast American saw the world with my eyes, felt it with my senses, perceived and became aware of it the way I wished myself to be as a role player for the role.

By the end of one year of preparation and numerous role-playing simulations, the contrast American and I had merged into one being—assimilated one into the other. The degree of assimilation was so intimate that my own person and my character could not be distinguished. Though distinct and separate personalities, we were comfortably and desirably entrapped within one human form.

> Bring yourself to the point of taking hold of a new role concretely,
> as if it were your own life. When you sense that real kinship to
> your part,...your newly created being will become soul of your
> soul, flesh of your flesh (Stanislavski 1963).

There was one fundamental reservation in ascribing my own activities and observations to the contrast American. While it was of utmost importance for me as an actor to have a knowledge of the American's predispositions, perceptions, and sensitivities, it would have been inappropriate for the contrast-American character to have such a highly informed and enlightened awareness. I had to draw a line where the actor-person would cease to be and the actor-role player would begin to exist. In the early stages of role playing, the drawing of this thin line posed a dilemma. However, with much practice the dilemma was overcome. This was done mainly by listing related concepts which may appear in the conversation and by predicting American behavior to the extent possible in the given situation. Yet, I must confess that whenever the dilemma persisted, it was to the detriment of effective role-playing performance.

Every role-playing exercise is a unique experience because the trainee is new. The actor encourages the trainee to expose his or her social and cultural characteristics in keeping with the research perspective. Training in cross-cultural communication takes place through self-realization. A similar kind of self-awareness occurs in the observer-participants because of empathy, which leads them to a vicarious experience. The manipulation is not done at the sacrifice of the validity of the role or the role-playing situation. Though the actor's performance is deliberately structured, it is incumbent on him to be natural, with an unforced manner and very real deliberation.

## Changes over Time

### Evolution of the Character

Following the days of HumRRO's research, the persona of the contrast-American character underwent change. A new persona has emerged which is more dramatic and loquacious than the previous one. While the character remains the same in form and nature, the presentation by Mr. Khan (as the contrast-American character is generally known) in simulated cultural encounters is different from the HumRRO-era presentation. The difference is a behavioral or performance change. One might say the change resulted in a depiction of a culture-contrast character rather than a contrast-American character not so much by design as to meet the demands of the workplace.

## Interpretive versus Manifest Culture Contrast

The change in Mr. Khan was brought about for several reasons, and I must say that change is for the better, at least for me. I can now use my versatility to express culture contrast without the prohibitions and restrictive structures of the HumRRO design. The HumRRO version was conceived to highlight the American value system more than non-American culture dispositions. A culture communication specialist interpreted Khan's culture, values, and beliefs with little opportunity for participants to become directly involved with Mr. Khan. I call the HumRRO version the interpretive contrast-American presentation or interpretive culture-contrast presentation.

Market trends appeared to indicate a desire for training programs in cross-cultural communication which would generate and promote more direct involvement between participants and Mr. Khan. This required a shift of emphasis on my part to perform the contrast-American role differently. I call this the manifest culture-contrast presentation. But this presentation cannot take place unless Mr. Khan enjoys the freedom to engage in a spirited conversation directly with the participants without depending on the interpretation of the trainer. The trainer's role in the manifest culture-contrast presentation is to validate and reinforce the ethos and the ethics of variant cultures in a general way. This is considered by some a violation of the contrast-American character, and HumRRO loyalists are aghast, perhaps with justification, at Mr. Kahn's explanation of his people's cultural values, customs, and traditions during the debriefing period.

The preceding discussion leads us to define the two kinds of role-playing presentations—interpretive culture-contrast and the manifest culture-contrast presentations. The interpretive culture-contrast presentation is subtle, less emotional, more abstract and general than concrete, with the implied or suggestive remarks requiring an astute interpretation by a cross-cultural communication professional. One could say that this style constitutes an objective/deductive approach. Expertise, experience, research, and scholarship are essential, since trainers play a major role and bear the burden of responsibility to interpret impeccably the mosaic of a culture-laden, role-playing interaction. In this instance an actor ought to adhere strictly to the HumRRO model, the contrast-American Mr. Khan.

The manifest culture-contrast presentation is defined as being very apparent and expressive, an interplay of abstract and concrete. This presentation depicts cultural characteristics that are clearly perceived and well understood without the assistance of the interpreter. One could say that this style represents a subjective/inductive approach. There needs to be an interdependency between the intercultural communication expert and the actor to highlight factors that control and affect the communication process and attendant successes and failures. Together, theirs is the force that can provide the intellectual knowledge (that is, theoretical and conceptual framework and undercurrents of assumptions, values, thought patterns, and so forth) as well as pragmatic learnings (that is, skill development) in correctly perceiving and interpreting the ongoing human interaction. The sociocultural expert and the actor are mutually inclusive in the training process, sharing equally their contribution to and responsibility for participants' growth in cultural awareness and enlightenment.

At times, I have moved even farther from the original HumRRO model. When teamwork between the two colleagues—the expert and the actor—was not possible, the simulation of a cross-cultural encounter took place with the help of the program administrator/coordinator/facilitator (not necessarily a communication expert). The underpinnings of an abstract foreign culture vis-à-vis American or Western cultures were extrapolated, not so much through scholarly analysis as through being simply based on human experiences and a general understanding of life itself. In this case, in a few small organizations, the guru made way for the practitioner.

Sometimes, because of restrictive schedules, the intercultural specialists who moderate the role-play exercises simply do not have sufficient time to analyze and discern the salient points of culture conflicts, delve deeply for explanations, or discuss misperceptions or misinterpretations. Hence the entire Khan exercise, that is, what takes place in a simulated cultural encounter between two role players, would be useless for the true depictions of each other's values, beliefs, traditions, and the like were it not clearly evident and understood. I suggest that in such situations one should resort to a manifest culture-contrast presentation, because the actor can at least demonstrate pitfalls and weaknesses as well as make known those areas of common interest to both parties.

Sometimes budget limitations cause an institution to use only one facilitator or presenter in the cross-cultural component of his or her training program. A call comes to me to present a culture-contrast experience through role playing for their trainees. Always the program design consists of an in-house trainer or an invited resource person for cultural sensitivity—a requisite for understanding value systems of both sides which precedes Khan's culture-contrast performance. In this situation manifest culture contrast is most appropriate.

## Training Design Trends

From the mid-sixties through the decade of the seventies my role playing entailed exclusively the HumRRO model of the contrast-American abstract culture presentation in cross-cultural communication workshops. With great pride I can say that the HumRRO model is still very valid even today, and it is ideally suited for cultural sensitivity training for those groups whose participants are assigned to work in different countries—not all going to the same country. In fact, with such a diverse group of participants, the abstract culture of Mr. Khan is the most effective instrument that exists today to bring about cultural awareness and consciousness of communication barriers, impediments, and obstacles, as well as commonly shared values and features that build cultural bridges. The HumRRO model is also very well suited in those training programs designed to generate a general and abstract cultural consciousness among participants in the early part of the program and, thereafter, to bring in role plays specific to a given society.

In the decade of the eighties, institutions have started to incorporate a new component in the intercultural communication workshops. They require trainers to write scenarios that display work-related, culture-specific issues pertinent to the country or region to which participants are going. (This derives from my experience with the Business Council for International Understanding (BCIU), American University, Washington, D.C., and a few other organizations.) This is especially true for American business personnel sent abroad to work either in joint ventures or wholly-owned subsidiaries or affiliates in a foreign country. Whenever the contrast-culture method was used for any group of trainees going to the same country, I brought cultural specificity to the training without identifying that country and its socioeconomic or cultural traits.

An actor such as myself can successfully manage to create the necessary company-oriented, work-related cultural realities. An actor can also portray aspects of that particular country experience that are specific to a company's tasks, problems, and procedures and are useful and applicable in the corporation's work within a foreign environment. An American businessperson, I was told, would rather tackle work-related problems with Mr. Khan than listen to theoretical, abstract discourse. This is clearly more difficult (perhaps impossible) when the cross-cultural communication specialist and the actor both are unfamiliar with the specific culture for which participants are being trained.

Usually, these program designs start with a cultural overview including a discussion of American cultural patterns, which sets the stage for Mr. Khan's abstract-culture role playing. These are followed by specific role-playing scenarios, sometimes performed by an actor role player who knows the foreign culture well, but also on occasion by myself. Despite some risks and potential pitfalls, these scenarios can be very successful when they emphasize aspects of human relations, public affairs, behavior and attitudes, management style, employment and hiring practices, efficiency and productivity, and other socioeconomic cultural traits.

## Role-Playing Dynamics

Anyone interested in making an avocation, if not a career, of role playing the culture contrast will require a good deal of discipline, training, and a certain amount of preparation before every role-playing session. Preparation means studying the scenarios for the relevant issues that may ensue in the simulation and visualizing a lesson plan for offering culture contrast in a gentle flow of conversation.

To be believable and credible you have to gain knowledge and develop an organic bond with the world of culture-contrast life. Before entering the simulation, to create a viable character, it is vital to free yourself from the trappings of your preparation and homework and from pressures and tensions. Let the inner energy and the force of mental and physical preparation (studying and rehearsing, trial role plays, analyzing them, and so on) freely flow through yourself—the creative instrument—unencumbered by the restrictions and controls which ought to serve as guides, not barriers, to performance.

Being foreign-born I have a quality of voice and speech pattern distinct from that of an American. As a result I sound different quite naturally. It makes me stand out among the Americans. As an actor, you would be well advised to develop a voice pattern and style of delivery that are markedly different from other Americans. In any case, if the trainee is pragmatic and to the point, Mr. Khan is more philosophic and meanders away, if only briefly, into a wonderland of lofty ideals and soaring grandeur.

While the actor becomes experienced as a role player and well acquainted with the scenarios, remember that the trainee is not. Whether or not one volunteers for the simulated encounter, there is a great deal of pressure upon the trainee to do well in front of peers and colleagues. It is incumbent upon the actor to make the trainee comfortable and at ease with words of welcome and greetings in the initial scenario. To break the tension of strangeness and initial awkwardness, inquire about the trainee's personal health and well-being and about his or her family. A general question such as "How have you been treated since arriving in this country?" can be effective in creating the right mood. Set up a comfortable pace and rhythm and create a congenial atmosphere that will promote confidence and self-assurance.

**Dealing with difficult people.** On the other hand, if the trainee treats the simulation as a frivolous activity and begins to play to the gallery—with asides or funny remarks, comical gestures, and the like, you must maintain your unruffled composure and bring the trainee back to the business of serious role playing. And this must be done in a manner that ensures your counterpart does not feel offended but quickly realizes the seriousness of this process for gathering training knowledge.

There will be times when a trainee breaks the role-playing interaction by calling a time-out for either some clarification from the trainer or to make an observation concerning the trainee's role or performance. This is a serious breach of the tradition of dramatization of the simulated encounter. When that happens, a thespian ethic dictates that you remain in character. Then, being in that state, try to bring the errant trainee to the simulated reality of the cross-cultural interplay. By making a discreet but pertinent comment which will counter the trainee's impertinence, you will avoid intervention by a trainer and the would-be distracting disruption. However, if a breakdown does occur, you must ignore it as if it had not happened and resume the ongoing conversation.

During the time of debriefing (processing of the simulation) you may find one or two participants in a group who will confront your presentation negatively and will try to hassle you to acquiesce in a noncontrast-American (or Western) point of view. Failing that, some may go even farther and question the authenticity of the contrast-American role's credibility and discount ensuing learning. With such people, you may have to use a kid-glove approach—flexible, compassionate, and tolerant but still holding firmly to the contrast beliefs and values.

When the simulation is over, reflect upon the content of the dialogue and be ready to discuss with the participants (when summoned for debriefing) whatever culture conflicts, contrasts, and value differences occurred in the simulation. As a general rule, be prepared for the unexpected. Stay in character in answering a question and maintain the role always.

**Levels of consciousness.** As the role-playing simulation progresses, many activities—tangible and otherwise, mental and physical—simultaneously occur. You need to be alert and attentive to opportunities in the conversation ripe for offering a culture contrast. From studying the scenario you already have an idea of the principal points or issues that are predicted to happen in the two-person interaction.

While being actively engaged in a give-and-take conversation you have to be conscious of various interrelated activities taking place at the mental or intellectual level. You have to discern what kind of idea or concept your American counterpart is enunciating and try to determine the rationale of the trainee for suggesting a particular idea.

At the same time, you have to conceive what kind of appropriate culture contrast you can present. You must be cognizant of the kind of language to use: a proverb, a wise saying, a metaphor, a lesson-oriented story told by a grandfather. You can create a culture contrast at any appropriate time during the course of conversation in a realistic, natural way at all levels of interaction. In the beginning, it is very difficult to grasp this subconscious phenomenon. But with practice, training, and experience it becomes almost second nature, so much so that selecting a response and timing its presentation are almost automatic.

At the physical level, watch for nonverbal signals like gestures, grimaces, facial expressions, sitting posture, physical movement (such as the shifting of body weight, delays, silences, and pauses), all of which reflect the state of inner being which may or may not correlate with what is expressed in words. At times, it may very well be that the nonverbal behavior gives a different message than that being communicated by speech.

## Considerations

There are times when the cross-cultural encounter becomes charged with heightened emotion. A lot of tension is created by frustrations vented through criticism. The role player may demean the integrity of the Mr. Khan character. In one instance I was derisively told "...it was *just plain stupid* that deadlines were not met one way or the other." Luckily, I did not respond in kind, thus avoiding an embarrassing situation. I simply said, "The torrential rain had flooded the roads, hence equipment and building materials did not arrive in time for the installation." Hurt feelings and wounded pride, if given expression, would detract from the business of educating and training. Allowances must be made for the trainee role players because they are in a hot seat in the presence of their colleagues.

Preserving the integrity of the trainees is of paramount importance. Sometimes they take a hard line to show they are in control, on top of the situation. Sometimes they are very patronizing and condescending. When they make a faux pas, it is important to smooth out the misstatement or the inadvertent mistake. For example, one role player was so enamored of Mr. Khan's sense of communion with nature that he seriously said, "He loves to watch the sunrise the whole day *long*." The class broke out in deafening laughter because sunrises last but for a short while. Mr. Khan quickly came to the trainee's rescue by responding, "Yes, the beauty of the rising sun is so overwhelming that it feels one is beholding the sunrise the *whole day long*."

# References

DeMello, Cajetan. "A Cultural Experience: And the Art of Acting as a Technique for Simulating Cross-Cultural Interaction Through Role-Playing in Communication." Unpublished master's thesis. Catholic University of America, 1975.

Kraemer, Alfred J. *A Cultural Self-Awareness Approach to Improving Intercultural Communication Skill.* Paper presented at the meeting of the International Studies Association, New York, March 1973.

Stanislavski, C. *An Actor's Handbook.* Translated by Elizabeth Hapgood, ed. New York: Theatre Arts Book, 1963.

# Facilitating the Contrast-Culture Method

## Paul R. Kimmel

When you use this training tool as part of and throughout a larger program, you have a valuable skill-building as well as a self-awareness exercise. To make a major impact on trainees' behavior, you need enough training time, good trainees, an experienced actor, and considerable facilitation skills. This chapter contains many suggestions and hints for successfully facilitating the contrast-culture method.

## History and Background

The contrast-culture training exercise was a key part of a training project commissioned by the U.S. Army to improve the interpersonal communication skills of its overseas military advisors. This training project was developed and carried out by the Human Resources Research Office (HumRRO) of George Washington University. The exercise (or simulation, as it was called) was first documented in HumRRO Technical Report 69-7, "Simulating Intercultural Communication through Role-Playing" (May 1969) by Edward C. Stewart, Jack Danielian, and Robert J. Foster. This report contains the theoretical background of the exercise plus the only recorded attempt to assess empirically its training impact. Much of this report appeared in the first edition of this sourcebook (Hoopes and Ventura 1979) under the same title. An alternative approach to the live role play using videos of staged conversations was later developed at HumRRO by Alfred J. Kraemer (see Technical Reports 73-17 and 74-13, July 1973 and June 1974, respectively, plus Kraemer's article in the earlier edition of this book).

The contrast-American exercise, or the Khan exercise as it came to be known (after the name originally given to one of the contrast Americans), has been used over the last twenty years by the Army; the Navy; the Peace Corps; the U.S. Information Agency; a number of religious, health, and educational institutions; the Foreign Service Institute; and, most extensively, by the Business Council for

International Understanding (BCIU) at American University. The exercise has been used primarily in programs to train Americans leaving for overseas assignments. All but two of these programs have been conducted in the United States.

## Context

While the original training exercise was designed to include six role-playing scenarios and took place over several days, it has since been used in a variety of other ways. Outside the military training programs, the typical approach has been to use the exercise as one part of an overseas departure program for American professionals, with the number of scenarios (usually one to three) adapted to the time available and the number of trainees. It is possible to adapt this exercise to other contexts. The 1969 Training Report suggested that it could be used at the beginning of a training program to open the trainee to future learning or at a much later stage for integrating knowledge and serving as a "testing ground." It might also be used as part of a selection program for overseas personnel or presented as a demonstration for marketing purposes.

In its original form, the exercise used two different contrast Americans who represented two similar but partially distinct contrast cultures. The great majority of the programs have used Mr. Cajetan DeMello as the contrast American (see previous article). I have been facilitating this exercise since 1966, principally at BCIU. To the best of my knowledge, no handbook for trainers exists for this exercise except for some general guidelines that appear in the section of TR 69-7 included in the first edition of this sourcebook (see Hoopes and Ventura 1979, 58-61).

Therefore, I will discuss facilitating the role-playing version of the contrast-culture method with which I am most familiar: as part of a training program for Americans preparing to go abroad to work and live. I have facilitated the Khan exercise as an experiential component of that part of the training program that deals with cultural relativity and intercultural communication. In the BCIU programs, this segment, titled "Adjusting to the Thought Patterns of Other Cultures and Workshop in Intercultural Communication," is usually at the beginning of the training.

I have used this exercise with as few as one trainee and as many as forty, the typical program having two to six trainees. Almost all of the trainees have been North Americans with a heavy preponderance of Anglo-Saxon couples. This demographic profile is not surprising, since the exercise is designed to examine the cultural assumptions and values of such trainees (middle-class American adults) and to draw attention to potential problems they will have in intercultural communication. The exercise has occasionally been used at BCIU with American adolescents (usually children of the couples) and with some Western Europeans. These trainees require different scenarios and some modifications in the behavior of Mr. Khan.

The facilitation process is similar for all types of trainees, however, since the issues of cultural relativity and adaptation are culture-general and the facilitation is adapted to the level(s) of intercultural awareness of the trainees. While there is no arbitrary limitation on the demographics of those who can be trained with the Khan exercise (except for the very young), I have found it easier to facilitate an exercise in which most of the trainees are at roughly the same stage of intercultural awareness (see Bennett 1986).

# Procedures

## Preparation

It has been my experience that the trainees benefit most from the exercise after we have discussed culture, cultural differences and their origins, and intercultural communication. In addition to providing a context for the exercise and its debriefing, this discussion also provides insights into the trainees' needs and experience. On those few occasions when I have used the Khan exercise with only a brief introduction, I have experienced more trainee resistance to taking part in the role play and more denials of its relevance and validity for their work and lives. Stewart, Danielian, and Foster (1969) had similar experiences with trainee reactions to the exercise. They wrote, "In general, the reactions were more positive when the audience had had prior instruction in the intercultural aspects of overseas work" (43).

In the discussion, I try to ascertain how much academic and direct experience the trainees have had with cultural differences and intercultural communication. Most of the trainees I worked with were going on their first overseas assignment and had only introductory courses in the social sciences. With such trainees, I begin the discussion with an explication of culture and its importance for human behavior. Most North Americans respond well to examples and anecdotes, so I provide stories about the impact of cultural differences. I encourage them to contribute their own stories and to question mine. One very important concept, especially for those who have not given a great deal of thought to these issues, is the idea that culture is learned. It is not difficult for most trainees to grasp this concept, which provides the needed groundwork for the more complicated idea of cultural relativity.

When I feel that the trainees understand what we mean by culture and acculturation, I illustrate the process by discussing the socialization of the individual in the United States, comparing this socialization with that in some other countries. Again, I have found anecdotes and examples to be very helpful in this discussion. The key concept here is that we all learn about our cultures in a similar way and that the content of our cultures is to a large extent arbitrary. This discussion helps the trainees understand how individual cultural differences originate. Often the trainees will want to know more about other cultures at this point. If they are in a BCIU training program, I let them know that later on they will be getting this information about the culture(s) they will be going to.

The comparative discussion of acculturation provides the trainees with the concept of cultural relativity. A further discussion of cultural change provides an historical context for different acculturation processes. For trainees with the least experience and knowledge of cultural differences, I usually end the introductory discussion at this point. For such trainees, an understanding of cultural differences and of their implications for individual behavior is a lot of learning for one session. For these trainees, the function of the Khan exercise that follows this discussion is to reinforce and make more tangible the idea of cultural differences, with an emphasis on the relativity of some of their own (American) values and assumptions. As Stewart, Danielian, and Foster (1969) put it, "The primary intention of such an approach would be to increase his awareness of the possible limitations of his own cultural frame of reference and of the possibility of alternative ways of perceiving a situation" (44). In terms of Bennett's (1986) stages of intercultural sensitivity, the goal of this part of the training program is to move these trainees beyond the denigration phase of defensiveness against cultural differences.

For trainees with more intercultural experience and knowledge of cultural differences, it is desirable to go further in the introductory discussion so that the Khan exercise can be used to analyze some of their own and Mr. Khan's values and assumptions and improve their skills in intercultural communication. I have found a model of intercultural information processing that Edmund Glenn and I developed to be very helpful for this analysis (see Kohls 1977, 1987). This model is based on Glenn's theories of cultural development (1981) and focuses on different ways of perceiving, knowing, and evaluating. Using this model, I summarize and integrate the discussions of individual and social development and then introduce intercultural communication in face-to-face situations.

**METHOD OF EVALUATING**

**UNIVERSAL**
Absolute
Axiomatic
Cognitive
Deductive

**METHOD OF UNDERSTANDING**

| **ASSOCIATIVE** | **ABSTRACTIVE** |
|---|---|
| Passive | Active |
| Global | Focused |
| Personal | Impersonal |
| Subjective | Objective |

**CASE PARTICULAR**
Relative
Pragmatic
Observational
Inductive

Two problems sometimes arise in using this model. One is the natural tendency of many trainees to try to classify countries, groups, or individuals on the two dimensions. To combat this tendency, I point out, using illustrations from their own country (the United States) to make the point, that people are too complex to fit permanently into such classifications. I also introduce the concept of stereotyping and some of its negative consequences. The key point here is that the model is only useful for the analysis of given intercultural communication *situations* and that the analysis of any intercultural exchange must start afresh with any change in situation (for example, a different issue, context, individual, group, or country).

The second problem that sometimes arises is that trainees feel that individuals, groups, or cultures categorized as more complex are in some way superior to those categorized as less complex. This bias comes from the Western value assumption that being economically or technologically more developed is "better." To combat this proclivity, I point out that to be more complex may entail more problems. I also ask trainees who are especially concerned with the issue of superiority if they think that an adult is better than an infant. The key point here is that differences in location on the dimensions of the model are just that, differences, and not judgments about better and worse.

When the trainees understand the model and its application, we discuss its potential for analyzing and improving their communication in difficult intercultural situations. I begin this discussion by giving examples of successful and unsuccessful interactions that involve cultural differences and analyze these in terms of the model. The trainees find these examples very interesting and become quite involved in using the model to look for those elements that contributed to the communicators' successes and failures. After the trainees have some familiarity with using the model as an analytic tool, I provide a detailed example of an intercultural communication situation that illustrates vividly many of the points made throughout the discussion. This illustration provides a dramatic summary of the discussion and sets the stage for the Khan exercise.

Some of the key points that are made by this illustration are:

❖ intercultural communication depends on context;

❖ language proficiency alone does not guarantee successful intercultural communication;

❖ nonverbal approaches can help when language is the problem, but are less successful when cultural differences are the problem;

❖ assumptions of stupidity or bad motivation on the part of the other are seldom accurate and never helpful;

❖ when a breakdown in intercultural communication is severe, it is usually necessary to leave the situation, physically or psychologically, in order to analyze it in a calmer context;

❖ assistance may be needed to locate the cultural differences involved in the breakdown and/or to work out ways to change one's message to take account of these differences;

❖ it is helpful to try out a new or revised message before returning to the problematic communication situation;

❖ success in an intercultural communication usually does not go beyond that situation, that is, communication alone does not produce major or lasting social/cultural change;

❖ there may be unexpected and possibly undesired side effects (such as loss of status or face) related to even the most successful intercultural communications.

## Conducting the Role Play

I always take a 15-minute break before beginning the Khan exercise during which we can relax and discuss in individual conversations anything that has not been clarified in the group interaction. The break signals a change in training approach from the cognitive to the more experiential. (I mention that we will be using these two different approaches at the beginning of the training segment.) When the trainees return, I ask for questions and go over anything of interest to all the trainees from any individual discussions (during the break). When all concerns have been covered, I pass out the first scenario for the Khan exercise.

The content of the scenario depends, of course, on the background of the trainees. The programs in which I have worked have developed a variety of scenarios to meet the needs of the trainees and their training programs. I have not been involved in the conceptualization of these scenarios, but in some cases have commented on them as they were being developed. The scenes should be realistic, not overly long or complicated, and culture-general. An overly complex or artificial scenario (or script) is likely to distract the trainees from the focus of the exercise on the cultural values and assumptions of the role players, and particularly on those of the American role player. If the role players have to concentrate on a number of unfamiliar issues and/or situations, they are not as likely to be themselves in the role play as they are when the issues and situations are simple and familiar. Since role playing, especially with an audience of peers, is unfamiliar and uncomfortable to many trainees, it is not wise to contribute further to their concerns by using an unrealistic or complicated script.

To further enhance the reality of the role play, I tell the role-play participants to play themselves during the exercise. They are to keep their own identities and not try to create a "character" (other than adopting the name of Mr. or Ms. Smith). The less the role players see the exercise as acting and the more they believe it is real life, the better the chances for learning. As Stewart, Danielian, and Foster (1969) noted, "It is only through the commitment demanded by a 'realistic task-oriented problem' situation that many trainees will confront and re-evaluate long-held assumptions and values about the nature of people and of the world" (28).

I prefer the scenarios to be culture-general (without the identification of a nationality or locale for Mr. Khan) to increase the focus of the trainees on the values and assumptions of the American. When Mr. Khan is given a specific cultural identity, the trainees tend to focus on their experiences with and feelings about that cultural group. Not only does this lead to stereotyping and, in some cases, denial of the validity of Mr. Khan's behavior in the role play, but it also shifts the focus of the trainees to Mr. Khan and the specific culture he is representing. Since Mr. Khan has been trained to represent an artificial culture that contrasts with the American value system and its underlying assumptions (see Stewart, Danielian, and Foster 1969 and the earlier edition of this sourcebook), it is unlikely that he will represent many of the values and assumptions of a specific "real" culture. Therefore, when Mr. Khan is given a specific cultural identity (as he has been in some training programs), I must spend more debriefing time dealing with the trainees' stereotypes about that culture. To the extent that you wish to work with stereotypes, this type of facilitation may have some value. I believe there are better ways to deal with such training issues, however, and find they distract from the Khan exercise emphasis on the cultural assumptions and values of the American role player and their implications for intercultural communication.

After the scenarios have been read, a volunteer is needed to play Mr. or Ms. Smith. Sometimes I have been instructed by the director of the training program to select a certain trainee for a certain scenario. I do this as offhandedly as possible so as not to raise questions about this selection process. More often, I ask for a volunteer and point out the training benefits of experiencing direct communication with Mr. Khan. I sometimes have a trainee in mind for the first role play (usually because I suspect he or she will be more at ease than the other trainees), and when I do, will ask if he or she would volunteer if my open invitation fails to produce Mr./Ms. Smiths. Of course, if I get a volunteer, I take that individual, and if someone I ask to take a role is firm in refusing, I respect that wish. Fortunately, very few of the trainees whom I have worked with have refused to take part in the role play after they have participated in the preparatory discussion. (As mentioned, there are more refusals when this discussion is brief.)

During the role play, my main occupation is taking relatively complete notes of the conversation between Mr./Ms. Smith and Mr. Khan. On rare occasions, an audience member will interrupt the role play (in spite of my instructions to be invisible) or a Mr./Ms. Smith will get out of the scene by asking (usually me) a question about what is going on. If possible, I let Mr. Khan handle these disruptions in character to preserve the integrity of the scene. When it is clear that this will not be possible, I deal directly with the question or interruption as briefly as possible. Of course, the involvement of the role players and the audience in the scenes depends primarily on the believability of Mr. Khan. The lack of disruptions over the twenty-five years I have been working with him attests to the superior abilities of Mr. DeMello.

The length of each role play is partially determined by the time available in the program and partially by the dynamics of the scene itself. Some role plays reach a natural conclusion within 10 to 15 minutes of their initiation. Others get bogged down or become repetitious in about the same amount of time; and so, in the role of a subordinate of Mr. Khan, I break in with a phone call and begin the debriefing after Mr. Khan leaves. In the great majority of cases, however, neither a natural conclusion nor bogging down occurs in the first 20 minutes, and I must decide how much new information about the values and assumptions of the role players will be generated by letting the role play continue. If there is enough time (which relates directly to the number of trainees), I tend to let the role plays continue up to 35 or 40 minutes if new information seems likely. If there are other trainees who would benefit from the experience of being Mr./Ms. Smith, or if the role play runs out of steam (no new information), I break in before this time. Seldom does a role play generate interest and information beyond 45 minutes.

More often the problem is not that scenes go too long, however, but that not enough time is available to do as many role plays as you or the program director would like. I have often been asked to squeeze in one more scenario than I think I can facilitate in the time available. Rather than dilute the value of all of the role plays by shortening them to allow for one more or giving a very brief experience to that one extra trainee who cannot properly be debriefed, I turn down such requests. It is important to allow enough time for each role play to be properly run and debriefed. Better to do two good role plays for three (or more) trainees, than three mediocre ones.

## Debriefing the Role Play

While the amount of time needed for the role play seems relatively stable (15 to 40 minutes), the amount of time needed for the debriefing varies a great deal. I have done adequate debriefings of role plays that ended naturally after 10 minutes. I have also debriefed particularly rich role plays for over an hour. Other trainers who use the Khan exercise at the very beginning of their sessions may devote over two hours to the debriefing and elaboration of one or two role plays. Also, if the role play is audio- or videotaped, as it sometimes was by HumRRO, additional debriefing time is needed for the playback of the recording. Since I do not record the role play and since my introductory discussion covers points that otherwise would need elaboration in the debriefing, I seldom find it necessary to debrief an exercise for more than an hour.

I usually begin debriefings by discussing the exercise with the people who play Mr./Ms. Smith. I focus this interview on their feelings about their own performance, especially in light of what they hoped or expected to do, and on their perceptions of Mr. Khan. To the extent that I can elicit comments about their motivations and perceptions and those they attribute to Mr. Khan, as well as their explanations of and reactions to what took place in the role play, it is easier to get at their values and assumptions. Most role players are verbal and articulate and have little trouble in providing this kind of information. Occasionally, I do some prompting based on my notes to help the role player recall parts of the exercise. Also, if there are other trainees, they can be helpful in recalling parts of the role play. (Some care must be taken, however, in involving audience members—especially spouses and colleagues—at this point, as they may get into evaluations of the role-player's performance that detract from his or her willingness to give more complete information.)

When the role player has provided enough information to discuss the main values and assumptions that have been exhibited, I ask the audience if they have any comments or questions that have not been covered. Getting them involved in the discussion not only brings up material that might otherwise be overlooked but, more importantly, usually provides additional information on American values and assumptions that may not have been exhibited in the exercise. I note the relevant comments of the role player and the audience on the same sheets on which I have recorded the conversation. Whenever possible, I group these comments under the American values and assumptions that they illustrate. During my note-taking on the role play, I also highlight specific comments in the conversation that illustrate American values and assumptions. To make this easier, I record Mr./Ms. Smith's comments and Mr. Khan's comments in separate columns on the page.

Since some scenarios are used frequently in the BCIU training program, patterns of comments from the role players and audiences begin to emerge in the debriefings. I have saved my notes from over five hundred role plays in hopes of doing a content analysis of these materials. Also, some American values and assumptions, such as social control through persuasion, reliance on self, status through achievement, individual responsibility, time as a quantifiable limited resource, frankness, task-centered judgments, loose role definitions, and a rational world, come up again and again. The comments that illustrate these values and assumptions are very similar. To guard against the possibility of thinking that a given comment means the same thing for a current trainee that it has for past trainees, I try to ascertain the reasons or motivations underlying even the most common comments during the debriefing.

If time permits and the circumstances are right, I sometimes bring Mr. Khan back into the debriefing. This can be especially helpful if the trainees are having trouble seeing the cultural differences between themselves and Mr. Khan. Stewart, Danielien, and Foster (1969) suggest that the most effective way to use Mr. Khan in the debriefing is to have him stay in character (32). Thus, playing the role of a friend and colleague, I interview him in his office. The focus of this interview is on his perceptions of Mr./Ms. Smith and their motivations and behaviors, as well as on his own motivations and reactions to the conversation. Although in some cases this requires more introspection than Mr. Khan should be able to provide, the contrasts between his views of the exercise and those of the trainees usually highlight the cultural differences and their influence for even the least experienced of them.

When the cultural differences have been appreciated and described by the trainees, I synthesize the preparatory discussion (with or without the Glenn/Kimmel model) and the role-play exercise. This is done in two different ways. First, I go over the American values and assumptions that were illustrated by the exercise and tie them in to the socialization processes discussed in the first part of the training segment. This integration can be done rather briefly and without much discussion. Second, I suggest some of the behaviors of Mr./Ms. Smith that facilitated or inhibited the conversation with Mr. Khan. Whenever possible, I relate these behaviors to the examples of effective and problematic intercultural communication that I used earlier.

If I have previously discussed the Glenn/Kimmel model, I ask the trainees to identify different styles of perception, cognition, and evaluation used by Mr. Khan and Mr./Ms. Smith. In addition to labeling these styles, we go over the clues from the conversation and debriefing that enabled them to make the identifications. For the more experienced trainees, this practice in using the Glenn/Kimmel model to analyze an intercultural interaction can be very valuable. The BCIU program director has said that many of the trainees he has visited overseas remember and find useful both the Khan exercise and the Glenn/Kimmel model.

## Conclusion

I am hopeful that some day a more formal assessment will be made of the impact of the Khan exercise on improving intercultural communication. Without such an assessment, using comparison groups and a longitudinal evaluation design, it is difficult to know in what ways to further develop this training tool. Such an assessment will require more funding and commitment from program planners than is currently available. Currently, the only feedback comes from trainee satisfaction forms filled out at the end of the training programs and the impressions of BCIU staff members when discussing the program with former participants on informal overseas visits.

It is my belief that this training tool has the most impact on the trainees' behavior when it is part of a larger program and if it is used throughout that program. Then it becomes a skill-building as well as a self-awareness exercise. To use it to develop skills requires small groups of trainees who are relatively homogeneous in levels of intercultural awareness. As I mentioned, the problems I have had using this exercise are usually attributable to a lack of time to introduce and debrief it properly and/or to differences in the levels of intercultural knowledge and experience among the trainees.

With enough training time, good selection of trainees, skilled facilitators, and well-trained and experienced actors, the contrast-culture method is a valuable technique for improving intercultural awareness and communication. The promise of this technique will be further realized as systematic, longitudinal, and evaluative research programs are conducted on the Khan exercise.

## Resources and References

Bennett, Milton J. "A Developmental Approach to Training for Intercultural Sensitivity." *International Journal of Intercultural Relations* 10, no. 2 (1986): 179-96.

Glenn, Edmund S. *Man and Mankind: Conflict and Communication Between Cultures.* Norwood, NJ: Ablex Publishing, 1981.

Hoopes, David S., and Paul Ventura, eds. *Intercultural Sourcebook: Cross-Cultural Training Methodologies.* Washington, DC: Society for Intercultural Education, Training, and Research (SIETAR International), 1979. (Out of print.)

Kohls, L. Robert. "Models for Contrasting and Comparing Cultures." Paper presented as part of the USIA's Tenth Annual Intercultural Communication Course, Washington, DC, September 6, 1977.

————. "Models for Comparing and Contrasting Cultures." Paper presented at the National Association for Foreign Student Affairs meetings, Washington, DC, June 1987.

Kraemer, Alfred J. "Development of a Cultural Self-Awareness Approach to Instruction in Intercultural Communication." (Technical Report 73-17). Alexandria, VA: Human Resources Research Organization (July 1973).

————. "Workshop in Intercultural Communication: Handbook for Instructors." (Technical Report 74-13). Alexandria, VA: Human Resources Research Organization (June 1974).

Stewart, Edward C., Jack Danielian, and Robert J. Foster. "Simulating Intercultural Communication Through Role-Playing." (Technical Report 69-7). Alexandria, VA: Human Resources Research Organization (May 1969).

# Simulation Games as Training Tools

## Dorothy A. Sisk

"Simulation games are experiential exercises which, like Alice's looking glass, challenge assumptions, expand perspectives, and facilitate change" (NASAGA 1991). Just as Alice experienced the manipulation of time and space in Wonderland and gained personal insight, players of simulation games gain insight as they turn the present into the possible future.

## Background and Definitions

The use of simulation games as training tools is not new. For years, law students have participated in moot courts, and student bodies have conducted mock political conventions; nevertheless, significant growth is being experienced in the development and use of simulation techniques in training. There are three major types of training simulations: (1) human interactive simulation, which can include role playing; (2) person-to-computer simulation, which tests human responses to simulated situations such as training airplane pilots, and (3) whole-earth models of economic, environmental, and other conditions.

Simulation can be defined as a general term referring to constructing an operational model that replicates behavioral processes (Zuckerman and Horn 1973) or a larger economic, environmental, or political system (Greenblat and Duke 1981). In other words, a simulation is an operating imitation of a real process.

A game can be defined as any contest (play) among adversaries (players) operating under constraints (rules) for an objective (winning, victory, or payoff). The term "game," according to Greenblat and Duke (1981), applies to those simulations in which outcomes are based wholly or partly on players' decisions. It also applies to simulations in which the environment and activities of participants have the characteristics of games: "...for example, when players have their goals, sets of activities to perform, constraints on what can be done and payoffs (good and bad) as consequences of the actions" (23).

A simulation game simply refers to a combination of a simulation and a game and functions as an operating model featuring the central characteristics of real or proposed systems or processes. Although there are many wonderful simulation games available, I have limited my illustrations and examples to those described elsewhere in this section of the *Intercultural Sourcebook* and to three briefly described in this chapter, *Parlé* (Sisk 1980), *Land of the Sphinx and Land of the Rainbow* (Sisk 1983), and *Tag Game* (Shirts 1985).

# Description of the Method

Simulation games provide interactive opportunities to practice new behaviors and experiment with new attitudes and points of view in a nonthreatening, nonjudgmental environment. They are particularly useful in intercultural training, since, in a very short time, they can stimulate cognitive and affective understanding and broaden participants' perspectives. To understand what a simulation game is, you have to look at each part: activity, simulation, and game.

**Activity.** As trainers, we are all familiar with exercises that can be processed so that trainees learn by doing. For example, if you ask a small group to put together a puzzle and give each person a few of the pieces, they would set about doing it. When you stop them and ask what they learned from this activity, they might discuss teamwork, leadership, cooperation, power, or strategic planning. This is an exercise.

**Simulation.** This exercise becomes a simulation when you ask participants what workplace roles would be appropriate for putting together the puzzle. They might suggest puzzle assemblers, frontline managers, executives, accountants, or possibly legal counsel. You could ask for volunteers to play each role and give them an identifying badge. Then they could continue to put the puzzle together using these new roles to relate to each other and get the job done. This is a simulation exercise.

**Game.** To turn this simulation exercise into a simulation game, you need to add gamelike elements and rules. In this case, you might give some of the puzzle assemblers specific constraints such as blindfolds or a rule that they can only touch inside pieces—no edges. You could give chips to the accountant to be used as rewards or give chips to the managers who need to pay the accountant when the assemblers make mistakes. You can give the executives the puzzle box with the picture of the completed puzzle. Or give the executives their own puzzle to complete. You can add payoffs by giving chips to assemblers or managers each time a puzzle is completed. You are now working with a simulation game that could produce a rich debriefing.

## Characteristics of Games

Simulation games can be compared across a range of characteristics. Those described below are significant factors to be considered in selecting an appropriate simulation game for a training program.

**Time.** A primary issue in training is the time available to play and debrief a simulation. Simulation games like *Barnga* can be conducted in an hour (Thiagarajan and Steinwachs 1990), or can take up to half a day, like *Markhall* (Youth for Understanding 1984) or *Ecotonos* (Nipporica Associates and Saphiere

1993) or *Land of the Sphinx and Land of the Rainbow* (described later in this chapter). The classic cross-cultural simulation game known to many trainers, *BaFá BaFá* (Shirts 1974), with its debriefing time, takes approximately three hours.

**Props.** Some games require only the instructions *(Land of the Sphinx and Land of the Rainbow),* some use simple props or artifacts such as paper clips and construction paper *(Tag Game)* or more sophisticated props and artifacts like those used in *BaFá BaFá.* In addition, simulation games can simulate whole cultures *(BaFá BaFá)* or only one or two aspects of a culture *(Parlé).* Facilitators must prepare or acquire these props well in advance of using the simulation.

**Number of participants.** *BaFá BaFá* is ideally played with sixteen to forty people, although recently I used it with over eighty in a cross-cultural seminar with participants from sixteen countries. It can also be played with as few as eight to ten people although much of the richness is lost. *Barnga* can be played with nine people but is more effective with sixteen to twenty. It can also be played in a huge room filled with tables and one hundred to two hundred people. Most games have an optimum number for playing but, with some ingenuity, can be shrunk or expanded to accommodate extreme numbers. One way to expand is to run several games simultaneously.

**Debriefing issues.** The most important part of any simulation is the debriefing. Each simulation tends to emphasize particular aspects of the intercultural experience. In debriefing intercultural simulation games, you can encourage participants to apply what the game simulates to specific real-life situations. For example, after playing *Barnga* you can ask participants to address what might be done when someone is placed in the predicament of not knowing the rules in a new culture—but thinking they do. *BaFá BaFá* raises, among other sensitive issues, the problem of adapting to another culture when perceptions of that culture are biased by one's own cultural view of, for example, the position of women in society or what constitutes appropriate interpersonal behavior.

Since process is the heart of any simulation game, debriefing usually focuses on what happened, what the consequences of actions were, how misperceptions led to mistakes, how certain strategies were effective, and the like. Content issues such as cultural baggage, values, and adaptation models can also be addressed.

## Understanding Simulation Games: Three Examples

Perhaps the best way to understand simulation games is to explore briefly three very different ones.

### Tag Game

This is a short, highly participative activity. It can be used as an icebreaker or introductory exercise to encourage a group to focus on similarities and differences so they can be openly discussed. Participants wear tags of different shapes and colors and walk around silently observing each other. Then they are instructed to, still silently, form groups. After at least four rounds of forming new groups, they trade their original tags for new, very unique tags. Again they observe, but do not talk, while they decide how to form groups during four more rounds. After the game, participants usually list obvious similarities and differences among people and eventually begin to identify deeper-seated, more intangible abstract similarities and differences. They also discuss the strong attachment people have to likeness rather than diversity. In-group/out-group issues can arise from this game and be discussed. The game and debriefing can take less than one half hour.

## Land of the Sphinx and Land of the Rainbow

This game was developed in 1983 to enable a group of psychologists to better understand learning styles and to explore the concept of cerebral differences. The setting is the year A.D. 2050 and two cultures are created: the Sphinx and the Rainbow. Each culture is challenged with the necessity of selecting three projects to shape its future; one in education, one in research, and one in environment. In small groups, participants identify their three projects. The citizens of the Land of the Sphinx are people who trust logic and objectivity implicitly and order is very important, as are schedules and routine. Conversely, the Land of the Rainbow is inhabited by people who are interested in a deeper, larger, all-embracing reality, and they follow hunches.

Before the game, a minimum of four travelers is selected to visit both lands during the activity period. The travelers are asked to display enthusiasm and curiosity and told to be bold, open, and courageous during their encounters with the natives of each land. These travelers experience different reactions to the questions they pose to members of the two lands.

In the debriefing, participants usually discuss whether or not they were comfortable in the different lands to which they were assigned, and then the travelers are asked to select a land where they might like to remain as a resident. Discussion centers on which environment is conducive to fulfilling aspirations, curiosity, and desires. Participants from different cultures often see similarities between the simulated cultures and their own cultures and openly discuss whether their land's simulated culture is shaping a future that they feel is desirable. This game can be played with as many as one hundred participants. Larger numbers require creating several Sphinx and Rainbow lands and adding sufficient numbers of travelers to make visits to all of them.

## Parlé

*Parlé* is a simulation game that involves players who are representatives of ten countries (Shima, Myna, Ila, Usa, Pam, Bonay, Shivey, Lani, Ranu, and Bili). Each of the countries has a variety of factors to be considered: defense, available resources, and demography. The major theme of *Parlé* is negotiation and interdependence among countries. Crisis incidents are introduced, such as a revolution in Ranu, as participants work toward solving global problems. In *Parlé* participants experience a variety of leadership roles and through the use of crisis cards they are asked to negotiate and make decisions on a variety of issues such as tribal war, famine, revolution. The point in time during which the game is played can be altered to reflect the past, deal with the present, or project to the future. The only way countries can win is by cooperating and pooling resources.

# Important Things You Need to Know to Use Simulation Games

In using simulation games, it is important that you, the facilitator, warm up the group with a brief introduction to the game and an explanation of the rules and patterns of play. Some participants may protest that they do not play games. Some trainers avoid the problem by calling a simulation game a learning activity or even referring to it as a simulation rather than a game. On the other hand, some trainers prefer to deal with the issue at the start of the activity. They develop a standard introduction for simulation games that briefly describes the role of both simulation and gaming in the learning process. Often when you express confidence, participants will not question this portion of a training program.

It is also important for you to start with a clear description of the game and then move on. A certain amount of confusion is characteristic of the beginning of any new activity, but the confusion is usually temporary. Clarity is essential, but it often comes as the activity progresses. While the participants are playing the game, you should be alert and observant but as unobtrusive as possible. When the participants are asked to halt the game to debrief, a simple bridge from the game to the debriefing can be: "Now let's talk about what happened during the past half hour or so...." Participants should be de-roled, consciously helped to give up their simulated roles and enter into a discussion about the experience.

One of the keys to organizing participants for simulation games is flexibility and imagination. The high degree of participant-to-participant communication requires an atmosphere that allows physical and intellectual mobility. To facilitate this, you need to develop a sense of pacing to know when it is appropriate to offer aid and support and when it is time to stop the simulation to process or debrief the action.

The processing, critiquing, or debriefing period is most essential for simulation games, because analyzing the experience allows participants to capitalize on the learning potential of the game. In the postgame discussion, participants inductively reach a consensus about the ideas that have been gleaned from the simulation experience. Your responsibility is to direct the participants' critical attention to the processes that were simulated and the concepts that lie behind them.

A debriefing format that encourages participants to share what they have experienced is useful. Initially they will need to *describe* what happened. It helps people to hear about others' experiences, as well as to share their own. As they talk about what they experienced during the simulation game, participants should be encouraged to *analyze* why certain things happened or what the basis is for certain observations or feelings. Then encourage participants to note the similarity and dissimilarity of the game to reality. With a little encouragement, debriefing sessions naturally move to summarizing, generalizing, and applying, which constitute the learning that has been achieved in the simulation game.

Still another effective technique is to ask participants to list or to share specific ideas that have emerged during the discussion. Ask them to develop generalizations based on these ideas and to draw conclusions. This approach is quite effective, since generalizations and conclusions are more meaningful to the participants when they come from the participants themselves.

You need to be aware that participants may become emotionally involved in the simulation and lose their critical sense. Games can trigger intense feelings, and occasionally arguments can lead to expressions of personal hostility. Use skill and sensitivity to help prevent harmful outbursts. Observe the group closely and make a special effort to resolve ill feelings as they become evident or during the debriefing. When there are disagreements, you can ask participants which rules were ignored and why, and encourage participants to analyze their own behavior during the game.

Finally, simulation games need to be culturally appropriate. Since participative learning is not practiced in all societies, it is important to be sure participants will be able to enter into the experience. This may require a careful introduction or it may mean a simulation is not to be the training tool of choice. Unfortunately, there is no rule of thumb for making the decision on whether or not to use a simulation game. I have seen games used successfully when I thought they never had a chance. The factors seem to be the facilitator's comfort level with the method, the manner in which sensitive topics are handled within the structure of the game, the degree of trust developed over the course of the training program, and the presence of an effective cultural broker who can help interpret the game in terms meaningful and relevant to the culture of the trainees.

## Designing a Simulation Game

Knowing something about designing simulation games can be helpful. It is a complicated process, not to be undertaken lightly, as there are many variables to consider. There are essentially six steps to the design process, each of which demands a great deal of thought and experimentation.

1. Decide what you want the game to teach.
2. Select the real-life situation you want the game to simulate.
3. Create the structure of the game. What roles, goals, resources, interaction, sequence of events, and external factors are to be considered?
4. Determine what props and artifacts can be used to enhance the structure of the game. Do you want to use a board, tokens, score sheets, tables, graphs, chance cards, spinners or dice, and so forth? This is the place to let your imagination fly but maintain some awareness of the practical aspects of acquiring or making these items.
5. Write the rules. What is the order of play? What do players do? How does the game end?
6. Review, test, and revise the final product for realism, validity, comprehensiveness, and playability. Redesigning an existing game may be preferable; it is certainly easier.

# Situations in Which Simulation Games Might Be Used

## For Young People

Simulation games are very effective for helping young people prepare for overseas experiences such as student exchange programs. Games can be equally powerful for preparing students for reentry at the end of an exchange program. At the Center for Creativity, Innovation and Leadership at Lamar University in Beaumont, Texas, simulation games have proved effective with graduate students from mostly Third-World countries as they prepare to return to their homelands after studying in the United States.

Several games are valuable training tools for students in political science, geography, history, and current affairs courses. *Parlé* illustrates the influence of geography and resources on foreign policy. It also confronts players with the central problem that has plagued foreign policymakers throughout history: the defense of a country surrounded by potentially hostile neighbors. Students learn the importance of personal diplomacy and individual responsibility that transforms international situations.

Very young children in multicultural classrooms can play *Rafá Rafá* (Shirts 1978), a variation of the adult *BaFá BaFá,* to help them understand intercultural issues.

## For Adults

The intensity of involvement in simulation games helps adults learn quickly, which makes this method a good choice for programs that need to illustrate some key points rapidly. Learning through experience is one of the basic tenets of adult learning theory.

For example, *BaFá BaFá* was used to help the host organization for an international business meeting understand the complexities of the host-guest relationship when more than one culture is involved. The organizers used their learning from the game to create the most successful meeting their international consortium had ever sponsored.

In another example, the simulation game *Talking Rocks* was used to help city council members in a small California community understand what it might be like to work with various candidates for city manager.

*Ecotonos* has been used in numerous international business environments where learning to function effectively in a variety of cross-cultural situations is essential. In one case, Japanese and American managers worked toward establishing business practices that would accommodate each group's culture and allow them to accomplish their work.

Although there are only a few specifically cross-cultural games, almost any game can be debriefed in a way that elicits the cultural dimensions of the situation or issue, especially when more than one culture is represented in the participant group. The game may be about city planning, aging, health, or any number of topics, but when cultural perspectives are contrasted by players during the debriefing, intercultural learning can take place.

## For Families

Games are great levelers. Families heading for an overseas assignment can play *BaFá BaFá* or other games as they become learners trying to penetrate a new environment. A simulation game gives families an opportunity to learn how they operate as a group. Family members become more aware of each other's strengths and weaknesses and how to help one another in a new situation.

# Benefits and Outcomes from Using Simulation Games

In discussing the use of simulation, Phil Phoenix, professor emeritus at Columbia University, related that play is one of the fundamental factors in the creation of culture, and simulation games provide a means for making the topic at hand relevant to current reality.

In a game where participants take on future roles in the limited time and space framework of the simulation game, choices are made to follow certain courses. For that moment, the players can turn the present into the future and sample the future. As a trainer, I find this manipulation of time and space one of the most meaningful aspects of simulation. Through simulation games, participants eliminate the interval between learning and applying; they tie the present, the future, and their skills, values, and knowledge together to make the ongoing situation relevant and useful.

Other major benefits derived from simulation games include:

**Critical thinking.** Simulation games motivate and reward critical thinking as participants analyze possible moves and probable consequences of those moves. Participants also must plan rationally and think through countermoves. Simulation games also encourage intuitive thinking as players make spontaneous decisions.

**Understanding the role of chance in life.** Simulation games demonstrate that life is not always affected by logical plans or even intuitive solutions. This is most apparent when chance is introduced in simulation games. We know from experience that we rarely are completely in control of our lives and, for that reason, most designers of simulations include chance variables.

**Multilevel learning.** Participants learn on three levels while participating: (1) learning information embodied in the context and dynamics of the game; (2) learning processes simulated by the game; and (3) learning the relative costs and benefits, risks, and potential rewards of alternative strategies for making decisions. Through information, processes, and strategies, simulation provides the participant the experience of operating on all three levels simultaneously and demonstrates that decision making is not a simple process.

**Social values**. Simulation games teach social values such as competition, cooperation, and empathy. In *Parlé* participants see clearly that players must cooperate in order to play and win. By cooperating on problems that affect the attainment of goals, participants come to understand the social value of cooperation.

**Personal responsibility.** Participants experience the way their decisions influence the future. In simulation games, players get to make decisions and, because of rapid feedback, see the consequences of those decisions immediately. They also learn that their actions affect others as well as themselves. Simulation games allow participants to recognize their personal responsibility in dealing constructively and effectively with the environment and in influencing plans for and actions in the future.

**Knowledge and skills.** Simulation games can increase the trainee's knowledge of specific terms, concepts, and facts and of structures and relationships. They build upon the knowledge and skills each participant brings to the simulation. In addition, you can help trainees develop certain intellectual and social skills and change attitudes toward certain behaviors and ways of thinking that were simulated in the games. Simulation games also encourage participants to think and ask the kinds of questions that help make sense of social systems in a global context and to experiment, trying new ideas and behaviors in a safe environment. With skillful debriefing, you can link game behavior to cross-cultural effectiveness. Moreover, according to James S. Coleman (1966), former director of the Johns Hopkins Center for Developing Simulation Games, the use of simulation reverses a common pattern of learning. Instead of being focused on absorbing content, the primary goal for the participant is doing well in the simulation game, which requires the mastery of certain processes in which the participant assimilates the material in order to be able to carry out action efficiently toward the game's goal.

**Group dynamics.** Simulation establishes a sense of community among participants as well as offering opportunities for self-awareness. Learning continues beyond the game as participants experience insights into their own lives and the lives of others. In a low-risk environment, participants are actively involved in problem-solving situations and engage in considerable interaction and communication, which fosters a sense of trust in the group.

**Motivation.** People enjoy playing games. Herman Kahn (1962) used simulation games at the highest levels of international policy study. He felt that since most people just naturally take sides, games create the feelings and zeal of partisanship. For example, taking the part of an Alpha in *BaFá BaFá* quickly makes devoted Alpha adherents of the members of that culture (and Beta partisans of the other culture). The role playing in a game engenders a more intense and thorough investigation, just as in a courtroom lawyers are likely to do a better job of raising the issues involved in a dispute than judges. These partisan feelings are a motivating factor in the complicated hypothetical situations often found in games. Most people will try to understand their own and others' reactions when they are forced to identify actively with one role or another. Thus, partisanship motivates participants to engage in and learn from the action in simulation games.

**Trainer/trainee dynamics.** Simulation games involve a close working relationship between the leader and the participants. Since the leader acts as facilitator and the rules of the game direct the participants, the leader is not viewed as teacher, judge, or jury but as an assistant in the process. Thus the leader is freed to focus attention on what is happening in the game while participants immerse themselves in the learning.

Trainers who successfully use simulation games tend to be highly enthusiastic about their potential for learning and report favorable outcomes. However, empirical evidence from rigorous, systematic testing of their claims is still limited.

## Comparison with Other Methods

When simulation games are compared to other instructional methods, their action and intensity become clear. Simulation games require a much more active response and involvement from the participants. Although the structure of the game is established, the actual play evolves as a result of players' behaviors and interactions. Simulation games are stimulating, offering a wide variety of ways of presenting information through the use of props and artifacts, furniture arrangement, and, as noted, player behavior and interaction.

In comparison with some other methods, such as critical incidents or case studies, games tend to require more time. However, the learning from simulation games becomes almost immediately apparent, continues after the event, and is available for further elaboration.

Simulation games are both trainer-dependent and trainer-independent. Since the play of a game takes on a life of its own, the play is trainer-independent. With a well-designed game, almost any trainer can get the play started and run the simulation. However, debriefing a simulation game requires strong facilitation skills and is much more complicated than processing a critical incident or culture assimilator. Processing a simulation game is highly trainer-dependent.

Being comfortable with this method requires a high tolerance for ambiguity. Even though the game has rules and parameters, you are never entirely sure how it will work out. In essence, responsibility for creating the learning is turned over to the participants. This is not as true when presenting a case study or showing a film, but it is similar to the trainer's experience in conducting a role play.

## Conclusion

Simulations have long been used in business, education, the health-care professions, the military, and many other organizational contexts, and their value as a training tool is substantial. They are easily applied to the study of social, political, and other kinds of issues, and they help participants learn to make intelligent life decisions by involving them in such things as interactive negotiation, communication, decision making, and creative problem solving. According to Fowler (1986), the "jolt" provided by a simulation game is often enough to start people learning how to learn about other cultures. The highly motivating nature of simulation games makes them complementary tools to well-integrated training programs.

# References

Coleman, James S. "In Defense of Games." *American Behavioral Scientist* 10 (1966): 3-4.

Fowler, Sandra M. "Intercultural Simulation Games: Removing Cultural Blinders." In *Experiential and Simulation Techniques for Teaching Adults: New Directions for Adult and Continuing Education,* no. 30. Edited by L. Lewis. San Francisco: Jossey-Bass (1986): 71-82.

Greenblat, C. S., and R. Duke. *Principles and Practices of Gaming Simulations.* Beverly Hills: Sage, 1981.

Kahn, Herman. *Thinking about the Unthinkable.* New York: Avon Press, 1962.

NASAGA (North American Simulation and Gaming Association). 30th Annual NASAGA Conference Announcement, Spokane, WA, 1991.

Nipporica Associates, and Dianne Hofner Saphiere. *Ecotonos.* Yarmouth, ME: Intercultural Press, 1993.

Shirts, R. Garry. *BaFá BaFá: A Cross-Cultural Simulation.* Del Mar, CA: Simulation Training Systems (formerly Simile II), 1974.

———. *Rafá Rafá.* Del Mar, CA: Simulation Training Systems (formerly Simile II), 1978.

———. *Tag Game.* Del Mar, CA: Simulation Training Systems (formerly Simile II), 1985.

Sisk, Dorothy. *Parlé.* Beaumont, TX: Center for Creativity, Innovation and Leadership, Lamar University, 1980.

———. *Land of the Sphinx and Land of the Rainbow.* Beaumont, TX: Center for Creativity, Innovation and Leadership, Lamar University, 1983.

Thiagarajan, Sivasailam, and Barbara Steinwachs. *Barnga: A Simulation Game on Cultural Clashes.* A SIETAR International Publication. Yarmouth, ME: Intercultural Press, 1990.

Vernon, R. F. *Talking Rocks: A Simulation on the Origins of Writing.* Del Mar, CA: Simulation Training Systems (formerly Simile II), 1978.

Youth for Understanding International Student Exchange and Resources Training Group. *Markhall: A Comparative Management Simulation.* Washington, DC: Youth for Understanding, 1984.

Zuckerman, D., and R. Horn. *The Guide to Simulation Games for Education and Training.* Cambridge, MA: Information Resources, 1973.

# Resources

Association for Business Simulations and Experiential Learning (ABSEL).

International Simulation and Gaming Association (ISAGA).

North American Simulation and Gaming Association (NASAGA).

*Simulation & Gaming: An International Journal of Theory, Practice, and Research.*
Edited by D. Crookall. Sage Periodicals Press. *Simulation & Gaming* is the official journal of the Association for Business Simulations and Experiential Learning (ABSEL), the International Simulation and Gaming Association, (ISAGA), and the North American Simulation and Gaming Association (NASAGA). The journal is devoted to research and applications in the rapidly expanding fields of simulation, computerized simulation, gaming, modeling, role play, and experiential learning.

# Beyond Ethnocentrism: Promoting Cross-Cultural Understanding with *BaFá BaFá*

## R. Garry Shirts

I magine the visceral impact of encountering a new culture. Imagine becoming suddenly mute, not speaking or understanding the strange language and gestures surrounding you. Imagine thinking you know what is going on and suddenly finding yourself ostracized for breaking a cultural rule. Imagine the relief of returning home, where everything is familiar. Imagine doing all this without leaving home at all. You do not have to imagine—you can play *BaFá BaFá\**.

## History

Dateline Greece, 1971: Two American sailors on shore leave bought identical souvenirs from a local merchant. Returning to the ship, one of the sailors discovered he had paid twice what his companion paid. Feeling cheated and outraged, the sailor returned to the merchant and severely assaulted him. The incident escalated in the local press until it threatened U.S. relations with Greece.

On the other side of the world, an American sailor on shore leave in Japan stabbed a taxi driver over a misunderstanding about his fare. Back in Greece, another American sailor caused a minor commotion when he tried to date the daughter of a village storekeeper.

The U.S. Navy was concerned, and rightly so. Greece, a linchpin in NATO's southern flank, was threatening to renege on its promise to allow home-port privileges to U.S. warships. Both the American and international press deplored our military personnel's inability to coexist with an alien culture. Naval administrators wanted to know why these incidents happened and, more importantly, how future incidents could be avoided. Clearly, something needed to be done.

---

\**BaFá BaFá* is a registered trademark of Simulation Training Systems.

After the first incident involving the assaulted Greek merchant, an acquaintance of mine at the Navy Personnel Research and Development Center who was familiar with my simulation *Star Power* (Shirts 1969), asked me to put together a simulation program that would give naval personnel a better understanding of Greek culture. As I was starting my research, however, the incident with the Japanese taxi driver prompted the Navy to ask me to redirect my program toward understanding Japanese-American cross-cultural differences. From *spanikopita* to *sushi* in one fell swoop! Yet just as things were getting under way with the new program, history once again intervened, and an already sensitized Greek government became involved in yet another incident of an American serviceman interacting inappropriately with local residents. So the Navy asked if I would go back to creating a simulation on Greek and American cultural differences.

Interestingly enough, the Navy had already provided me with some pamphlets that spelled out some of the differences between American and Greek culture. In Greece, as in most Mediterranean cultures, the customer is expected to negotiate with street merchants for the best price. Suitors are expected to become friends of the family before they pursue an unmarried daughter.

Why were Navy personnel failing to use this readily available information when interacting with other cultures? I realized the problem went beyond ethnocentrism and that simply educating one culture to the ways of another solves only part of the problem. It was necessary to create a need to learn by developing an awareness of culture itself and the profound impact it has on human affairs. Only then could we expect to motivate people to learn how to interact effectively within any cultural milieu, no matter how different from their own.

So, I went back to the Navy and said, "Let's make the simulation about the idea of culture itself and then follow up the training with culture-specific learning about Greece and Japan." The Navy agreed, and I began to work on the simulation game that would eventually become *BaFá BaFá* (Shirts 1974). The training program included not only the simulation, but an entire package that contained a comic strip, language tapes, and several other learning modules. The star of each one of these modules was "Brent Folsum." I chose that name because it sounded like the sailors I had met who I knew would be going through the training. When we illustrated the "foreign" language used in the simulation, we used the example of Brent Folsum saying the number "four," or "Ba Fa Ba Fa," and thus the game was named.

*BaFá BaFá* teaches that what seems irrational, contradictory, or unimportant to us in our culture may seem rational, consistent, and terribly important to a person from another culture. Since it was first published in 1974, *BaFá BaFá* has been used by many different groups for many different purposes. In 1978, I developed a version for elementary schoolchildren called *Rafá Rafá*. A professional version of *BaFá BaFá* for business and government organizations was released in 1993.

# Description

*BaFá BaFá* begins with an introduction describing what happens in the simulation. The group is then divided into two cultures: Alpha and Beta. In separate rooms each group learns the rules specific to its own culture. Alpha is an in-group/out-group, touching culture, and Beta is a foreign-language-speaking, task-oriented culture. Once participants learn and practice the rules of their own culture, observers and visitors are exchanged. After each exchange, participants return and try to describe their experiences in observing and interacting with the other culture. When everyone has had the opportunity to visit the other culture, the simulation is ended. Participants from the two cultures are brought back together to discuss and analyze the experience.

## Sample Insights Reported by Participants After Playing *BaFá BaFá*

"We tried to understand the other culture by using our own culture as a frame of reference. For example, when the observer returned we asked, 'Did they stand close together? Do they have a hierarchical system?' Consequently, most of the questions we asked and the observations we made about the other culture missed the mark. We tend to do the same thing when we talk about the behavior of people who are from other real cultures."

"When our observer returned he said, 'They're weird.' Similar words were said by our visitors when they returned. The remarks made our group feel closer; it relieved tension and reduced the threat of the other culture. But such pejorative terms have many negative effects for understanding. First, it makes it legitimate for members of the group to call the other culture names. And because the people who use derogatory terms are often rewarded with laughter it encourages other people to do the same. Second, it discounts legitimate aspects of the other culture so one doesn't have to try to understand that aspect of the culture. Third, it makes it difficult to say good things about the other culture. Those who say good things are often seen as being disloyal to the home culture."

"Good intentions are not enough. It is possible to have the best intentions in the world and completely misunderstand and offend the other culture."

"We'll begin to make progress toward understanding one another when we realize that most of us are from different cultures in some way. Some of us are marginalized because we are a different gender, or because we are physically different, or because we grew up in a particularly difficult home, or we don't have the right degree from the right school, and so forth."

"Even when you think you have done well you may have offended the other culture. I proudly displayed a card that the people in the other culture gave me and it turned out that it was not a gift as I thought but an insult."

"When I learned that the orange wristband meant that I had lower status, I was disappointed. But then when I had the opportunity to be declared the leader, I didn't want that either. I realized that I have to look at how I feel about status and power."

"It is important to find out about other cultures from reliable sources. We relied on the visitors and inherited their prejudices."

"The amount of personal space one demands or allows others is one of those subtle cultural elements that is difficult to identify or talk about because you don't know what is making you feel uncomfortable. You just know you are uncomfortable when you are around this person. The person who is standing close may not be aware that he is doing something that is different than other people do."

"I felt invisible when I was in the Alpha culture. As a woman I often feel invisible, especially when I am meeting with the engineering department."

"When you go into the culture with preconceived beliefs about what the other culture is about, you tend to look for behaviors that support your theory. We thought the Betans belonged to three different classes because the first person who went into Beta observed that there were three clumps of people. She thought they represented three different strata of people. So when a Betan refused to trade with me, I thought it was probably because he was a lower-class person and wasn't allowed to trade. In fact, he didn't trade with me because I didn't have the cards he wanted."

"Let's be honest about this diversity issue. It's not easy. Getting people to value people who are different is not something that most people do easily. Most of us would prefer to work with people who talk like us, have the same values as us, and who look like us."

"If we understand the other person's culture but we don't understand the other person's language, we can get by. If we understand the language but don't understand the culture, we will not be able to really communicate or relate to people in the other culture."

"When two people aren't communicating, *both* have a responsibility to try to solve the problem."

"If we observe but don't ask, we're likely to misunderstand the other person's behavior."

"Understanding is not accepting or condoning. I might understand why a person behaves in a certain way and at the same time believe that the behavior is not appropriate for the workplace."

"Alphans were interested in keeping their culture pure. They excluded people who did not support Alpha values. This feature of their culture makes it unlikely that they will learn much from other cultures."

"When dealing with people from other cultures we must realize that much of what is going on is not visible to a stranger. On the surface the Beta culture seemed less complicated than the Alpha culture. In fact, the Alpha culture only *appeared* less complicated. Underneath it was *more* complicated."

"There are probably people in the workplace who feel the way we did when we visited the other culture, but until you feel it yourself, you're likely to discount it as unimportant or insignificant."

"In Beta we didn't want to stop to learn about the other culture because we were so competitive. Unless it can be shown that learning about the other culture is going to help us be more competitive, many businesspeople will not want to learn about other cultures or people who are different."

"Gestures often look silly to an outsider but seem very natural to the person who is using the gesture."

# Procedure

To conduct the simulation, you will want to take the following guidelines into consideration.

### Preparation

- ❖ *BaFá BaFá* requires two trainers. Discuss with your cotrainer how you want to run the simulation. Decide on timing and responsibilities, plan the introduction and debriefing, the questions and approach you will use to discuss and analyze the experience.
- ❖ Arrange the cards for each culture so they are ready to distribute.
- ❖ Make sure you have two rooms, one filled with chairs and the other without chairs or with the chairs pushed to the side.

### Activity

- ❖ During the introduction, tie the game to its context by linking it to the goals you are trying to achieve. Follow the introduction in the Trainer's Manual or provide one that suits your style and the needs of the trainees.
- ❖ Once you become familiar with the simulation, I recommend that you use the tapes for the Beta instructions, but give the Alpha instructions in a warm personal manner without the tape. In Beta culture use a chart to help illustrate the Beta language, and in Alpha culture chart the Alpha transaction. Be sure to remove or cover the charts before the observers arrive for their visit.

### Processing

- ❖ Use the questions in the manual to develop the descriptive portion of the debriefing.
- ❖ Develop some questions of your own to address your trainees' needs. For example, if your goal is to help participants understand some of the dynamics of cross-cultural communication, then you might ask what communication barriers exist in the game. You can follow that by asking what happened in the game that suggests strategies for overcoming such barriers in the real world.

## Contexts in Which *BaFá BaFá* Has Been Used

The simulation has been used by many different groups for many different purposes. For example:

- ❖ By schools, corporations, and government agencies to help manage a culturally diverse workforce.
- ❖ By corporations, the Peace Corps, educational exchange programs, the AFS Intercultural Programs, and other international groups to prepare and sensitize people to work and study overseas.

❖ By service organizations such as banks, utilities, the US. Forest Service, and hospitals to better serve their multcultural clients and improve internal communication within a multicultural workforce.

❖ By corporations preparing diverse departmental "cultures" to communicate with each other (for example, engineering and marketing).

❖ By anthropology and sociology professors teaching students about the meaning of culture.

❖ By deans interested in preparing students to live in multicultural dormitories or to learn in a multicultural environment.

❖ By corporations as part of their new employee orientation programs to convey the message that they take diversity very seriously.

## Points to Remember

1. **Be prepared.** It is important to be well prepared to run the simulation. This means reading the instruction manual carefully, preparing the materials well before the simulation begins, and, most importantly, having questions and activities ready for the discussion and analysis at the end of the simulation.

2. **Give a concise orientation.** It is generally best to give the overview as outlined in the instructor's manual and get on with the simulation. Too often, a novice director sees the introduction as a way of helping the participants know what they are going to experience, how they are going to feel, and what they should learn from it. There are two problems with this type of introduction. First, the participants hear what the director is saying, but they rarely understand. The experience is generally so different from anything they have done before, they have no personal experience to relate to what the director is saying. For most people, the introduction is useless; it is only when they start doing the simulation that they can understand how the simulation works. Second, such an introduction robs them of the opportunity to draw their own conclusions, interpret their own feelings, and draw from the experience in their own ways. Giving an overly detailed introduction is like telling someone who is going to see a movie what they will see, when they will see it, and how they should feel about it.

3. **Allow participants to spend an appropriate length of time in the other culture.** The primary purpose of the simulation is to give the participants a visceral feeling of what it is like to live in another culture and thus to understand the profound impact that culture itself has on behavior. Because these are not real cultures, but simulated ones, it is important to allow the participants to be in the other culture an amount of time that simulates an actual visit. This can be much shorter than most trainers intuitively want to allow. If participants are allowed to stay in the other culture too long, the impact of the simulation is reduced.

4. **Follow up with appropriate activities.** *BaFá BaFá* was designed to create an awareness of the importance and impact of culture in general; it was not

designed to teach about any specific culture. To meet most objectives, it needs to be followed up with discussion, specific training modules, and other didactic types of training.

## References

Shirts, R. Garry. *Star Power.* Del Mar, CA: Simulation Training Systems (formerly Simile II), 1969.

———. *BaFá BaFá: A Cross-Cultural Simulation.* Del Mar, CA: Simulation Training Systems (formerly Simile II), 1974.

———. *Rafá Rafá.* Del Mar, CA: Simulation Training Systems (formerly Simile II), 1978.

## Resources

Bredemeier, M. E., G. Berstein, and W. Oxman. *"BaFá BaFá* and Dogmatism/ Ethnocentrism: A Study of Attitude Change Through Simulation-Gaming." *Simulation and Games: An International Journal* 13 (1982): 413-36.

Bredemeier, M. E., and C. S. Greenblatt. "The Educational Effectiveness of Simulation Games: A Synthesis of Findings." *Simulation and Games: An International Journal* 12 (1981): 307-32.

Bruin, K. "Prejudices, Discrimination and Gaming Simulation: An Analysis." *Simulation and Games: An International Journal* 16 (1985): 161-73.

Fowler, Sandra M. "Intercultural Simulation Games: Removing Cultural Blinders." In *Experiential and Simulation Techniques for Teaching Adults: New Directions for Adult and Continuing Education,* no. 30. Edited by Linda Lewis. San Francisco: Jossey-Bass (1986): 71-82.

Greenblatt, C. S. "Extending the Range of Experience." In *Communication and Simulation: From Two Fields To One Theme,* edited by D. Crookall and D. Sanders. Clevedon, England: Multilingual Matters, 1989.

Lashutka, S. "Using Cross-Cultural Simulation as a Predictor of Cross-Cultural Adjustment." *Simulation and Games: An International Journal* 8 (1977): 481-82.

Moses, Y. T., and P. J. Higgins. *Anthropology and Multicultural Education: Classroom Applications.* (Report No. 83-1). Anthropology Curriculum Project. Athens: University of Georgia, 1990.

Noesjirwan, J., and K. Brujin. "Culture, Prejudice and Simulation/Gaming in Theory and Practice." In *Communication and Simulation: From Two Fields to One Theme,* edited by D. Crookall and D. Sanders. Clevedon, England: Multilingual Matters, 1989.

Petranek, C. K. F. "Knowing oneself: A symbolic interactions view of simulation." In *Communication and Simulation: From Two Fields to One Theme,* edited by D. Crookall and D. Sanders. Clevedon, England: Multilingual Matters, 1989.

Shirts, R. Garry. "Ten Secrets of Successful Simulations." *Training,* October 1992.

Tiene, D. *"BaFá* and after: Exposing teacher trainees to the world of simulation games." *Simages* 3, 1981.

Ting-Toomey, K. S. "Intergroup communication and simulation in low- and high-context culture." In *Communication and Simulation: From Two Fields to One Theme,* edited by D. Crookall and D. Sanders. Clevedon, England: Multilingual Matters, 1989.

## Availability

All of the resources required to run the simulation are contained in the *BaFá BaFá* simulation package available from Simulation Training Systems (formerly Simile II), P.O. Box 910, Del Mar, California 92014 or call (619) 755-0272 or 1-800-942-2900.

Most people purchase the simulation and run it from the directions without any outside help. Should you like to speak with someone who has successfully used *BaFá BaFá,* the Simulation Training Systems staff will be happy to put you in touch with a person in your area. Call for more information.

# *Barnga:* A Game for All Seasons

## Barbara Steinwachs

On a beautiful autumn day in the mountains of North Carolina, nearly one hundred higher education faculty and administrators working in international programs meet together for a statewide conference on issues and methodologies relevant to their work. After the usual academic welcomes, they are asked to sit at tables of six and learn a new card game. The game is extremely simple, so they learn and begin practicing it quickly. The group leader then takes away the printed game rules and announces a card tournament, one with a twist—no verbal communication, no spoken or written words. The tournament begins in stillness, participants fairly serious but relaxed, although somewhat puzzled. Suddenly the room is filled with murmurs of frustration, with chuckles, with fists banging on tables.[1]

Another autumn day, in a rural area of New York State. Dozens of high school students from surrounding towns arrive by bus for a conference on problems facing youth today. Most of the day will be spent in small concurrent sessions, but the first meeting is a general session on some of the causes underlying communication problems. It starts with everyone sitting in small groups, learning a new, very simple card game. As soon as they have mastered the rules, the written instructions are taken away, and they are told there will now be a tournament during which they no longer can speak or write words, although gesturing or drawing pictures is OK. The tournament begins with curiosity kindled and talking stifled with some difficulty. Suddenly efforts to repress talking are replaced by murmurs of frustration, by chuckles, by fists banging on tables.

An early spring day in Washington, D.C. Twenty long-term visitors to the United States, primarily from Arab and African countries, attend a week-long orientation to U.S. culture. They have spent most of the week doing orientation exercises, listening to lectures on American culture, and going on field trips. On this, the last day, they are asked to sit in groups of four and learn a card game

[1] I would like to thank Intercultural Press for allowing me to use and modify for this chapter parts of the manual *Barnga: A Simulation Game on Cultural Clashes* which they published in 1990.

which will help them adjust to living in another culture. Some have never played cards in their lives. But the game is easy; they soon learn it. Then the instructor tells them a tournament is about to start, during which they will not be allowed to talk or write any words. As the game rules are taken away and the tournament begins, the initial uneasy silence suddenly is broken by murmurs of frustration, by chuckles, by fists banging on tables.

What is going on here? Each of these groups is playing a short, simple, easy-to-use simulation game, so versatile it can be played by any number of people beyond a minimum of nine. Despite its simplicity, it generates experiences that lead to a very rich follow-up discussion on the difficulties of understanding and communicating with persons different from oneself in situations where the rules are different from the familiar ones, but it is not known that they are different.

## History

All the groups described above were playing *Barnga* (Thiagarajan and Steinwachs 1990), a simulation game designed by Sivasailam Thiagarajan, affectionately known to all as Thiagi (tee-ah´-gee, with 'g' as in get). A prolific designer of simple simulation games, Thiagi's supple mind combines a respect for instructional-development theory with creative spontaneity.

Thiagi developed *Barnga* in the early 1980s as a "flexim," which he defines in his original (unpublished) instructions as "a flexible simulation game providing a rich learning experience in a short period of time. *Barnga*," he explains, "induces the shock of realizing that in spite of many similarities, people from the other culture have differences in the way they do things. You have to understand and reconcile these differences to function effectively in a cross-cultural group" (Thiagarajan 1984, 2).

He likes to tell the story of his own experience in a West African town named Barnga, where he was developing educational materials with a group of Africans who shared a knowledge of the subject matter and basic principles about instructional development. "Or at least it seemed so during our analysis of the curriculum and preparation of the materials," he says. "However, when I came down with a bout of malaria, my counterparts suggested that squeezing the juice of a tobacco leaf into my left nostril would relieve my symptoms. I never did check out this cure, but my perception of the other person's perception of the world underwent a major change. I had to understand and accept our cultural differences before we could function as a collaborative team" (Thiagarajan and Steinwachs 1990, 4).

At the heart of *Barnga's* design is the premise that "cultural differences exist in more or less subtle forms...often swamped by obvious similarities." The game helps us understand that "unless we recognize and respect the different assumptions underlying our interactions, we run into interpersonal conflicts" (Thiagarajan and Steinwachs 1990, 5). This insight—that cultural differences may bring more of a clash when hidden amidst apparent similarities and therefore unexpected and unprepared for—is a source of the rich follow-up discussion the game generates among its players.

Thiagi's original design was elegant in its simplicity, yet he encouraged users to modify it at will. Several simulation game facilitators including myself have experimented over the last few years with a variety of modifications, most of which turn out to make little difference in how the game is experienced and debriefed. To some extent, the power of the game can be attributed to its simplicity.

## Procedure

As noted above, *Barnga* is a short, easy-to-use simulation game. The procedure is straightforward, the game almost immediately involves all its players, and supplies (card decks and instruction sheets) are easily procurable. Careful planning of the debriefing period helps assure that all participants will become aware of and reflect on the learnings of the exercise.

The game works like this. Players (any number greater than about nine, although twelve or more is better) form small groups of four to seven players each. Each group sits at a separate table and receives a modified deck of normal playing cards (each deck containing only the same few cards) and a sheet of rules for playing a new card game called "Five Tricks." They have a few minutes to study the rules and practice playing the game. Once everyone has the hang of it, the rule sheets are collected and at the same time a strict command of "no verbal communication" is imposed. This means that players may gesture or draw pictures if they wish, but may neither speak (orally or by signing) nor write words. Clearly, communication, should it be needed, is going to be more difficult. Since the game is so simple and so short, this artificial barrier to communication forces the players, within the simulated setting, to be as creative and alert as possible.

Frequently at this point there is a little nervous laughter, some stifled words, and finally a settling into playing "Five Tricks" without the written rules and in silence. A tournament is then announced, during which some players leave their home table and move to another, some from that other table have moved to yet another, and so on. They sit down at their new tables, look around, and begin at once playing "Five Tricks." Shortly thereafter an almost imperceptible change is felt in the room, then come the expressions of uncertainty, murmurs of frustration, chuckles, and fists banging on tables described above. The tournament, with more movement to other tables, continues for another ten minutes or so amidst growing uncertainty, frustration, laughter, banging on tables. Sometimes one player is ready to claim a trick when someone else reaches out and takes it. Sometimes a player makes an effort to draw a picture to clarify an uncertainty. Sometimes whoever was first at the table prevails, sometimes whoever is more aggressive wins out. When the game is over and the debriefing begins, players are asked what might have been going on. Someone is likely to take another player to task for not learning the rules correctly. Someone else confesses that she never was very good at cards. Someone else speaks about others trying to cheat. And several suggest that each table originally had been given a different set of rules. Some are sure of this; others think it might be true; a few had not considered it.

In fact, at the beginning of the game each group had received a slightly differ-ent version of a basic set of rules to "Five Tricks." In one set, for example, ace is high; in another, ace low. In one set diamonds are trump, in another spades, in another no trump at all. In one set, trump may be used at any time; in another, only when the player does not have a card of the suit which was led. Variations on these rules are the only differences, no matter how many groups are playing.

This is the beauty of *Barnga*—everything appears to be the same because, in fact, almost everything *is* the same, yet great confusion, uncertainty, misunder-standing, and misjudgments fill the room because of just a few differences. Even those who understand that the rules are different are not always able to bridge the communication barriers to work out a solution. These concepts spark the energy generated by the game and provide the starting point for a discussion rich in observations of how things that happened during play are analogous to what happens in real life.

Once again, a simulation game has done what this learning methodology does so well: provided the group with an experience they can participate in with energy and enthusiasm and draw learning from, rather than being told what they are expected to learn. This experience, unlike other individual experiences in their lives, is common to each person present and serves as a model against which they can compare their other real experiences, analyze them, and under-stand them in new ways. All this happens in a safe, time-compressed setting, much as a fire drill lets people explore behaviors needed for mass exits or as a flight simulator lets pilots practice flying in safety. And because this simulation is also a game, allowing human players to take action as they wish, it is challenging and fun.

## Contexts for Use

Since *Barnga* simulates misperceptions and consequent communication difficul-ties, it is equally at home in learning situations exploring cultural clashes and in countless other learning situations focusing more generically on understanding and bridging conflicts. It can be readily integrated within a training design wher-ever an experiential activity is appropriate. Whether the focus is heightened aware-ness for entry-level cross-cultural experiences, or analysis of day-to-day growth in cross-cultural settings, or exploration of the relationship of everyday commu-nication barriers to cross-cultural ones, this exercise will work, even for the inex-perienced simulation game facilitator.

### To Demonstrate Simulation Gaming

The beginning of this chapter described three learning settings using *Barnga* successfully. The first one, in North Carolina, demonstrated the value of experien-tial learning. Participants (faculty and administrators involved in international pro-grams in their respective colleges and universities) played the game and then ex-plored how they might use it in faculty or student academic and social settings where persons from more than one culture interact. Few games are short and simple enough to be played in their entirety in a demonstration context; too often players become so immersed in the game's subject matter that it is difficult for them, within the same time block, to shift gears and begin reflecting on possible uses. Because of its shortness and simplicity, *Barnga* is an ideal demonstration activity.

## To Explore Communication Difficulties

The second experience described at the beginning of this chapter used the game with high school students to explore generic communication difficulties. Many problems examined in cross-cultural learning situations can be analyzed from the perspective of the difficulties of human communication. Some people contend that even at the individual level we all are cultures unto ourselves, each operating out of our own set of rules and struggling to understand the other's rules and to bridge the gap. At the group or organization level, when organizations are merging or endeavoring to form a coalition or attempting to interact, the same cross-cultural struggle to understand, bridge, and communicate occurs.

After playing *Barnga,* participants can examine their simulated situation to determine what communication barriers were operating, noting that these barriers are greater when the differences are unexpected. They can look at the strategies they developed for crossing these barriers and assess which ones worked in the game. From here, it is a natural next step to find similarities and differences in their real life and to consider what strategies they might use to bridge them.

## To Prepare for Cross-Cultural Adjustment

The third example described a cultural orientation where participants from African and Arab countries were being briefed on adjusting to life in the United States. I have used *Barnga* in such a setting several times at the Washington International Center of Meridian House International in Washington, D.C. Even those persons for whom card playing was a new experience played with gusto and debriefed with insight once the initial hurdle of learning the "Five Tricks" card game was passed.

One reason *Barnga* is particularly effective with these groups is that much of the actual play period passes without verbal communication, thus eliminating—for a little while—the need to communicate in a language which, while common, is for most not their primary language. The language burden can be further lightened by translating the short player guide sheets into languages with which the participants are more comfortable. Similarly, players can be grouped by primary language for the initial descriptive phase of the debriefing, although the large group will have to reconvene to continue the discussion. The participants with whom I work enjoy drawing analogies to experiences they have actually had since arriving in the United States and suggest several simple but workable strategies they might employ to better understand and respond to difficulties arising from cross-cultural differences.

In much the same way, *Barnga* offers U.S. groups about to embark on journeys to other countries the opportunity to examine experiences in their own lives where misunderstanding has impeded communication and to use their reflections to prepare for similar experiences that are likely to arise when they are in a different cultural environment.

Truly a game for all seasons, *Barnga*—versatile, simple, and brief—can be used effectively in countless learning situations. Applications for matching real-life situations with this experiential tool are limited only by our imagination.

# Modifications

### Using *Barnga* as a Game-within-a-Game

The United Way asked me to design a simulation game to help players understand the intricacies of engaging effectively in community development. They wanted an exercise which not only would walk players through the basics of needs assessment, coalition forming, and careful planning, but also would give them an actual experience of perceiving and diagnosing needs. The result was a simulation with a kicker. A number of outside groups—funding bodies, community resource groups, and media—were assigned the task of developing solutions and seeking needed resources for problems they recognized in the community. The kicker was that no one told the players in the outside groups what the community problems were. Instead, a group of people in the middle of the room, "members of the community," played *Barnga* as it ordinarily is played. The outside groups, observing the play, knew nothing about what was going on. When the frustration, chuckles, and banging on tables began, it was up to them to try to understand and analyze the needs being expressed by "members of the community" and devise recommendations that would address them.

This experience was different from bringing in a homeless person or a pregnant teenager to talk with the group. That would enable participants to probe a specific problem area. The simulation game with *Barnga* in the middle gave participants a generic grip on what it means to try to understand a problem and then develop a strategy for responding to it. Since the "needy" were their peers right in the middle of the room, it was easy to check whether the understandings and strategies the outside groups developed were considered out of touch or patronizing or effective by those in need. Once again, *Barnga*'s brevity and simplicity made it ideal as a core game within a larger context. It lent itself easily to creating a sort of minilaboratory within which others could examine and experiment with alternative solutions.

### Procedural Changes

Thiagi's original game suggested forming groups of four players each, each group using a "deck" of twenty cards modified to contain only ace through five. For the United Way variation, I experimented with two modifications:

❖ Changing four players per group to six per group (and twenty cards per deck to twenty-eight cards per deck) in order to use the game with a large number of players but a manageable number of groups. This led to the discovery that the number of players per group is more or less irrelevant and can in fact change spontaneously at any time during play without affecting the operation of the game.

❖ Adding more specific rules governing tournament movement—namely, that those who win the most hands during a round move up to the next highest-numbered table, while those who win the fewest move down. This addition, suggested by Fred Goodman of the School of Education at the University of Michigan, introduces aspects of social mobility into the game. It also adds complexity, making for a bit more to be worked out among the players as they struggle with their communication barriers. Nevertheless, it actually affects the basic process and its impact little if at all.

While the changes noted above worked well, the value of adding any complexity should be carefully considered before implementation, since any complexity however intriguing may detract unnecessarily from the elegant simplicity of the game.

### Other Modifications

Richard Dukes of the University of Colorado at Colorado Springs experiments with an added "last round" of the game by removing the no-talking constraint and asking each group to agree on one set of rules they will follow at their table. This added step gradually makes explicit the only-guessed-at conflicts of the game and opens a path for attempted resolution of these conflicts by consensus. Pierre Corbeil of CEGEP (Collège d'Enseignement Général et Professionnel) of Drummondville, Québec, developed a version of the game for very young children using even simpler artifacts. He is exploring at what age children are able to move beyond simply getting angry or frustrated with one another and realizing that a breakdown of common cultural rules is behind what is happening.

## Considerations for Use

The game is so well designed that it practically runs itself. During play, you need only remain comfortable with the flow, and hang loose—no matter what happens.

This game depends on the gimmick of each set of rules being slightly different. You must take care not to reveal the gimmick too soon and not to become uncomfortable with it. Even though its gradual unfolding is what makes the game work, some players might resent having a trick played on them. To defuse any latent resentment, the gimmick issue can be raised during the debriefing by asking players if it was OK to have done this to them. It can also be pointed out that people understand and adjust to cultural differences at differing paces, just as understanding occurred at different times during the game.

Even persons not used to learning in a participative manner are quickly caught up by *Barnga,* probably because the initial interaction is so simple and straightforward, and the hidden gimmick emerges as something of a mystery to be unraveled. The restriction on verbal communication during play assures that people are bursting to talk by the time this restriction is lifted.

While the game aspect is practically foolproof and participants always are eager to begin the follow-up debriefing discussion, best results are obtained when care is taken to integrate the simulation within a total training context and to strategically plan the debriefing to focus on and draw out ideas about specific aspects relevant to the participants. Such preparation helps assure involvement by each member of the group and a rewarding exploration of the meanings and applications the game holds for them.

## References

Thiagarajan, Sivasailam. *Barnga: A Flexim on Cultural Clashes.* Original unpublished instructions. Workshops by Thiagi, 4423 East Trailridge Road, Bloomington, IN 47401, 1984.

Thiagarajan, Sivasailam, and Barbara Steinwachs. *Barnga: A Simulation Game on Cultural Clashes.* A SIETAR International publication. Yarmouth, ME: Intercultural Press, 1990.

## Resources

The *Barnga* manual referenced above contains an edited version of Sivasailam Thiagarajan's original *Barnga* instructions with thorough guidelines for preparation, facilitation, debriefing, and modification as well as master copies of participant handouts in three languages (English, French, and Spanish). The user must make the copies needed and supply the playing cards and table signs.

# Markhall: A Comparative Corporate-Culture Simulation

## Judee M. Blohm

The simulation *Markhall* involves two companies with different and contrasting management styles and corporate cultures. One, the Creative Card Company, is organized according to practices characteristic of large Japanese corporations. The other, the Ace Card Company, is based on American corporate models. Participants are divided in half and assigned to one or the other of the companies, where they engage in the creation, production, and marketing of greeting cards (such as Christmas, wedding, Mother's Day). In the several hours the simulation runs, the participants, playing employees of the corporations, experience many aspects of corporate life, including those related to production specifications and deadlines, changing markets, the use of new materials, reduction in capital, sales meetings, celebrations, deaths, retirements, and promotions.

## Development of the Simulation

Developed in 1983 for Youth for Understanding International Exchange (YFU) by Training Resources Group, *Markhall* was designed to be used in a reentry or follow-up program for American exchange students returning from Japan. The simulation was intended to meet two separate goals of the reentry program. The first goal was to study a contemporary issue of particular importance to Japan and the United States. The highly publicized differing management styles in Japan and the United States suited that aim. The second goal was to assist the students in career planning. To meet this goal, the simulation enabled the students to experience different organizational structures and management styles and relate them to the quality of work life they imagined would best meet their own needs, interests, and values.

### Field-testing

During 1983, *Markhall* was conducted on five separate occasions with groups of forty to sixty young people between the ages of 16 and 22. Different trainers conducted the simulation, approximately sixteen high school social science teachers assisted and/or played, and another ten educators and corporate donors to the exchange program observed as guests or participated. The results of these field trials were gratifying and some were unpredicted.

First, the Japanese-American connection with the companies did not become immediately apparent or influence the students' thinking during the debriefing. This was surprising, since they had recent, firsthand experience in Japan and tended to focus on "things Japanese." In fact, many students felt that either management style could or did exist in both countries, and many variations of these styles were part of their own experiences. On the other hand, they were able to identify basic cultural values of each country which might make certain aspects of the management styles more readily acceptable to employees in that culture.

Second, the simulation was exceedingly successful in creating very different corporate cultures rapidly. The need to produce and sell a product in short periods forced workers to perform according to the structure in their company. Trainers, visitors, and employee/participants who had moved from one company to the other easily noted specific corporate cultural differences, which were discussed during the debriefing.

Third, some of the stresses involved in a manufacturing business surfaced, and participants talked openly about them. In some runs of the game, employees talked to their supervisors about changes in communication or operating procedures to try to relieve some of the stress. Many participants identified aspects of work, such as repetitive tasks, which, given a choice, they would not want in a career.

And finally, corporate guests had interesting observations related to their own work situations. Some of the guests identified in the simulation examples of problems their corporations faced in reality. They commented on how educational it was for them to observe the participants playing both employees and managers in a neutral situation—that is, in a simulation where they were not involved in real decision making.

The result of these trial runs was a decision to prepare *Markhall* for publication in two forms: one for educators and one for management trainers. The differences in the two forms are ones of detail for the trainer and in the introduction and debriefing, not in the actual playing of the game. The leader's guide for educators focuses more on career development and corporate cultural issues. The leader's guide for management trainers provides additional information on how to use *Markhall* with various groups within a corporation to raise consciousness about how their own structures and systems affect production and morale and to form the basis for developing action plans for making changes in the corporation's management practices.

## Description

As mentioned in the opening paragraph of this chapter, the simulation sets up two contrasting organizations with different management styles and organizational practices: the Creative Card Company, based on the practices of some of the larger Japanese corporations, and the Ace Card Company, derived from an American industrial model. The principles around which the two companies were organized are listed below.

| Ace Card Company | Creative Card Company |
|---|---|
| Leader-centered decision making | Consensus or participative decision making |
| One-way (up or down) communication | Two-way or "all-way" communication |
| Short-term employment | Long-term employment |
| Specialized work/tasks | Nonspecialized work/tasks |
| Segmented work/social situations | Integrated work/social situations |
| Individual responsibility/accountability | Collective responsibility/accountability |

Since variations of both styles can be found in each country, and to minimize the possibility of inappropriate stereotyping, the company was not identified as American or Japanese. During the debriefing of the simulation, the corporate values that emerged during the simulation are discussed and participants explore which values are more likely to be acceptable in one culture or another. Also discussed are participants' own experiences in the United States and Japan that reinforce the varieties of styles possible and used in both countries.

# Procedures for Conducting *Markhall*

## Space and Materials

A minimum of two rooms and an adjoining hallway or other space are needed. One room needs to be large enough to hold the entire group, and a second room large enough for half of the group. Ace Card Company requires a divider screen to separate the two working units or a separate adjoining room. The hallway or other area is needed for the Buying Committee. Worktables are needed for each room. Three tables need to be reserved in the dining area if the simulation continues through lunch.

The *Markhall* materials consist of the leader's guide, multiple copies of each company's Philosophy and Operating Practices, role cards for each manager or director, and for other employees in each company. There are also role cards for members of the Buying Committee. Additionally there are instruction cards for each step in the simulation for each company, such as Marketing Target Cards, Cost Reduction Cards, Personnel Change Cards, and Rumor Cards. All cards are color-coded by company.

## Simulation Leader, Assistants, and Staff Preparation

The simulation leader introduces and debriefs *Markhall*, keeps time, and provides the instruction cards to assistants at designated times. There should be three additional facilitators. One is assigned to each company to help employees initially understand the organization of the company, including selecting their own positions in the company, and the product specifications of the company. The two assistants working with the companies monitor the trial run and help the managers follow the company philosophy. Throughout the game they will deliver the instruction cards to the managers and keep time for the company. They do not advise or intervene unless the company is straying from its stated philosophy and policies.

A third facilitator monitors the activity of the Buying Committee and makes sure the sales representatives have results to report back to their companies.

It is useful to have two or more observers with no responsibilities other than to move from company to company and note specifics to be used in the debriefing.

The simulation leader needs to be well versed in the entire game. An hour meeting prior to the beginning of the game is sufficient to brief assistants on the flow of the rounds; to have them read the philosophies, product specifications, and role cards for the companies; and to learn how they will receive instructions throughout the game.

## Flow of the Simulation

The game has three major parts: the introduction, the game, and the debriefing. The introduction includes setting the climate; presenting the goals of the game; assigning people to companies; learning company philosophy, structure, and tasks to be completed; and assigning and learning roles.

The introduction may take up to 50 minutes. The game phase is 2 1/2 hours plus the optional lunch period. This phase includes a 15-minute trial run, three 35-minute rounds, lunch (up to an hour), and a 15-minute final sales meeting and celebration. An hour is the minimum recommended for the debriefing; an hour and a half is more productive.

Divide the participant group in half on a random basis. Assign half as members of the Creative Card Company and half as Ace members. They should then be assigned to their separate rooms or physically divided working space.

The following list samples events that happen during the game:

*Trial Run.* Companies learn to function by producing Valentine cards; members practice roles and learn to use the materials.

*Round One.* Marketing targets of Christmas and New Year's cards are announced; a promotion takes place in Ace; and employees prepare for the first sales presentation of completed cards.

*Lunch.* Ace has a lunch table designated for management; Creative has its weekly lunch where management and workers eat together.

*Round Two.* Marketing target is changed to wedding, Mother's Day, and get well cards for teachers; sales meetings take place simultaneously while new production is in progress; cost reduction must be achieved (Ace lays off worker who is reassigned to Creative); report from sales meeting and preparation of new samples for sale.

*Round Three.* Sales meeting takes place while production for new marketing target begins; new materials are introduced; death of middle manager and promotion to fill position; different Rumor Cards introduced in each company.

*Final Sales Meeting and Celebration.* Final sales meetings proceed while each company has a celebration; final sales totals for the entire game are announced.

Since the debriefing should correspond to the goals established for each use of the game, the debriefing will vary from game to game. However, regardless of other aspects of the debriefing, allocate at least 30 minutes to exploring each company's organizational values and practices (communication channels, decision making, rewards, and the like) and strengths and weaknesses. Participants can relate these simulated management styles to ones they have experienced, further analyzing the strengths and weaknesses in actual work situations. One trainer reported, "Having had leadership jobs myself, the game helped me discover the interrelatedness of structures and policies and how these affect worker productivity and satisfaction."

Debriefing might also include the further analysis of those elements of corporate cultures that were selected to be part of the game. If appropriate for the participants, an exploration of comparative business practices can be included. Though American and Japanese styles are contrasted in the trainer notes, the American/German styles and Danish/Scandinavian styles might be compared if the game were used in Europe. Building an "ideal" organization is another potential follow-up that might be based on the debriefing.

Personal applications of information gained from participating in a simulation are always important. If the game is used for in-house training in a company, action planning for improving company systems or cultures may be added to the debriefing period. However, this would require more time, possibly adding another half day to the activity.

## Successful Uses of the Simulation

*Markhall* has been used in its original form and modified to fit specific needs. As noted earlier, it can be used successfully in career development seminars with high school and college students. In these instances, the focus is on understanding different management styles and how these affect the work climate, including the effect on work-task pressures experienced and the evaluation of one's own work experiences, and the preferences one expresses when making career decisions. Likewise, it can be used to stimulate a deeper study of American and Japanese (and other) management styles. In this usage, the simulation cannot stand alone; it must include prior or follow-up reading (or both), other methods or presentations, drawing in the personal experience of the participants, and organized discussion in order to prevent the oversimplification and stereotyping of these styles.

*Markhall* has been adapted for other audiences. For example, it was used in Denmark with graduate business students to give them practical insight into how

organizations function and to illustrate various dimensions of organizational culture and the effects of different management styles. In this setting, Buying Committee membership had interesting educational value itself. The Danish graduate
students in business considered themselves specialists in marketing. However,
when they served on the Buying Committee in the simulation, they found it does
not always come naturally to apply good theories. In action, they became prod-
uct-oriented instead of market-oriented, which provided for interesting debriefing.

In another situation, the different management styles embodied in the game
were used to help managers of a multinational corporation understand how some
of their headquarters' directives might be received and handled in branch companies in other countries.

## Considerations for Use

Five potential challenges to the effective conduct of *Markhall* need to be considered. They are space, number of participants, number of facilitators and assistants, time, and culture.

The *space* required if a large number are participating is significant. Ideally,
four separate working spaces are needed where participants cannot overhear or
see what is going on in other areas.

*Fifteen participants* is the minimum number required to make the companies
function (forty is the ideal maximum). Creative Card Company can run with six
people but a minimum of nine is required for the hierarchical structure of Ace.
Outsiders who are not program participants can compose the Buying Committee.

The number *of facilitators* depends on the size of the group, the amount of
control desired in keeping the companies true to their philosophies, and the
amount of observation desired. A minimum of two, a simulation director and an
assistant, can manage the game, with each helping one of the companies. With
only two facilitators, however, it is more difficult to monitor how well the companies adhere to their management philosophies and to be sure the Buying Committee is making timely decisions. Less time is available to make and note valuable observations as the game progresses. A director and three assistants are the
optimum staff for the simulation.

The amount of *time* required for the simulation is its biggest drawback. To
play out all of the steps (with the exception of lunch) requires a minimum of four
hours. A little time can be eliminated in the introduction, but less than 60 minutes of debriefing seriously jeopardizes the learning potential of the game. The
dynamics introduced through the lunch scene can be modified for a shorter coffee break. Decisions to significantly reduce the playing time require dropping
one round of the game or choosing to eliminate some of the aspects of corporate
life introduced in the various rounds. Another possible alternative is to change
the task or the product to make it possible to have something to sell or evaluate in
less time.

The final challenge occurs if you use the game in a *culture* where American-style greeting cards are not common. Though greeting cards are now on the market in places where they were previously unknown, the extent to which they are promoted and the events for which they are produced are not universal. This is not an insurmountable problem; it was overcome in the case cited earlier of using the game in Denmark. Examples of greeting cards were shown in the introductory portions of the game, and some of the production targets were changed to be more culturally appropriate.

## Resources

*Markhall* is available from:

>Youth for Understanding International Exchange
>Orientation and Training Services
>3501 Newark Street N.W.
>Washington, DC 20016

# Ecotonos: A Multicultural Problem-Solving Simulation

## Dianne M. Hofner Saphiere

"I came to observe *Ecotonos*. But once we got into it, I found even me, jaded as I am about simulations, getting really excited. *Ecotonos* transcended my ability to remain objective; in this sense, it's reality."

"Nobody didn't get it. And nobody got all of it. The process in *Ecotonos* itself demonstrates the value of diversity. There is always more to be gained."

"The Delphenian culture didn't come naturally to me and in fact I felt like an outsider in it. Once I got into the multicultural group, however, I saw myself clinging to other Delphenians."

These quotes are from people who have experienced *Ecotonos*, a simulation in which participants confront the realities (both positive and negative) of problem solving in multicultural groups. *Ecotonos* allows participants to discover their cross-cultural strengths and styles and to improve their performance in intercultural contexts. The simulation requires one hour plus about two hours for debriefing, and it can be used with a variety of audiences and with groups of people with very different learning styles.

Participants in *Ecotonos* learn how communication styles, values, expectations, and thought processes create power imbalances that allow some people to contribute meaningfully to the group task while others are disenfranchised. Participants learn to actively seek solutions which prevent such power imbalances from occurring, thus improving team productivity and strengthening members' self-esteem and commitment.

# The History and Rationale of *Ecotonos*

## Background

Since the early 1980s some colleagues and I have been working with international business teams involved in transferring technology, managing projects, constructing facilities, developing products, identifying resources, establishing distribution and marketing networks, and delivering customer services. Our intent was to enhance client productivity using an intercultural and systemic perspective. Our projects were always tailored for specific clients and were, therefore, very labor-intensive, and we were frequently brought into tense intercultural situations.

After many years we began to realize that although each project we conducted appeared unique, there were a number of core ideas and processes that were common to almost everything we did. We wondered if there were some way to condense our experience and package the process, refining it to a higher level than we were able to do when designing it anew for every project. A package design would allow us to focus our learning and transfer our knowledge to other facilitators, and it would free us to further customize program designs. The design of *Ecotonos* began by analyzing several key dimensions of our work. These dimensions are:

❖ **Task focus.** Our client teams were frequently cross-functional groups whose members had come together to complete a task; the task was all they had in common. They were concerned about deadlines and budgets in addition to the quality of the final outcomes of their task. That would determine their success. We therefore designed *Ecotonos* around a central task, which enabled it to be different each time it was played, preventing the facilitators from getting bored and allowing participants to assess their progress by playing it at several different points in time.

❖ **Real issues.** In our work we found that a powerful way to introduce cultural issues was to get group members to discuss their own expectations and styles. ("I want to have a clearer idea of expected revenue; you seem to want to develop a friendship first.") This avoided the dangers of stereotypic generalizations (for example, Americans tend to be "bottom line") and allowed individual and regional differences to be taken into account. In *Ecotonos,* we wanted participants to experience the realities of attempting a task in a multicultural group. We wanted the simulation to be emotionally involving and to illustrate participants' personal tendencies in dealing with differences.

❖ **Group process and individual abilities.** Our experience had convinced us that no matter how committed and talented a work team might be, it would be evaluated as underachieving if its members were not open to learning about group processes and were unable to generate new solutions creatively for the benefit of all concerned. Therefore, *Ecotonos* was designed to allow participants to focus on the impact of the problem-solving *process* as well as on the abilities each team member could contribute.

❖ **Personal effectiveness.** We believe that there are certain components and patterns of culture which, once learned, allow a person to become a Cultural Detective* and find his/her own most effective way to interact in other cultures. Rather than design *Ecotonos* with defined, predetermined cultures, as some cross-cultural simulations do, we wanted to allow behaviors and values to be assembled in random combinations so different effects could be created. Valuing assertiveness when combined with a logical, persuasive communication style is quite different from valuing assertiveness combined with an intuitive, hesitant communication style. In the latter, one may appear to contradict the other, but every culture has its inherent contradictions. The members of a culture manage those contradictions in different ways, and it was that which we wanted our participants to understand. We wanted the simulation to teach our clients the components of culture they would find in differing combinations in the real-world cultures they encountered.

❖ **Many types of "multicultural."** It was our belief that the skills and strategies for effectiveness in multicultural situations varied with the composition of the group. For example, a minority member of a group might need different competencies than a majority member, and members of a group with a mix of several cultures would need different abilities than members of a group representing only two cultures. We wanted to structure *Ecotonos* in a way which would allow us to explore this hypothesis.

## The Development Process

Starting in 1990, we tested *Ecotonos* with over 2,000 people in many different situations, and each time we recorded and integrated our findings. We encouraged colleagues to use the simulation in return for their feedback on how we might make it better. *Ecotonos* was used extensively by Sony and by Nipporica in Japan, in both Japanese and English, and in U.S. international academic settings, intercultural marriage counseling, multicultural communities, and business.

**Alternating between theorizing and doing.** Once we had analyzed these dimensions, we discussed the factors which most often interfered with problem solving in multicultural groups. These included: (1) approach, (2) listening style, (3) treatment of differences, (4) attitudes regarding teamwork, (5) beliefs about leadership, (6) customs regarding space and touch, (7) gestures and eye contact, (8) focus on and use of time, (9) explanation or speaking style, and (10) past, present, and future orientation. These became the categories of the cultural rule cards for *Ecotonos*.

From this base we selected a name for the simulation and names for the culture groups and produced the visual images, rules, and culture group buttons. We reviewed children's picture books, comics, ornithological and horticultural drawings, legends, dictionaries, and thesauruses to find the images we wanted:

---

*Cultural Detective* is a Nipporica trademarked process for learning to read the clues presented in an unfamiliar situation and thereby make sense of it.

images which were evocative and yet as culturally neutral as possible. We also made an effort to include in each rule a concrete behavior based on anthropological fact. Originally we used statements of values or assumptions that were too theoretical and abstract; participants spent so much time defining their cultures that it detracted from the flow of the simulation.

# Procedure for Using *Ecotonos*

## Overall Process

*Ecotonos* is a multicultural problem-solving simulation in three steps: acculturation, monocultural group problem solving, and mixed or multicultural group problem solving. Both monocultural and multicultural groups work to solve the same problem. The debriefing deals first with participants' emotions and then focuses on the processes and skills for solving problems in multicultural groups.

## The Simulation

Usually three facilitators conduct *Ecotonos*. Participants are given one of three culture badges: Aguila, an eagle on a teal background; Delphenius, a dolphin on a maroon background; or Zante, a daisy on a yellow background. Acculturation takes place through each group choosing cultural rule cards (usually three, but up to ten). These become the rules for their culture. Each group discusses the meaning of their rules, how they fit together, and how the group will manifest them. Then, using their rules, the group creates a story about how its culture came into being.

Once the groups seem comfortable with their cultures, the same task is assigned to all groups. This might be a case study with an issue to be solved, or it might be a more physical or creative task such as making a tower or a paper airplane. The groups are given ten to twenty minutes to work on the problem. They are stopped in the middle of their task and reassigned to form multicultural groups composed of members of the three groups described above.

The three multicultural groups continue working on their task for another ten to fifteen minutes. The facilitators play a crucial role during this stage, as participants may be so involved in the task that they forget to be attentive to their problem-solving process. To illustrate the dynamics of the three different multicultural situations, one group may have a balanced number of people from two cultures, one a majority/minority composition, and the third a diverse mix of people from all three cultures.

## The Debriefing

Helping participants make sense of their experience can be done in many ways. One facilitator who runs the simulation often has participants write down how it felt to be in their monocultural and multicultural groups and what in their discussions went well and what did not. Once the reactions are recorded, he leads all participants in a debriefing. In this manner he is able to conduct the simulation by himself.

My preference is to employ three facilitators and have each debrief one of the multicultural groups, discussing their experiences in both their monocultural group and their multicultural group. Participants can then analyze a specific topic, such as what enabled the mixed group to create a common, workable culture and what drove the members of the group apart. Small-group reactions and learnings are then shared with all participants, and the lead facilitator weaves them together and emphasizes the key learnings.

In a third type of debriefing, the lead facilitator conducts most of the discussion in a large group, with both participants and cofacilitators offering details on the small-group experiences as appropriate. This is the preferred way to debrief when using inexperienced cofacilitators.

An important though optional part of the debriefing is to ask the participants of each multicultural group to draw or diagram their problem-solving process. These drawings take many forms, but are usually quite revealing. The drawings can be shared with members of the other multicultural groups and the dynamics of their diverse situations compared. Participants might also be asked to depict in drawings their concept of the ideal processes, skills, or procedures they would need to realize such ideals.

To maximize learning during the debriefing, participants must be helped to separate themselves from their roles. They should speak as themselves *about* how it was to be a Delphenian or Zantean. This level of objectivity or removal from the emotions of the game is an ability participants need to be able to achieve in their everyday lives.

## Contexts in Which *Ecotonos* Has Been Used Successfully

Though *Ecotonos* was developed primarily from our experience with international business teams, it has also been valuable in domestic diversity contexts and in academic, nonprofit, and community venues. No matter what the context, the facilitator must understand the situations, experience, needs, expectations, and learning styles of the participants and present the simulation accordingly. *Ecotonos* itself is very flexible; the facilitator can determine how complex the cultures will be, the amount of structure imposed versus the "discovery" that is permitted in the process, and whether to focus the introduction and debriefing on problem-solving skills, power structures, or the decision-making process.

**With language teachers.** One of our colleagues conducts training for professionals who teach English to non-native speakers. He feels that unless these teachers have themselves attempted to learn in mixed groups, they will be unable to empathize with their students. At the beginning of his teacher training courses, he conducts *Ecotonos*. His debriefing focuses on what the teachers have discovered about themselves and how they might create more supportive language-learning environments.

**With study abroad and foreign students.** Another colleague uses *Ecotonos* in orientation programs for students bound for locations worldwide. He wants to help them prepare for their overseas experience by reflecting on what they will feel and how they will manage their experience. As the students learn to observe the dynamics of "process," they discover and come to better understand aspects of their own styles of learning and expression and are able to compare these with the styles of others in the group. This educator values *Ecotonos* because he feels it goes beyond individual behaviors to issues of group cooperation.

**With multicultural communities.** *Ecotonos* can be valuable in helping members of service organizations, special-interest groups, and citizen representatives of multicultural communities understand one another and work together to appropriately serve all members of a community.

**With continuous-improvement/total-quality teams.** One trainer related a story of a team of thirty European-American males on a manufacturing team with two African-American males. She had been hired to conduct a team-building session to facilitate implementation of total-quality and continuous-improvement concepts. Team members saw no need for a team-building session. The trainer believed there was such a need and felt the answer lay in an activity which would create an awareness of the differences within apparently homogeneous groups. She conducted *Ecotonos* using a case study about a current problem on the organization's production line. She felt the simulation made all the difference to her own success both with the subsequent team building and with the team's successful implementation of total quality. *Ecotonos* helped the members to see in a meaningful way the enormous complexity of communication and cooperation and to broaden their definitions of multiculturalism beyond issues of gender, birthplace, and skin color.

**With international business executives.** I once worked with an international, cross-functional team of executives who were building a production facility in Asia. Although the project began smoothly, eight months into it the national subgroups began doubting one another's intentions, developing many hidden agendas in the process. Playing *Ecotonos* helped them, among other things, to realize how necessary their differing perspectives and skills were to the success of the project. They renewed their motivation to work together to bring the project to completion.

**As a benchmark for acculturation/a program evaluation tool.** When graduates of intercultural training programs participate in *Ecotonos*, the simulation provides a good measure of what they have learned and have integrated into their behavior. Several colleagues have said they see visible behavioral changes when using *Ecotonos* for pre/posttest purposes. When it is used in conjunction with a behavioral skills list, *Ecotonos* provides concrete feedback on participant progress.

## Considerations for Use

You should encourage participants' personal involvement in the process of *Ecotonos* by using facilitation techniques which are culturally appropriate for the participants.

**Preparation.** Experience any simulation before you attempt to conduct it. This is especially true of *Ecotonos*. Read the manual thoroughly. Talk to others who have done it. Be very comfortable with the entire process before conducting the simulation. If it is possible, speak with each participant prior to the simulation. At the least, spend some time in the introductory phase getting to know them. This will help you gauge their needs, experience, and learning styles; create a relationship with them; and prepare them and your cofacilitators for the types of emotional and cognitive reactions participants might experience.

**Facilitation.** One of the risks of almost any simulation is that the outcome cannot be predicted. You can prepare and organize, but the key to success is your ability to work with the participants' reactions and pull the learnings from their experience—to help participants make sense of what happened. While a facilitative approach is necessary, participants in *Ecotonos* tend to make a wide variety of discoveries about themselves and about multicultural groups. It takes strong focus and leadership to weave the disparate individual learnings into coherent learning for the group as a whole.

**Movement of participants.** *Ecotonos* involves the creation of three cultures and the mixing of members of these cultures into multicultural groups. There are several phases of debriefing, including both small- and large-group discussion. Participants must move physically and psychologically. It is important to remember to:

1. Focus on the participants and the process; do not get distracted by the logistics. If groups are not evenly divided, for example, the simulation will still work well.

2. Prepare ahead of time so you know who will be in which culture group and who will transfer to which multicultural group. Sign-up sheets work well for this; you can also transfer people from group to group simply by naming them off and directing them.

3. Have a room large enough to conduct the game and the debriefing so that each group can meet by itself without overhearing the others. One large room will also facilitate the transfer of participants between groups.

**Create a comfortable and familiar atmosphere.** It is your responsibility to conduct the simulation in such a way that participants are comfortable with and able to learn from it.

1. Arrange the physical space and props such as newsprint and blackboards to simulate the type of meeting or group-work situation with which the participants are most familiar.

2. Introduce the simulation so that participants realize the emotions and the insights that may arise, but also in a way which does not overwhelm. When introducing the simulation I once talked about how much fun *Ecotonos* was, and then my participants did not take it seriously. I have also gone too far in the other direction, talking about how intense the experience can be and how much learning can occur; participants felt intimidated.

3. Use a case study or task which is suitable to the participants and which deals with the issues they encounter in their daily lives. This will help them be themselves within the context of their *Ecotonos* culture.

**Discussing too many points.** *Ecotonos* is a rich experience which produces a variety of complex learnings. It is your responsibility to help the participants hold on to two or three of the most meaningful of these.

1. Introduce a couple of skills or concepts before the simulation, and ask participants to watch for or try to practice them during the simulation.

2. Elicit participant feedback, validating feelings and comments, but concentrate the debriefing on one, two, or three key themes to synthesize and focus participants' comments.

3. Proceed with the debriefing layer by layer, spending time to help participants understand the basics if necessary. Because *Ecotonos* is so real, participants often fail to maintain their objectivity. Even sophisticated audiences well-grounded in intention/perception theory can get caught up in the emotion of the experience and attribute blame if you proceed too quickly.

**Coordination with cofacilitators.** *Ecotonos* is best conducted with three or four facilitators. At least one person, the lead facilitator, should be skilled at processing or debriefing the experience. The others can stay with the culture groups and could be volunteer assistants from the group.

1. Meet with the cofacilitators prior to the simulation. Be sure that each person understands his/her own role and the roles of the other facilitators. Discuss what they should watch for, at which points they should intervene in the small-group process, and how they should participate in the debriefing.

2. Have one facilitator stay with each group throughout the simulation. The insights gained and the observations which can be shared with the participants later will be invaluable.

## Conclusion

*Ecotonos* comes in a colorful box with an instruction manual, metal cultural name pins, thirty sets of laminated rule cards, and three prewritten case studies. The manual includes instructions for creating tasks for specific groups. *Ecotonos* was created by Nipporica Associates and is published by Intercultural Press. An *Ecotonos* UserGroup has formed to share information about uses and adaptations of the simulation. This is an independent group of users representing many disciplines. Facilitator Certification Workshops are held periodically to enhance facilitator skills with *Ecotonos*. Contact the publisher for information on either of these services.

## Resources

Adler, N. J., and J. L. Graham. "Cross-Cultural Interaction: The International Comparison Fallacy." *Journal of International Business Studies* 20, 1989.

Bales, R. F. *Personality and Interpersonal Behavior.* New York: Holt, Rhinehart and Winston, 1970.

Fodor, E. M., and T. Smith. "The Power Motive as an Influence on Group Decision Making." *Journal of Personal and Social Psychology* 42, 1982.

Fontaine, G. "Support Systems for International Microcultures." Paper presented at the International Society for Intercultural Education, Training and Research Annual Conference in Montreal, May 1987.

Heskin, A. D., and R. A. Heffner. "Learning about Bilingual, Multicultural Organizing." *Journal of Applied Behavioral Science* 23, 1987.

Martin, J. N., ed. "Intercultural Communication Competence" [special issue]. *International Journal of Intercultural Relations* 13, no. 3, 1989.

McCann, D., and C. Margerison. "Managing High-Performance Teams." *Training and Development Journal* 43, 1989.

Nipporica Associates. *Ecotonos: A Multicultural Problem-Solving Simulation.* Yarmouth, ME: Intercultural Press, 1993.

Parnell, M., and J. Vanderkloot. "How to Build Cross-Cultural Bridges." *Communication World* 6,1989.

Reagan, P. and J. Rohrbaugh. "Group Decision-Process Effectiveness: A Competing Values Approach." *Group and Organization Studies* 15, 1990.

Schwartzman, H. B. "Research on Work-Group Effectiveness: An Anthropological Critique." In *Designing Effective Work Groups,* edited by P. S. Goodman and Associates. San Francisco: Jossey-Bass, 1986.

Schweiger, D. M., W. R. Sandberg, and P. L. Reohner. "Experiential Effects of Dialectical Inquiry, Devil's Advocacy and Consensus Approaches to Strategic Decision Making." *Academy of Management Journal* 32, 1989.

Wood, J. "Alternative Methods of Group Decision-Making: A Comparative Examination of Consensus, Negotiation and Voting." In *Emergent Issues in Decision-Making,* edited by G. M. Phillips and J. Wood. Carbondale, IL: Southern Illinois University Press, 1984.

# The Critical Incident as a Training Tool

## Albert R. Wight

Over the past thirty years, critical incidents have proved to be one of the most useful and effective training tools. They have been used in a wide variety of training programs—not just cross-cultural—where achievement of increased understanding of human attitudes, expectations, behavior, and interaction (one's own as well as others') is an important goal. Relatively easy to develop and to conduct, they never fail (if written and used properly) to engage participants at a meaningful, personal level in examining attitudes and behaviors that might be critical to their effectiveness in the role for which they are preparing.

## History

Apparently, critical incidents were first used by Flanagan (1954) for task analysis in developing job descriptions; later they were used to assess training needs and to evaluate training programs (Morton and Wight 1963). To my knowledge, the first use of critical incidents in a cross-cultural situation was in the culture assimilators developed by Harry Triandis and associates at the University of Illinois in the early 1960s and in situational tests developed at the University of Utah in 1964 by Michael Tucker, Gary de Mik, and myself for use in selection of U.S. Peace Corps volunteers (Taylor et al. 1967).

In 1965, I converted the critical incidents and other situational tests we had developed at Utah into instrumented, experiential exercises for use in Peace Corps training at Utah State University and Southwest Texas Teachers College (Wight 1967). The Critical Incidents Exercise (CIE), a series of individual, small-group, and large-group activities in which a number of critical incidents are analyzed and discussed, was included as one of the principal exercises in the *Guidelines for Peace Corps Cross-Cultural Training* (Wight and Hammons 1970) and has been used widely by the Peace Corps since that time. Aside from its application in the training of Peace Corps volunteers, the CIE has been used in a variety of settings to prepare persons to live and work in other cultures. It is still part of Peace Corps staff training, and I have incorporated it in cross-cultural training programs for VISTA, Job Corps, New Careers, New Start (Canada); in the training of teachers to work on or near American Indian reservations; and in the training of managers and their families to work and live in cultures different from their own. (CIE will henceforth signify any concentrated series of critical incidents used in cross-cultural training.)

# Description of the Method

Critical incidents used in cross-cultural training are brief descriptions of situations in which there is a misunderstanding, problem, or conflict arising from cultural differences between interacting parties or where there is a problem of cross-cultural adaptation. Each incident gives only enough information to set the stage, describe what happened, and possibly provide the feelings and reactions of the parties involved. It does not explain the cultural differences that the parties bring to the situation. These are discovered or revealed as a part of the exercise.

I have never used only one incident in training, and it is unlikely that I ever would. Instead, a number of incidents, describing different situations and revealing different aspects of the culture, are used in the CIE. There are many ways critical incidents can be included in training. A number of incidents can be grouped to illustrate a concept or process, like the conflict-negotiation example presented by Milton J. Bennett in this volume. It is also effective to teach trainees to write critical incidents from their own experience, as demonstrated by William Dant (this volume). The CIE can be used as the central activity in a short training program, then followed by role plays or situational exercises to provide skill practice in cross-cultural interaction. The CIE can be presented as a case study that delves deeply into a given area (Wight and Hammons 1970) or as one of many complementary exercises in a longer training program.

## Purpose and Objectives of the CIE

The purpose of the CIE is to confront participants with examples of the kinds of difficult, confusing, frustrating problems or conflict situations they can expect to encounter in interacting with persons from another culture or adjusting to a new culture. Objectives of the exercise are to:

❖ Increase participants' awareness of their own typical, idiosyncratic, or culturally determined interpretations and explanations of others' behavior and their own attitudes and responses in situations such as the ones described.

❖ Draw out, compare, and analyze the various interpretations and perceptions of participants, resource persons, and staff.

❖ Clarify the cultural differences in the incidents that might have contributed to the misunderstandings, problems, and conflicts or influenced the various interpretations and explanations of the participants and resource people.

❖ Assist participants in understanding the diversity among members of each culture as well as normative differences between the cultures.

❖ Help participants achieve the understanding necessary to behave more appropriately and effectively in similar situations.

❖ Enlarge participants' awareness of the kinds of things they need to learn and motivate them to continue learning.

❖ Provide the basis for engaging in role plays that will build skill in handling problematic cross-cultural situations.

## Selecting Critical Incidents

Ideally, incidents are based on actual experiences of the writers or persons interviewed by the writers, but any given incident might represent a composite of a number of related situations. In thinking back over one's experience, it usually is not difficult to recall in some detail those situations that were most difficult or perplexing. When developing case studies through interviews, it helps to ask the interviewees to recall situations in which they thought they were particularly effective and situations in which they were ineffective, and why. Some of the people you interview have probably kept a journal, which is a good source of incidents. Hypothetical incidents should be used only as a last resort.

In developing or selecting incidents for a given program, you should identify the nature of the participants' assignment and the kinds of cross-cultural interactions they can anticipate. Select incidents based on their relevance, breadth of coverage of important situations, and insight into fundamental cultural differences and the kinds of problems and misunderstandings that arise from these differences. When you are training supervisors or counselors, you might focus on the fundamental phenomena of human behavior (in addition to cross-cultural problems) and the interaction and relations between supervisor and employee or counselor and client. Over time you will acquire a collection of incidents which can be adapted for use in new training programs.

The number of incidents selected for a CIE will depend to some extent on the time available for the exercise, but generally it is better to have too many incidents than too few. With too few, important situations may go unexplored. My preference is to use between ten and fifteen incidents representing various situations and cultural differences.

## Writing Critical Incidents

**The incident.** Having selected the situations and behavioral or cultural concepts you wish to present, you now have the task of writing the incidents. Each incident should be brief and succinct, providing only the information needed for the exercise. It should not be too complex. It should focus on one issue or problem or a few related issues. It should provide enough background information to set the stage and should describe what happened, *but not why it happened.* No clues should be given to help a reader unfamiliar with the culture understand why the person from the other culture behaved or reacted as he/she did. The reactions of the person from the participants' home culture should be authentic, what might reasonably be expected to occur in a similar encounter within the home culture. The incident can end with an action taken by one of the parties in the incident or with a dilemma the reader has to resolve. When using real incidents, names and any other identifying features should be changed to maintain anonymity. In summary, the incident should:

❖ identify the main actors in the incident;
❖ give only enough background information to set the stage;
❖ indicate when and where the incident occurred, if it is helpful;
❖ describe briefly what happened, the sequence of events;
❖ describe how the person from the participants' culture reacted, his or her feelings, thoughts, and actions—depending on the point to be made with the incident;
❖ if appropriate to the situation, describe *how* the person from the other culture reacted, but not *why.*

Once written, an incident should be checked by persons familiar with the culture to make sure it is plausible and typical and that names and terms are accurate. Incidents should also be checked for clarity and succinctness and examined as a collection to ensure that the important cultural differences are covered and that each incident is unique in its representation of potential problems.

**The questions.** Follow each incident with questions that require participants to analyze what happened, give their interpretations, and indicate what they feel would be appropriate attitudes and behavior in such a situation. Asking participants to identify with the person from their own culture results in increased cultural self-awareness; identifying with the person from the other culture results in increased awareness of the other culture and empathy with persons from that culture. Questions similar to those below might be asked.

1. To what extent do you agree or disagree with _____ (name the person)? (I usually use a scale from "totally agree" to "totally disagree.")
2. Why do you agree or disagree to the extent that you do?
3. If you were _____ (name the person), what would you have done?
4. How would you feel if you were _____ (name the person)?
5. Why do you think_____ (name the person) reacted (or felt) as he/she did?
6. If you were _____ (name the person), what would you do now?

It is advisable to use a separate page for each incident, with the questions and space for answering the incident on the same page as the incident. Different questions might be used with different incidents, depending on the points to be made.

## Location in a Training Program

**At the beginning.** The CIE can be used early in the program to confront participants with perplexing incidents they probably will not understand. This is a very effective way of getting their attention, convincing them of the importance of learning more about the other culture, and motivating them to do so. It also is a way (and I feel this is particularly important) of eliminating any expectation of being taught by "experts" and orienting them toward problem solving and doing their own thinking in an experiential program.

Using the exercise at the beginning of the program is also an effective way of eliciting typical, habitual, culturally determined ways of interpreting and dealing with such situations and demonstrating how inappropriate and ineffective such behavior is in the cross-cultural context. It helps the participants recognize the importance of learning more about themselves as products of their own culture, others as products of their culture, and the dynamics of interaction when the two come together.

**Later in the program.** Alternatively, the CIE can be used later in a program to build on the cultural understanding participants have achieved through other means, to provide more specific examples of situations in which cultural differences will be manifested, and to test participants' ability to apply their cultural understanding. When used as examples or illustrations of cultural differences identified earlier in the training, the incidents are more reinforcing than illuminating (which can be important). Whether used earlier or later in a program, it is best not to use incidents that are directly repetitious of points made or examples given in other exercises.

## Procedure

**Individual work.** At the beginning of the exercise, ask participants to work individually on the incidents. Send the assignment in advance or introduce it when the participants arrive for the training program.

Following a brief written or verbal introduction to and overview of the exercise, ask the participants to read the incidents and answer the questions following each one. If participants are on site at the beginning of the exercise, review the instructions orally. Suggest that they not write lengthy responses to the questions, since the answers will be primarily for their own use in group discussions. Be sure to ask them not to discuss their answers with anyone until the scheduled group discussion. This is particularly important if you give it as a homework assignment. (See Example 1, page 137, for typical instructions for the individual activity.)

If individual work is done in the session, inform participants how much time they have to read and respond to the incidents, so that they will read quickly and write only a brief response to each question. Sufficient time should be allowed, however, for slow readers to read all the incidents. It helps to schedule a coffee break at the end of this period to allow extra time for participants to complete the work. If it appears that some might not be able to finish even with this extra time, ask them to skim through the remainder of the incidents quickly but not to take time to write out their answers.

Occasionally a participant will complain that a situation is not described in sufficient detail to answer the questions. Point out that this represents reality. They probably will be faced with many situations in which they have limited knowledge, do not know where the other person is coming from or what he or she is thinking, and have to make decisions and react with little or no time to reflect or to collect additional information. (See Example 2, page 138, for an example of a critical incident used in a counseling or supervision training program.)

**Small-group discussion.** The second part of the exercise is small-group discussion. How this is handled depends on the number of participants, availability of resource persons, and whether or not staff decides to participate in the discussions. Discussions are more effective in a group that has a sufficient number of participants to provide a variety of views and opinions but small enough to allow each person to participate actively. My experience suggests this to be no less than five or six persons and no more than eight or nine, not counting resource persons. With more than nine persons, it is better to break into two small groups, unless your number of resource persons is insufficient. With more than eighteen persons, break into three groups, and so on. The small groups should be as heterogeneous as possible.

It is not essential that you, the trainer, or other staff members take part in the group discussions. It might be easier to achieve open participation if you do not. With written instructions given to the group (see Example 3, page 139,) and reinforced orally, participants are fully capable of managing and monitoring their own discussion. *Do not assign a group leader,* regardless of how uneasy you might be about the possibility that the discussion will be uncontrolled. The group will function more effectively without a group leader, and everyone will be free to participate. Tell the groups they will be asked to share the results of their discussions with the other groups in a general meeting. Who represents them in the large group is a decision that should be left up to them. They might even choose to have more than one spokesperson.

When giving the instructions, you might tell the participants one way to start the discussion of each incident is to record quickly the scale values selected by the participants (if you used a scale). These should be recorded on a chalkboard or newsprint, where everyone can see the range of responses. If there is a wide range, the group might want to start with the extremes. If there appears to be a lot of agreement, they might choose to go around the room with each person giving his or her response to the particular question being discussed.

**Resource persons.** It is important that one or more, preferably two or three, resource people from the other culture be present in each small group. With only one resource person in a group, only one view from the other culture is available. With more than one person, more than one view might be revealed, particularly if one is male and one female, one is older and one younger, one supports a particular political perspective and one an opposite view, and so on. Variety in terms of views and experience should be considered in the selection of resource persons. If you do not have sufficient resource persons to include at least one in each small group, it would be best to save their participation for the general meeting following the small-group meetings. It is important to give copies of the exercise to the resource people in advance, so they will have an opportunity to study the incidents carefully before meeting with the participants. They can review the incidents while the small groups are meeting or discuss them with you and other staff as well.

Brief the resource persons separately before the exercise, to give them time to think about their role and to ask questions. If this is not possible, explain their role as you give the instructions for the small-group activity. It should be made clear that the resource persons are not instructors but rather participants, all of whom are analyzing, discussing, and explaining what happened in the incidents from their cultural perspective and seeking understanding of what was happening from the other cultural perspective. It is quite common for resource persons to report that they have learned a lot about their own culture, and themselves, as well as the participants' culture during the discussion, just as the participants do.

When giving the instructions, suggest to the group that regular participants give their views for each incident first, followed by the resource people. This helps participants become aware of how much or how little they know about the other culture and forces them to think more deeply about the issues before they hear from the resource persons. It is important that the resource persons explain how they think the people from their culture in the incidents felt and why they behaved and reacted as they did.

The CIE can also be used in programs with multicultural groups in which people from different cultures are learning to work together. Here resource persons are not needed, because the participants become resources for each other. If the exercise is used for team building, with people who will continue to work together, participants are learning skills they can continue to use after training.

**Facilitator's role.** You should monitor the small groups to see how they are doing and remind them occasionally how much time is remaining for the discussion. Observe for a while in each group, but avoid participating. This keeps you in touch with how well the discussions are going. If you do decide to participate, make sure you are not drawn into an expert role. You might, if you choose to do so, ask questions that are not being asked, but with the realization that this is likely to be more of a hindrance than a help, since it takes the initiative away from the participants.

If it appears that all the incidents will not be discussed in the allotted time, you should suggest that the group prioritize the incidents, based on those they are most interested in, and proceed in the priority order established. You might also decide that it would be worthwhile to continue the discussion beyond the scheduled time and shorten another activity. It is more important to make effective use of the time than to adhere to a schedule.

If you have enough people for only one group, it would probably be better if you remained with the group, in the role of facilitator, not expert. It is essential that you understand the facilitator role, however. You should do only as much talking as required to keep the analysis and discussion going, making sure that all participants remain involved. Recording scale values and seeking clarification of positions taken by individual participants are useful things you can do. You should encourage the exploration of various perceptions, interpretations, explanations, and possible consequences. When you feel the time is right, ask the resource persons to share their reactions to each incident and to the discussion. If you feel you have something to add toward the end of the discussion of an incident, do so, but more as a participant giving other views, clarifying or elaborating, than as the expert with the final answers.

Another thing you might do as facilitator is to keep a running record on newsprint of the cultural differences identified during discussion of the incidents. You can then review these as a part of the summary toward the end of the session.

**Summary discussion.** When the small groups have completed their discussion of the incidents, the results are shared in a general meeting. It is not necessary to discuss each incident again, only those that were particularly perplexing. The highlights of what was learned should be stated briefly, particularly insights into the cultures. Each group should report, but it is good if this develops into a general discussion rather than formal presentations. You should record the cultural differences identified (just as suggested if you have only one group) where they can be seen by all participants. These should then be reviewed in the summary and duplicated and given to each participant.

Resource persons should be free to participate along with the others in the summary discussion. As facilitator, you should draw them in if they do not readily contribute. If you do not have enough resource persons to meet with each small group, structure the summary discussion so the small groups report on a given incident before the resource persons give their reactions.

Resource persons may not always agree on the perceptions and interpretations of the attitudes, feelings, and reactions of people in the incidents who are from their own culture, or on the reasons for their reactions. This can lead to a very productive discussion and reinforce awareness of differences within the culture. Differences among resource persons also help to prevent stereotyping and might be pointed out as a demonstration of the fact that we are dealing with cultures in transition (our own as well as the other culture). Differences might also reveal that a given problem is more likely to occur with people from particular age, social, education, or regional groups. Or they might indicate that a resource person is out of touch with his or her own culture and might have become too Westernized. This might be discussed, but discreetly. It could also be worthwhile to examine how people with a lot of exposure to other cultures differ from more traditional people in the culture.

You should be careful not to disagree with a resource person in front of the participants, even if you are sure the person is mistaken. It is important to build the credibility of the resource persons and not to cause them to lose face. You might ask questions for clarification or examples, particularly if you think the person did not understand the question or the issue. If the statement is important enough to correct, you should find another time and a way that does not discredit or embarrass the resource person. You might want to discuss the issue with him or her when it is convenient, away from the participants.

The summary processing of the critical incidents, particularly when used early in the program, is an appropriate time to discuss attribution theory. Point out that if we do not have sufficient understanding of another culture, we have no choice but to rely on our experience in our own culture to interpret what is happening. However, when we attribute motives, intentions, feelings, reactions, and objectives to the other person on the basis of what is appropriate in our own culture, we may be making a mistake that has serious consequences. It could reduce our effectiveness in the interaction and damage our relations with that person. The critical incidents allow us to examine many of these possibilities in the safety of the training program and, one would hope, help participants avoid making mistakes in real life.

# Comparison with Other Methods

### Case Studies and the CIE

The primary difference between a CIE and a case study is that the former is made up of a number of incidents relating to different situations and actors whereas the latter involves a series of related incidents within a single situation involving one set of actors, somewhat akin to comparing a collection of short stories with a novel. While a case study goes into greater detail and depth in one situation, a CIE gives broader coverage through a variety of incidents in unrelated situations.

Selection of one versus the other depends on whether the objective is to achieve depth of understanding in one situation (case study) or broader understanding of a variety of situations (critical incidents). Given the limitations of time and the broad objectives in most cross-cultural training programs, the CIE usually is the more useful, but there is no reason why both could not be used in the same program. The technique of the two is similar. In fact, I modeled the CIE to some extent on the case study, after several years' experience with case studies in management training.

### Culture Assimilators and the CIE

The CIE is similar to the culture assimilator in that both are based on critical incidents and present a variety of situations representing a wide range of significant differences between two cultures. It is the way in which the exercises are developed and used that is different, but it is a critical difference. The culture assimilator follows the design and assumptions of programmed-learning methodology, the CIE those of experiential-learning methodology. It is important to understand the difference.

In the culture assimilator, each incident is followed by three, four, or five interpretations. The trainee chooses one of the interpretations, then checks to see whether it is the preferred interpretation. If not, additional choices are made until the most preferred interpretation is found, accompanied by an explanation for why this particular response is best. The preferred interpretation has been selected by the experts designing the assimilator, based on research they have conducted. The other interpretations might seem plausible to someone unfamiliar with the culture but not to someone who is familiar with it.

In the CIE, participants are not given interpretations from which to choose but are required to come up with their own. This forces them to give more thought to the situation and requires them to identify their own personal interpretation and what they would be likely to do if they were in that situation. They have to decide what they feel would be appropriate or effective behavior, and they have to make a personal commitment by explaining and defending the interpretation and solution they propose. In the culture assimilator, the participant has to choose the correct response. Thus, the culture assimilator is like a multiple choice test, whereas the CIE is more like an essay examination.

With the culture assimilator, an individual is often (but not always) working through the exercise alone with no opportunity for discussion. With the CIE, participants discuss and compare their responses with those of the other participants and resource persons. Discussion is an essential part of the exercise, is more involving than working alone, allows participants to develop cross-cultural problem-solving skills, and leads to deeper understanding of the unknown culture. There is no limit to the number of interpretations that can be examined in the CIE discussion, and participants have the opportunity to question, disagree, clarify, and elaborate, whereas with the culture assimilator they often do not. In the CIE, the interpretations are those of real persons from both cultures taking part in the discussions, not hypothetical persons or experts who are not available to the trainees.

The argument is sometimes made that nonexperts discussing a critical incident might not come up with an accurate interpretation, but in my experience they usually arrive at the same conclusions an expert might, along with a much better understanding of the nuances of the situation and the variation that exists within both cultures. That is the main reason for having resource persons in the program. In the final summary discussion, trainers can add their own views, but usually this is unnecessary. Participants become aware of ways in which their culture has conditioned them (not some hypothetical person) to react in situations such as those described. Participants then discover how effective or ineffective these reactions are within the other culture and can change or modify their attitudes, expectations, and behavior. This learning is less likely to be achieved with the culture assimilator.

The CIE is much easier, less time-consuming, and less costly to develop than a culture assimilator, since it does not require the same amount of research. In developing a culture assimilator, it is necessary to make certain that the less preferred interpretations are genuinely typical of the trainee population, interpretations they might see as plausible, and that there is general expert agreement on the preferred interpretation. Done properly, this is a time-consuming, costly process, whereas an experienced trainer, familiar with the target culture or with access to persons familiar with the culture, can develop a CIE in only a few hours.

The culture assimilator might be more useful in training one person at a time where there is no opportunity for analysis and discussion. With more than one person and with time for discussion, it is my opinion that the Critical Incidents Exercise is much more effective.

**Example 1**

# Critical Incidents Exercise Instructions for Individual Work[1]

The incidents in this packet are taken from real situations. The names and any features that might identify the people or place from which they were taken have been changed.

The first part of this exercise is an individual activity. Read through each incident quickly and answer the questions following the incident, without discussing it with the other participants. There are no right or wrong answers, so please respond according to your personal feelings. You will be given an opportunity to discuss and compare your answers with the other participants later in the program.

The first question after each incident will ask you to indicate the extent to which you agree or disagree with one of the characters in the incident. To do so, use the following scale:

| | |
|---|---|
| Totally disagree | 1 |
| Disagree very much | 2 |
| Disagree more than agree | 3 |
| Agree as much as disagree | 4 |
| Agree more than disagree | 5 |
| Agree very much | 6 |
| Totally Agree | 7 |

**Please work quickly.** You will have approximately twenty-five minutes to complete this portion of the exercise. Write very brief notes in response to the questions at the end of each incident. These will be for only your use in the discussions.

TURN THE PAGE AND BEGIN

---

[1]Hypothetical instruction sheet, typical of the kind I use with critical incidents exercises.

**Example 2**

# Critical Incident[2]

Louis and Julie were a senior couple, in their early sixties, in an overseas agricultural extension program. They seemed ideally suited for such a program. They had operated their own farm for over thirty years. When they were children they both lived on farms without indoor plumbing or electricity, so the living conditions in their host country were not new to them. In addition to being a good farmer, Louis was handy with machinery and could repair almost anything. Julie was a traditional farm housewife, accustomed to helping with the chores, tending the garden, preserving vegetables, etc. Both were friendly and outgoing and seemed interested in using their experience and skills to help the people in their host country.

Their biggest problem in training was with the language, but they left on their assignment with acceptable proficiency. Julie was having some medical problems after they arrived—minor stomach upset, diarrhea, infections from scratches that were slow to heal, and a continuous cold. According to the doctor there was nothing seriously wrong. The problems didn't bother Julie much but they began to worry Louis. Finally, after one month at their site, they came into the office and told Chris, their supervisor, they were terminating. Louis said that since the doctors couldn't tell them what was wrong with Julie, they were going home. In further discussion, Chris found that there were many other problems and surmised that the physical ailments were only a symptom. Their house wasn't ready and they had to live with a host family. They didn't like the lack of privacy and loss of control over their own lives. They didn't like sharing the bathroom with strangers. They didn't like eating the local food prepared by their hosts. They didn't like the unsanitary conditions in the market—flies on the meat, people handling the food with dirty hands. Although they were used to farm smells, they didn't like the smell of open sewers. It was a real struggle having to use the language all the time. It wasn't clear what their job was supposed to be.

Chris could see they were really upset and decided there was no point in trying to talk them into staying. She helped them process their termination as quickly as possible.

1. To what extent do you agree or disagree with Chris?

   Totally Disagree   1   2   3   4   5   6   7   Totally Agree

   Why?

2. If you were Chris, what would you have done?

3. What are the main issues in this incident?

---

[2]Developed by Albert R. Wight for use in training Peace Corps staff to work with senior volunteers. Used by permission.

**Example 3**

# Instructions for Small-Group Discussion

When everyone has completed reading the critical incidents and has answered the questions, you are to discuss each incident in your group. The objective is to try to arrive at agreement (consensus, not majority rule) as to:

- What the problem is.
- Why it is a problem—the real issues involved.
- The extent to which you agree or disagree with the person in the incident.
- How you might prevent this kind of problem from happening.
- What might be done that would be effective if it did occur.
- Other concerns or considerations.
- Policies or practices you might establish to deal with such problems.
- Ways in which you might prepare yourself to deal with such problems.

Make certain that everyone has a chance to be heard and that all views, perceptions, and interpretations are examined. It helps to be able to see these problems from different perspectives.

You have ten incidents to discuss in two hours and fifteen minutes. That is a little over ten minutes apiece. Some may require more time, some less, but watch your time so you will be able to finish discussing all incidents within the allotted time.

# References

Flanagan, J. C. "The Critical Incident Technique." *Psychological Bulletin* 51 (1954): 327-58.

Morton, R. B., and Albert R. Wight. "Critical-Incidents Evaluation of a Human Relations Laboratory." Presented at American Psychological Association Meeting, Los Angeles, CA, 1964. Sacramento, CA: Aerojet-General Corporation, 1963.

Taylor, C., et al. *Development of Situational Tests for Selection of Peace Corps Volunteers.* Salt Lake City: University of Utah, 1967.

Wight, Albert R. "Use of Situational Tests in Instrumented Laboratory Training for the Peace Corps." In *Development of Situational Tests for Selection of Peace Corps Volunteers,* edited by C. Taylor et al. Salt Lake City: University of Utah, 1967.

Wight, Albert R., and Mary Ann Hammons. *Guidelines for Peace Corps Cross-Cultural Training.* Washington, DC: U. S. Peace Corps, 1970.

# Using Critical Incidents as a Tool for Reflection

## William Dant

The critical-incident exercise is well known as a ready-made training tool in which one is asked to react to described situations. Another way to work with the concept is to train sojourners, in this case alumni of a student exchange program, to generate and learn from their own critical incidents in the process of reentry adaptation.

## Background

This approach to using critical incidents was adapted by Judith M. Blohm for Youth for Understanding (YFU) from a process used at The Experiment for International Living and originally described in the first edition of *Beyond Experience* (1977). Some of the directions developed at The Experiment were adopted by YFU, but considerable adaptation was necessary for the exercise to work with YFU students. At the same time, this method works well with any type of sojourner. Although the description is drawn from experience with youth exchange students, you can easily substitute "sojourner" for "student" throughout this chapter.

The approach is easier if the sojourner or student keeps a journal, but this is not obligatory. The journal can become an important confidant for youth exchange participants, who, at their young age, usually have the most intense intercultural experiences, living as a member of a host family and attending a local school. A journal is sometimes the student's only outlet for honest reflection about and reaction to the host culture. Soon after events and experiences take place, the student records and, to some extent, reflects upon them. Many students say that keeping a journal was a great support in coping with the stresses of their experience. A quick review of days and weeks past gave them the courage and confidence to know that things get better. Little victories from day to day ultimately provide a sense of accomplishment, and some things which seemed unbearable felt easier to deal with after they were described on paper.

With journal material to refer back to later, the personally generated critical incident can become an effective tool for working with returning students. People are full of anecdotes and experiences to share, but sometimes at a loss to know what they really learned, when and how they learned it, and how this learning can help them in the future.

The objective in this type of critical-incident exercise is to invite the reentering sojourner to find some situation or interaction which, in retrospect, appears to have opened doors of understanding and stimulated personal insight or better integration into the host culture. Because of the name of the exercise, students often begin by looking for the dramatic or the exciting, yet the really critical moments of learning are to be found in some small or banal situation. Our experience shows that to grasp the true objective of the assignment, students need some clarification of what is meant by "critical."

# Procedure

At Youth for Understanding, students develop their own critical incidents through a process ending in a session entitled "It Happened to Me" (Blohm and McDermott 1985). The exercise begins when the student receives, along with an invitation to attend the alumni reentry orientation, the following instructions for writing the critical incident.

### Writing a Critical Incident

> **What it is:** A critical incident is a description of a situation that took place while you were overseas which helped you better understand or appreciate the cross-cultural experience.

To write a critical incident, complete the following five steps (the five steps follow closely Don Batchelder's in *Beyond Experience* (149):

1. Identify the event or situation as clearly as possible, the problem to be solved, the issue involved, and so forth.

2. Describe the relevant details and circumstances surrounding the event, so that readers will understand what happened. (What? When? How? Why? Where?)

3. List the people involved; describe them and their relationships to you and to one another. (Who?)

4. Describe your own role in the situation (that is, what you did and how you acted) and identify the particular cross-cultural skill or skills involved. How well or badly did you understand the situation? How well or badly did you use the skill involved? What would you do differently the next time? Describe your interpretation of events.

5. Write a brief analysis of the incident, telling what you learned from the experience.

> Your paper should be refined down to one page, or not much longer than one page. This paper must be done before you arrive at the Alumni Workshop.

**How it will be used:** Your paper will be used for group discussions during the weekend to help heighten the consciousness of returnees to cross-cultural issues. In the session called "It Happened to Me," you will be asked, as will others, to share the experience you wrote about. It will help to set the tone for the weekend/workshop.

# A Sample Critical Incident

Here is what one student wrote:

My critical incident took place in the most ordinary of places—at the dry cleaner's just around the corner from my host family. After wearing my corduroy jacket almost daily for several weeks, I realized that I needed to get it cleaned, and my host mother told me where to go.

I went into the small establishment and dropped off the jacket, asking to have it back as soon as possible because I needed to wear it to stay warm as the autumn days became chillier. The attendant promised me it would be ready the next day.

Following school the next day, I stopped in on my way home to pick up my jacket. It was ready and quickly was folded and wrapped up for me in paper, a different procedure from what I was used to in the U.S., where I'd get it back on a hanger. "This is a different system," I thought, "but it has its advantages: no waste of hangers going back and forth as we have back home." I was feeling accomplished in my observational skills and ability to see the pros and cons of a small difference across cultures.

As I was about to leave, she held up her hand, asking me to wait, she'd forgotten something. She opened a drawer under the counter and pulled out a small, sealed envelope. *"Voilà vos boutons"*—here are your buttons! Totally mystified, I opened the envelope to discover the six braided leather buttons that used to be on my jacket.

"You must have forgotten to remove them before bringing them in, monsieur," she explained. "Fortunately, we noticed that before your jacket went into the machine."

My earlier confidence about how attuned I was to small everyday subtleties seemed to vanish. *This lady cut the buttons off my jacket and now she's just giving them back to me to deal with. What kind of service is that?*

My anger about what had been done wrong paralyzed my abilities to explain in French what was bothering me. For about half a minute I sputtered something, not feeling I could explain myself clearly. Meanwhile, the person in the back who had done me the good deed of removing the buttons was brought out to explain to me again how lucky I was that she'd caught it and lectured me on the fact that I should think about doing this before-hand next time, because sometimes there is too much dry cleaning to allow them to double-check such things.

Defeated, I left the shop and walked around the block three times before I could go back home and face my host mother. I headed in, greeting her as she was going out to run errands, and went into my room to sit and suffer my defeat in peace.

An hour later, my host mother came back, knocking on my door. "I hear you might need some help with sewing on some buttons," she said to me with a gentle smile. As it turned out, the dry cleaner was on her errand list, and the owner had related my performance to her. We had a little chat about it and I learned all about how careful one must be with leather goods sent to the dry cleaner—that the owner was right that I should have thought to remove those buttons. At that point, it seemed useless to try to explain that I'd sent that jacket to a dry cleaner's half a dozen times back home and that I'd never taken off the buttons then, and they seemed to have survived....

Ultimately I realized that my first observation about a cultural difference—folding the jacket up in paper, saving on hangers—was a "safe" insight I'd been able to make based on what I'd learned through my cross-cultural orientation. But *that* was external—I wasn't really involved and didn't have much to lose one way or the other. After I'd thought over the rest of the situation, I realized that, yes, I was really involved here as a person and that I had to be ready to have others assume that my actions were possibly as erroneous (despite being based on my own safe assumptions about "how things are" back home) as those that I was criticizing as the outsider.

## Procedure

At the reentry weekend, the workshop leader takes the following steps to facilitate discussion of the incident:

**Introduction:** The leader begins with a short introduction, including observations such as:

❖ All of you experienced certain incidents during your summer or year overseas that, upon reflection, were very important.

❖ These were situations which helped you better understand or appreciate the cross-cultural experience.

❖ Perhaps there was an experience that demonstrated to you the variety of ways in which we can communicate or an uncomfortable situation that vividly showed your lack of understanding of the host culture.

❖ By becoming more aware of the cross-cultural issues you have faced, you can now begin to identify the skills you developed to deal with those issues.

**Personal example:** The leader can begin with a personal critical incident (sample follows) in order to set the tone for discussion and provide a model for presentation. The incident itself should be short (no more than three minutes to relate). This incident follows closely Don Batchelder's in *Beyond Experience* (150).

> I have always been a night person. I enjoy staying up late and talking with friends, and relish having the quiet peacefulness of the night to myself. I prefer sleeping in late in the morning.
>
> Soon after I settled in with my host family, I went out one night with friends I'd met through my family there, and came home at about 10:00 P.M., relatively late for a small town over there, but usually about the hour I would begin to sit down to study back home.
>
> Once I'd settled in at my desk in my room to study and write letters, the hours passed by quickly, though I had no concept of the time. Just as I was re-reading a long letter I'd written, I heard some stirring noises in the hallway, and suddenly, with a loud click all of the lights went out!
>
> I was in total darkness, confused, unprepared, trying to understand why they would be so cruel as to turn the lights out that way—just to conserve electricity?! The next day, my host mother explained to me what had happened—that my host father had awakened in the night, saw the light under my door, and assumed I'd fallen asleep without turning off the lights. In order to be "correct" he decided to cut off all the lights in the apartment rather than look in on me.
>
> I was apologetic, explaining I was awake but had just lost track of time, and I promised it wouldn't happen again, thinking with dread that I'd be sacrificing my hours of solitude.
>
> This incident made me realize that I would have to change my hours and habits to comply with those of my host family. My commitment to being a part of the family and pleasing them helped me to adjust to their way of living, even if it meant giving up something I enjoy very much. This sacrifice helped me understand more about myself, my values, my habits and how they differ from those of my new family.

**Discussion issues.** List the following issues on newsprint to use as a guide during the discussion of the incident:

1. What I learned from the incident: about myself, my host country, and the United States
2. How I dealt with the situation
3. How I could have dealt with it
4. What cross-cultural skills resulted from the experience

**Group work:** Now ask the students to form small groups. Instruct the groups as follows:

First choose a recorder who will take notes on your discussion. You will each be able to share your own incident and discuss it with the other group members, using the four questions shown on the newsprint. The recorder should keep track of the major issues and skills mentioned, in order to report them to the full group when we come back together.

Then choose a group leader. Group leaders should monitor the clock so that each student has time to recount his or her incident. They should also encourage all group members to participate in the discussion, drawing out various points of view and individual differences. Leaders should help the group focus and summarize their discussion so the recorder can spot the major issues and skills to be reported.

**Report:** All the groups reassemble and recorders report on their discussions.

**Closure:** In summary, the leader should emphasize the importance of what students have learned, highlight the skills they have developed, and reiterate the fact that these skills can be valuable assets in the future.

## Reflections on Using This Method

Alumni of the exchange program from the past three years are invited to participate in the reentry orientation. The reporting out of the exercise allows older alumni an opportunity to reflect again on their experiences and to provide to the discussion the kind of insight that comes from distance, while the newer returnee brings a fresh, immediate view. When incidents are read at the reentry orientation, the insights of one student often trigger similar or related ones for others. It is not unusual to find that a small detail of one person's experience throws light on unnoticed aspects of other students' experiences, which then can be identified and analyzed as critical points of learning.

The facilitator performs an interesting role in this exercise—staying out of the way of participants' learning but making sure that it occurs. The participants provide the content for the workshop and have a lot to learn from each other. However, without a skilled facilitator, important insights might be missed, and the full value of the overseas experience might not be realized.

## References

Batchelder, Don. "Developing Cross-Cultural Learning Skills." In *Beyond Experience: The Experiential Approach to Cross-Cultural Education,* edited by Don Batchelder and Elizabeth G. Warner. Brattleboro, VT: The Experiment in International Living (1977): 145-53.

Blohm, Judee, and J. McDermott. *Preparing and Delivering Alumni Re-Entry Orientations.* Washington, DC: Youth for Understanding International Exchange (1985): 39-41.

# Critical Incidents in an Intercultural Conflict-Resolution Exercise

## Milton J. Bennett

This example of using critical incidents describes the modification of a conflict-resolution exercise for intercultural applications. Advantages of this type of exercise in group-training situations are described, the modifications are explained, and a complete guide to using the modified exercise is given. The author's cotrainer, Janet M. Bennett, participated in all aspects of modifying the exercise.

## History

The original exercise, developed by University Associates (Simpson 1977), used critical incidents drawn from an organizational context to illustrate some typical conflict situations and to help participants explore appropriate responses. Five possible actions listed after each incident represented a variety of conflict-resolution "styles" as follows:

### Styles of Conflict Resolution

**Denial.** Existence of the problem is ignored.
*Advantage:* If the issue is not very important, this style avoids "making a mountain out of a molehill."
*Disadvantage:* If the issue turns out to be important, this style may allow the problem to build into a worse problem.
**Suppression.** The importance of the problem is played down, generally in an effort to smooth over differences.
*Advantage:* If the issue is transitory, like a bad mood, this style preserves harmony while time passes.
*Disadvantage:* Important issues may be evaded by this strategy, and others may feel that their concerns are being made light of.

**Power or Authority.** Authority, positional power, majority rule, or threats by a special-interest group settle the conflict.
*Advantage:* This style can be more efficient than others, for instance, in emergencies. Also, the style may be appropriate to situations where an authority has the responsibility to control behavior of others (for example, prison guards).
*Disadvantage:* This is a win/lose strategy, and the loser may try to get even in the next disagreement. Losers may not feel they are responsible for the solution.

**Compromise or Negotiation.** Everybody gives up something to meet halfway in the solution.
*Advantage:* This style is less likely than "Power or Authority" to create bad feelings of being the loser in a conflict.
*Disadvantage:* Positions may be inflated in anticipation of this style of negotiation. Also, the solution may be interpreted as lose/lose, with both parties ending up unhappy.

**Collaboration.** Open discussion of the conflict occurs in a direct encounter.
*Advantage:* All positions are taken into account to come up with a win/win solution. Parties to the conflict feel responsibility for the resolution.
*Disadvantage:* This style demands time, commitment to the process, and communication skills in problem solving. If these ingredients are missing, the process may lead to greater frustration.

(Adapted from "Handling Group and Organizational Conflict," *The 1977 Annual Handbook for Group Facilitators,* University Associates.)

In the original exercise, individual participants rank-ordered the five approaches in terms of their appropriateness for each of several incidents. Small groups were used to discuss individuals' rankings and to achieve a consensus on the rankings. The trainer then explained each style in the large group and received the reports of the small-group rankings. Follow-up discussion explored the advantages and disadvantages of each style for various communication contexts and purposes.

I have used this exercise in various forms with a wide variety of groups, ranging in age from high school students to adults and in occupation from line-level employees and teachers to high-level managers and administrators. In many cases, new critical incidents drawn from the work context of the participants were created for specific programs. In all cases, the exercise was successful in achieving the following goals:

**Appreciation of diversity in style.** Awareness of different approaches to conflict resolution allowed participants to interpret the behavior of their colleagues in a more positive light. Participants recognized that different styles might be appropriate in different circumstances, that no one style was always the right one, and that difference in style could be a resource rather than an impediment to problem solving.

**Self-assessment of preferred style.** Participants became more aware of their own preferred approach to conflict resolution, and they were able to compare their preference to that of others in both the small and large groups.

**Effective group communication.** The opportunity for individual work, small-group discussion, and large-group debriefing helped to develop effective two-way communication in the training programs. Group cohesion was served by participants interacting with each other, and enthusiasm was maintained by coupling the presentation of concepts with the participants' own consideration and discussion of the incidents.

**Immediate personal and professional application.** By creating incidents for the exercise that were relevant to the lives of the participants, I could easily guide discussion into consideration of actual conflicts. Participants were able to see how the different styles could be used in approaching the resolution of the real problems they faced.

## Intercultural Modification of the Exercise

Using the conflict-resolution exercise modified for intercultural situations achieves all the goals noted above, plus some others. Both the styles and the incidents needed to be modified. The addition of styles used in cultures other than that of European Americans (white North Americans) makes the exercise more appropriate for culturally mixed groups. Participants gain awareness of cultural as well as personal differences in style, and the exercise is more easily applied to issues of intercultural communication and negotiation.

## Intercultural Styles

We modified the list of conflict resolution styles by combining "Denial" and "Suppression" from the original list. The distinction between these two styles was already obscure for European Americans, and it seemed that it would disappear altogether for people of other cultures. The main thrust of this style is inaction, whether it be because the problem is being ignored ("Denial") or for reasons of maintaining harmony ("Suppression").

The "Third-Person Intermediary" style was added to accommodate many Asian, Pacific, African, and Arab cultures where conflict may be handled with a go-between. In European-American culture, this style is often seen as hypocritical, so it offers an interesting cultural contrast. It is illuminating for European Americans to hear this style discussed as an effective tool for dealing with relationships.

The "Group Consensus" style was added to address some Asian, Hispanic, and African-American patterns that make extensive use of family and friends for discussion of conflict. European Americans tend to be open with the direct participants in a conflict, but they are often reticent in revealing such problems to their friends. In contrast, some other cultures are more open with friends and family than they are with the direct participant. Discussion of this cultural contrast reveals that openness may occur in different social contexts.

The original name "Collaboration" was changed to "Direct Discussion" to stress the European-American value of openness in dealing with conflict. The "Direct" style often seems extreme or selfish to people from many non-Western cultures. This negative evaluation of the consistent American preference for directness can fuel an interesting discussion of cultural difference.

These changes resulted in the following list of cross-cultural styles of conflict resolution.

## Cross-Cultural Styles of Conflict Resolution

**Denial or Suppression**. Person tries to solve the problem by denying its existence. Differences are played down and surface harmony is preserved.
*Advantage:* If the issue is relatively unimportant, this style allows a cooling-off period or simply lets time heal the problem.
*Disadvantage:* If the issue is important, this style allows the problem to build into a more severe situation that is more difficult to resolve.

**Power or Authority.** An authority, position, majority rule, or a persuasive minority settles the conflict. Power is used to impose a solution.
*Advantage:* When speed or efficiency is most important, this style may be effective. It also demonstrates the status of the person or group in authority.
*Disadvantage:* The people who lose the conflict may feel devalued and/or they may cause disruptions in the future to get even.

**Third-Person Intermediary**. Two or more people who are having a conflict use a third person as a go-between to convey messages to each other. Direct mention of the problem to involved people is avoided, but the go-between is aware of everyone's position.
*Advantage:* This style allows the preservation of surface harmony while still addressing the conflict and possibly resolving it.
*Disadvantage:* The conflict may become confused and more complicated because of misinterpretations by the third-person intermediary. Persons involved in the conflict may not think their feelings have been sufficiently understood.

**Group Consensus.** A group is used to share ideas about resolving a conflict and coming to a decision on action that is agreed to by the whole group.
*Advantage:* A group may come up with better ideas for resolving the conflict than could an individual alone. Agreement of the whole group to a resolution is a powerful, nonauthoritarian influence on the people in the conflict.
*Disadvantage:* This style is usually very time-consuming. The group may avoid facing the difficult issues and concentrate on a relatively unimportant aspect of the conflict.

**Direct Discussion.** Individuals involved in a conflict talk openly with one another about their perception of the problem, their feelings about it, and possible solutions.
*Advantage:* The conflict is clear and understood by the involved people. Resolution of the conflict is supported by the participants, since they came up with it.
*Disadvantage:* Involved individuals may not have the skills to engage in constructive confrontation, and they feel worse after it. Time and commitment to this process may be lacking.

## Intercultural Incidents

In creating critical incidents for this exercise, it is important to make them intercultural. For the sake of clarity, there generally should be only two parties to the conflict, and each of them should be from a different culture. In the example provided, Case 1 involves an American and a Chinese person. In Case 2, an American family acts as one party, and a Japanese visitor is the other party.

The situation in Case 3 is more complicated. The conflict has two levels; one is the dispute between Nasser (from the Middle East) and Jeff, and the other is the role Jennifer should play in helping to resolve the situation. Should Jennifer alter what might be her own preference to be more culturally sensitive to Nasser? If she does that, will it mean that she is not being sensitive to Jeff's preference? This case addresses the dilemma faced by supervisors and managers of multicultural groups.

The sample exercise provided here was created for international education professionals. Different critical incidents should be created for other applications. For instance, if the training is for American students preparing for homestays in France, all the incidents should relate to potential conflicts between an American student and French family members. If the application relates to ethnic rather than national cultural differences, care should be taken that the incidents do not unnecessarily elicit legal or political issues of prejudice. The point is to explore differences in interpersonal style, not to address concerns involving legal rights, which are equally important but not the primary focus of this exercise.

## Cross-Cultural Conflict-Resolution Exercise

**Case 1.** The American foreign student advisor, Tom, had developed an idea of how to help Chinese students in his school. His Chinese colleague Liu knew that the idea would be very insulting to the Chinese. If you were Liu, you would (rank-order):

_____ Talk to other members of your family and friends about how to handle this situation.

_____ Just keep quiet. It probably won't be a problem.

_____ Go to a person in authority and tell him or her your concerns about this possibly insulting project.

_____ Talk to Tom and tell him honestly about your concerns. Tell him you can help him work out a better solution.

_____ Go to an older friend who is also a friend of Tom's. Maybe he can talk to Tom about this problem.

**Case 2.** The Alder family is hosting Noriko for this school year. The family is very pleased to have a Japanese visitor, and they constantly try to persuade her to study less so she can join in more of the family's activities. Noriko is very worried because she likes her host family but also feels as if she must study many hours every day to complete her degree. If you were Noriko, you would (rank-order):

_____ Not discuss this with your family, but keep on studying. After all, they mean well and they'll get over it if you can't always join them.

_____ Speak directly to your family, and discuss what can be done to solve this difference.

_____ Talk to the group of Japanese friends in other homestays and see how they feel about it.

_____ Go to the host family coordinator and tell her that you have to switch families unless your family can change their attitude.

_____ Plan to meet with your host sister's best friend. Explain your worries to her; perhaps she can talk to your host sister.

**Case 3.** Jennifer is an assistant in the international residence hall on her campus. Nasser is a Middle Eastern student who is observing the dawn-to-dusk fasting for the holy month of Ramadan. His American roommate, Jeff, has complained to Jennifer that Nasser's pre-dawn rituals are extremely disturbing. If you were Jennifer, you would (rank-order):

_____ Talk to Nasser and tell him about the problem. Arrange a meeting with Jeff for all of you to sit down and talk about this conflict.

_____ Assume that this minor problem will gradually go away when Ramadan is over, and everyone will forget about it.

_____ Discuss this issue with your supervisor, who will tell Nasser and Jeff what to do.

_____ Discuss this with the other resident assistants and see what the group thinks about the situation.

_____ Talk to another Muslim friend of yours and see if he or she will go talk to Nasser about the problem.

# Conducting the Exercise

1. **Individual participants complete rank-ordering of styles.** Distribute the instruments to participants with minimal introduction.

    **Directions:** "Each incident has several possible approaches or solutions to the conflict. Rank-order only these alternatives. Other alternatives are possible, but they are not part of the exercise. No tied ranks. Try to assume the perspective of the person in the incident, not your own."

    **Possible problem:** Some people may not finish, because they do not read English well, they are unfamiliar with this type of instrument, or they are very reflective. Help, encourage, but, in the end, send them off to groups without finishing. Completion of this step is not crucial. Some participants may complain that they don't know enough about the other cultures. Encourage them to make a "best guess" based on what they have learned so far. Such guesses are "working hypotheses," not stereotypes.

    **Time:** 5 to 10 minutes.

2. **Group discussion and consensus.** Make sure groups are culturally mixed. Groups of four or five members are best; more than seven members increases the time and decreases the participation severely. Supply each group with one clean copy of the instrument marked "Group 1," and so on.

**Directions:** "Share your individual rankings and agree as a group on a single ranking for each case. Try to achieve consensus on the ranking. If consensus is impossible, use whatever other means necessary (such as voting) to achieve a group ranking. Choose a recorder to complete the group-ranking form."

**Possible problems:** Though it rarely occurs, intractable arguments may develop. Encourage the group to compromise or allow a dissenting opinion. It is important that this step be completed. Groups may want to rewrite solutions, which should not be allowed.

**Time:** 20 to 30 minutes, with active encouragement from the trainer.

3. **Describe styles in large group and label the approaches.** This step of the exercise combines a lecturette describing the styles of conflict resolution with the identification of which approach represents which style.

While participants are in their small groups, prepare on a chalkboard, whiteboard, or other wide surface a large grid with five rows, one wide column entitled "Styles," a number of columns corresponding to the number of incidents titled "Case 1," "Case 2," and so on, and two additional columns entitled "totals" and "combined ranks" (see figure 1). When the large group has reconvened, begin the lecturette by describing the "Denial/Suppression" style, mentioning its advantages and disadvantages, and explaining how the style might be appropriate in different cultural contexts. Write the name of the style in the first column of your grid as you begin to discuss it. (You won't use the other columns until the next step of this exercise.)

**Figure 1**

# Sample of a Completed Grid

| STYLES | CASE 1 | CASE 2 | CASE 3 | TOTALS | COMBINED RANKS |
|---|---|---|---|---|---|
| Denial or Suppression | - + | - -- / -- | -- -- / -- | -11 | 5 |
| Power or Authority | -- -- | + | - - | -7 | 4 |
| Third-Person Intermediary | + ++ | - ++ | ++ ++ | +8 | 2 |
| Group Consensus | ++ + ++ | ++ ++ + | - + | +10 | 1 |
| Direct Discussion | -- | -- + - | + ++ + | 0 | 3 |

After your description of the style, ask the large group which approach in Case 1 seems to fit the "Denial/Suppression" style. Confirm a correct response, and have the recorders write the name of the style next to that approach on the group-ranking forms. Quickly repeat this question for each of the other two cases, and remind the recorders to label those approaches with the name of the style.

Continue this procedure for each of the remaining styles. Total time per style for lecturette and group identification of approaches should be about 4 minutes.

> **Directions:** "The approaches you have just ranked represent particular styles of conflict resolution. After I discuss each style, I will ask you which approach in each case might represent that style. The group recorders should write the *name* of the style next to each approach as we identify it."

> **Possible problems:** Sometimes cuing is necessary to identify the style with an approach in the first case. Thereafter, the group usually can identify the parallel solutions in other cases. Occasionally, someone will want to argue about a classification. Now is not the time for it. Interaction with the group needs to move very fast in this section.

> **Time:** 20 minutes.

4. **Comparison of small-group ranks and computation of large-group ranks.** Ask the recorder of one group to name the style it ranked first in Case 1. In the cell corresponding to Case 1 and the first-ranked style, enter a "++" (double plus) (see figure 1). Continue this procedure with the same group for Case 1: in the appropriate cell in the Case 1 (see figure 1) column, mark a "+" (plus) for the second-ranked style, a "-" (minus) for the fourth-ranked, and a "--" (double minus) for the fifth-ranked (entering the third-ranked style is unnecessary, because it emerges automatically in the final tally).

Staying with Case 1, move on to the other groups and enter their ranks in the appropriate cells of the Case 1 column. When all groups have reported their ranks for Case 1, move on to Case 2. Enter data into cells in this same way for each small group and for each case.

At the end of data entry, totals are easily made by counting, for each row corresponding to a style, the number of pluses less the number of minuses. Enter this number (some will be negative) in the total column for each row. In the final column, mark #1 for the largest (positive) number, #5 for the lowest (negative) number, and appropriate numbers for the ranks in between.

> **Directions:** "Recorders, please be prepared to give me the *names* of your group's first-, second-, fourth-, and fifth-ranked styles for each case. Leave out the third rank. Group number one, please begin for Case 1—which style did you rank as first choice?"

> **Possible problems:** Recorders may have forgotten to write the style name down for ranked approaches, so be prepared to supply the name. You should practice thinking through the grid before doing

the computations in a group. The grid procedure allows the computation to go very fast; if the trainer lags, the group may get bored. Be sure to include all groups for Case 1, then move on to Case 2; debriefing all cases at once for each group can be boring for the other groups.

**Time:** 10 minutes.

5. **Discussion and debriefing.** The following questions have proved stimulating in debriefing this exercise:

❖ In Case 1 (or 2, or 3), *why* was the first-ranked style chosen? Discussion should move through all groups for each case. If one style was routinely ranked high by all groups for all cases, cases can be combined in a general discussion of the style, but each group should have a turn for input.

❖ Why was the lowest-ranked style chosen?

❖ What examples of cultural difference in approach to conflict resolution were evident in the small-group discussion of the styles?

❖ What style was used *in the groups* to resolve conflicts about ranking? Was that related to cultural difference?

❖ How does an awareness of differences in style help explain a real-life interpersonal or intercultural conflict?

❖ How might you alter your preferred style in situations demanding cultural adaptation?

**Possible problems:** Americans may tend to dominate discussion. Be prepared to direct specific questions to members of other cultures.

**Time:** 20 minutes.

# References

Simpson, Donald T. "Handling Group and Organizational Conflict" and "Conflict Styles: Organizational Decision Making." In *1977 Annual Handbook for Group Facilitators,* edited by John E. Jones and J. William Pfeiffer. San Diego: University Associates, 1977.

# Resources

Borisoff, Deborah, and David Victor. *Conflict Management.* Englewood Cliffs, NJ: Prentice-Hall, 1989.

Brislin, Richard, Kenneth Cushner, Craig Cherrie, and Mahealani Yong. *Intercultural Interactions: A Practical Guide.* Beverly Hills: Sage, 1986.

DeBono, Edward. *Conflicts: A Better Way to Resolve Them.* New York: Viking Penguin, 1986.

Folger, Joseph, and Marshall Poole. *Working Through Conflict: A Communication Perspective.* Glenview, IL: Scott, Foresman, 1984.

Pfeiffer, William, and Arlette Ballew. *UA Training Technologies* Series. San Diego: University Associates, 1988.

Pusch, Margaret, ed. *Multicultural Education: A Cross-Cultural Training Approach.* Yarmouth, ME: Intercultural Press, 1979.

Wilmot, Joyce, and William Wilmot. *Interpersonal Conflict.* Dubuque, IA: Wm. C. Brown, 1978.

# The Intercultural Sensitizer/ Culture Assimilator as a Cross- Cultural Training Method

## Rosita D. Albert

The Intercultural Sensitizer (ICS) is an instrument specifically constructed to sensitize persons from one cultural group to the assumptions, behaviors, norms, perceptions, interpretations, attitudes, and values—in short, the subjective culture (Triandis 1972)—of persons from another cultural group.

## History and Description

The ICS was first developed at the University of Illinois by Fiedler, Osgood, Stolurow, and Triandis in 1962, when they were seeking a way to improve communication in culturally heterogeneous work groups. It was then called the Culture Assimilator (Albert and Adamopoulos 1976, Fiedler, Mitchell and Triandis 1971). As our experience and knowledge about the instrument evolved, we renamed it the Intercultural Sensitizer (Albert 1983) to avoid the suggestion that trainees might have to give up their own culture and assimilate into another culture. Actually, concern over this issue is unwarranted. If anything, the instrument helps trainees become more aware of their *own* cultural patterns. But the new name is also more descriptive, since to sensitize people to another culture—and through contrast, to their own culture—is exactly what the instrument does.

Although primarily a cognitive method of culture training, both the process and the content have behavioral and affective components. The instrument is very versatile and can be used with a wide variety of groups to teach many different aspects of culture. It can also be used in many different training situations.

Some key features of this method are that it:

❖ exposes trainees to a wide variety of situations in the target culture;

❖ simulates important aspects of the experience of entering a new culture, such as uncertainty about what is going on or what certain actions mean;

❖ centers on critical incidents and on key cultural differences between the trainee's own culture and the target culture;

❖ focuses on differences in perceptions and interpretations of behaviors, differences which are important to the success of intercultural encounters yet difficult for the trainee to observe directly;

❖ fosters the active involvement of the trainee.

In addition, this method is:

❖ **Efficient.** A typical ICS gives the trainee a good grasp of the main features of a culture in a matter of a few hours.

❖ **Theory-based.** It derives from work on attribution theory, which posits that we constantly make attributions about the behavior of others. The purpose of the ICS is to teach the trainee to make isomorphic attributions, that is, to interpret events as persons from the target culture do.

❖ **Research-based.** As the methodology for ICS construction has evolved, the instruments have been increasingly based on painstaking research into actual situations and the reactions of persons from the target culture as well as from the trainee's own culture.

❖ **Effective.** Numerous evaluation studies have shown it to improve not only the trainee's understanding about patterns of behavior and thinking in the other culture, but also task performance and adjustment.

### The Instrument

The instrument consists of several dozen episodes depicting potentially problematic situations. Each episode has the following components:

**Critical incidents.** These are short stories depicting situations that have the potential for creating misunderstandings or that signify key differences between the two cultures. They represent things that can actually happen when persons from the two cultures interact or when a trainee from culture A goes to a country or region where culture B predominates. The incidents are obtained through careful research with persons from both cultures and are written by experts in those cultures.

**Attributions.** Each story is followed by one or more questions about the behavior, thoughts, or feelings of the person from culture B in the story. After that come four (occasionally three or five) possible attributions or alternative interpretations which might be given in response to the question.

Trainees must select the attribution or interpretation that makes the most sense to people living in culture B. The goal is to train the reader to see the situation from the perspective of persons from culture B, that is, to train them to make isomorphic attributions.

**Feedback and explanations.** Once trainees have chosen an attribution, they are instructed to turn to a given page in the book that discusses the interpretation they chose to determine if it is the attribution made by persons in culture B. If the attribution selected was not one favored by persons in culture B, trainees are told so and are asked to go back to the story and make another choice. They keep doing this until they select the attribution which is preferred overall by persons in culture B; at that point they are given an explanation for the behavior and additional information about culture B.

## Example of an ICS Episode

The following example is an episode from an ICS for Americans who are learning about the culture of Hispanics or Latin Americans (Albert 1986a):

Miss Kelly is teaching her class about American history. She is about to tell her students something very important and she says to them, "Now, I am only going to explain this once, so please pay attention." However, after she has finished the explanation, Amparo asks Miss Kelly if she would repeat what she said. Miss Kelly becomes angry and says, "I told you I would only explain it once. You should have listened." Why did Amparo ask Miss Kelly to repeat what she had said?

Amparo asked Miss Kelly to repeat because:
Choose the alternative preferred by Hispanics more than by Anglo-Americans (page numbers cited are from the original ICS):

1. Amparo was not paying close attention.
   Go to page 82.
2. Amparo wanted to be sure she had understood what the teacher had said.
   Go to page 83.
3. Amparo thought that it would be good for the class if Miss Kelly repeated important ideas at least twice.
   Go to page 84.
4. Amparo was a slow learner.
   Go to page 85.

If the trainee selects number one as the preferred alternative and turns to page 82, he or she will find the following explanation, derived largely from my research on Hispanic-Anglo interactions with Hispanic and Anglo-American teachers and pupils (Albert 1986a):

**You have chosen number 1 which says:**

> *Amparo asked Miss Kelly to repeat because Amparo was not paying close attention.*

> Although this is certainly possible in this situation, this alternative was *not* chosen by Hispanics more frequently than by Anglo-Americans. In fact the opposite occurred: Anglo-American teachers and students preferred it more than the Hispanics in our sample.

> Go back to the story (page 81) and try to select the alternative that Hispanics preferred more than Anglo-Americans.

If the trainee selects number two, he or she will turn to page 83 and will find the following:

**You have chosen number 2 which says:**

*Amparo asked Miss Kelly to repeat because Amparo wanted to be sure she had understood what the teacher had said.*

This interpretation seemed to make a lot of sense to most of our respondents. It was the most frequently chosen interpretation by *both* Anglo-Americans and Hispanics. (In fact, it was most frequently chosen by teachers from both cultures.) Since people from both cultures preferred it, however, it does not differentiate between the two cultures. There is another alternative which does and which the Hispanics preferred more than the Anglo-Americans. Can you identify it?

Go back to page 81.

Trainees who select number three will turn to page 84 and find:

**You have chosen number 3 which says:**

*Amparo asked Miss Kelly to repeat because Amparo thought it would be good for the class if Miss Kelly repeated important ideas at least twice.*

Very good! This is the alternative which was chosen more frequently by Hispanic teachers and Hispanic pupils than by Anglo-American teachers and pupils. Two possible cultural themes run through this interpretation; one is an interest in the collective good. There are a number of research findings which point to a greater amount of cooperation among Hispanics and relatively more competition among Anglo-Americans. (Some studies have shown that Anglo-American children are so used to competing that they may adopt a competitive strategy even in situations where they will lose by doing so. Hispanic children, on the other hand, tend to show the opposite tendency: namely, to cooperate even when, at times, this may not be the optimal strategy.) There are probably many reasons for, and correlates of, this cooperativeness. For example, it may be related to the fact that many Hispanics have grown up in large extended families, where the collective good may be viewed as relatively more important than individual gain. In the story we are considering, the cooperative orientation was expressed by Amparo's desire to have everyone in the class benefit, not just herself.

The second cultural theme is the importance of repetition. In a culture where many standards (of behavior, of information) are strict, repetition ensures better learning of those standards.

Go to page 86 (next story).

Trainees who select number four will find the following on page 85:

**You have chosen number 4 which says:**

> *Amparo asked Miss Kelly to repeat because Amparo was a slow learner.*

> It is interesting that relatively more students (both Hispanic and Anglo) than teachers chose this interpretation. In spite of this, it was *not* a preferred alternative for either Hispanics or Anglo-Americans. Please make another choice.

> Go back to page 81.

Although the above example is culture-specific, ICSs can also be culture-general. The original intention was to make the ICS culture-specific and to tailor it to the needs of the particular group. For example, when young Americans were going to Honduras to work in health-care clinics as volunteers, an ICS was developed for them using stories which depicted situations in clinics in Honduras. But culture permeates all aspects of life, and usually persons from one culture have to deal with those from another culture in a variety of settings. Consequently, general aspects of the particular culture as well as aspects which are specific to that setting are incorporated into the episodes of an ICS. A culture-general ICS which does not focus on any particular culture has been developed by Richard Brislin and associates and is discussed in a separate chapter in this volume (Brislin, et al., 1986). The culture-specific and culture-general ICSs have somewhat different goals, but are complementary and may be used together.

# Culture-Specific Sensitizers

To date, culture-specific ICSs have been developed for use in two contexts. One is by persons going to or interacting with persons from other countries, the other for interactions between people from mainstream cultures and members of subcultural groups. Thus, there are ICSs for Americans interacting with Arabs, Greeks, Hondurans, Iranians, and Thais. In addition there are some ICS episodes for foreign exchange students, particularly Latin Americans, focusing on gender roles in the United States, as well as ICSs for Chinese students and scholars and for Japanese visitors to the United States. There is also an ICS for Australians focusing on Japan.

In addition, there are ICSs for the following:

❖ Mainstream or Anglo-Americans interacting with Hispanics or Latin Americans

❖ Hispanic pupils interacting with mainstream Anglo-American teachers

❖ Mainstream or Anglo-American pupils interacting with Hispanic pupils

❖ Mainstream American social workers interacting with Mexican-Americans

❖ Whites in the U.S. Army interacting with black soldiers

❖ Economically disadvantaged blacks interacting with white supervisors

❖ White supervisors interacting with disadvantaged blacks

❖ People from other areas interacting with U.S. Southerners

❖ White nurses interacting with Australian Aborigines

❖ Non-Navajos interacting with Navajos

As mentioned earlier, the use of an ICS does not have to be limited to the specific context for which it was written. For example, the Hispanic ICS was developed from the experiences of mainstream Anglo-Americans and Hispanics in educational settings. Yet a high-level public official told me that he found many of the same cultural issues operating when mainstream Americans and Hispanics interact in work settings. Of course one must always be extremely careful when generalizing to other settings. This should only be done after careful research to ascertain those aspects of the culture that are exhibited across settings. For further description of many of the culture-specific ICSs and information on how to obtain them, see Albert (1983) and the resources listed at the end of this chapter.

## Training Situations for Which the ICS Is Appropriate

Because of its flexibility, the ICS can be used in many different training situations. The following are some of the most pertinent:

**With a variable number of trainees.** The ICS can be used as effectively with one person as with a large group of people.

**With trainees who have varying levels of knowledge about a culture.** The ICS can be used with trainees ranging from naive to those who are quite sophisticated.

**With trainers who have varying levels of knowledge about the target culture.** Knowledgeable trainers will be able to provide more context or expand on the responses as they use particular episodes as examples or demonstrations of cultural differences. Although we do not recommend it, an ICS can, in an emergency, be used by trainers who may not be particularly familiar with the culture at hand.

**When there are variable time constraints.** The ICS can be used when trainees are pressed for time or don't learn that they are going to another culture until the last minute, since it takes only a few hours for trainees to read and respond to all the episodes in a typical assimilator/ICS. On the other hand, it can be used when there is plenty of time, since episodes can then be read and discussed at length over a number of sessions, delving deeper into the cultural issues that have been revealed.

**When impact and vividness are desired.** Because an ICS gives the trainee concrete situations to work with, it can have more impact than providing generalized information, such as telling the trainee that in culture X the family is very important.

**Whenever the training is needed or desired: before a sojourn, during the early stages of a sojourn, or prior to a second sojourn.** The ICS has been used successfully in all of these situations and is especially effective when a person has already been in the target culture and experienced some of the situations personally.

Besides ease of administration, portability, and efficiency, the method has the following advantages: it is nonthreatening, particularly good for teaching nonobvious aspects of a culture, and well suited to situations in which wide coverage of a culture is desired. It can be used with people from most cultures (since all cultures use stories to instruct people) and can be combined with other methods.

In short, the ICS can be productively used in almost any training situation. It can also be used in a variety of *ways*. For example, a trainer can:

❖ ask trainees to read the incidents, tally their choice of alternatives on newsprint, and then have them turn to the feedback pages

❖ assign chapters of the ICS for reading between training sessions

❖ ask trainees to describe the cultural themes represented in the episodes

❖ ask trainees to role-play the incidents

❖ lead a discussion based on the feedback from the episodes

❖ provide the ICS for trainees to take with them and use while they are abroad or in contact with members of the target culture

(Reminder: trainers wishing to copy sensitizer materials for training use need permission from the author and/or publisher.)

### Considerations for Using the ICS

Users of ICSs should be cautioned that although the behaviors and attributions in the episodes represent general cultural patterns, not every individual in the target culture will behave in the same way or have the same perceptions. In every culture there are individuals who differ from the dominant pattern of their culture. Thus, although as a rule the Japanese are considered to be more collectivistic while Americans are considered more individualistic, there are some Japanese who tend to be more individualistic, just as there are some Americans who tend to be more collectivistic. Trainees need to understand the dominant cultural patterns, but should also be alert to the possibility of deviation in individual cases. The role of the ICS is to sensitize trainees to *likely* or *possible* cultural differences, not to create stereotypes.

Trainees should also be reminded that behavior will vary according to a number of factors, including the context in which the cross-cultural encounter occurs, and the role, sex, age, and other characteristics of the participants. Giving your trainees some examples of these variations will be useful. As an example of the influence the context exerts on a given behavior, one can point out that while in American culture it is acceptable for a boss to give gifts to his or her subordinates at a Christmas party, it is not acceptable—in fact, it would be considered bribery—for the same boss to give gifts to government employees with whom he or she does business.

One way to drive home the importance of these variations is to use *all* of the episodes in the ICS rather than just a few. This exposes trainees to a wide variety of situations, permitting—indeed requiring—them to make finer distinctions, giving them a glimpse of the complexity of behavior, and allowing them to interpret the behaviors in different contexts. The complete ICS also sensitizes learners to the interrelatedness of different aspects of a culture. Trainers therefore should resist the temptation to use isolated episodes. Just as a paragraph taken out of context can completely change the meaning of a given statement, so a few epi-sodes taken out of the ICS can give a lopsided and inaccurate view of the culture.

Trainers should keep in mind that the important thing is for trainees to be-come aware that a new or different way of looking at events may exist in the other culture. Above all, trainees need to learn *not* to assume automatically that a given behavior is interpreted the same way in the target culture as it is in their own culture. It may or may not be. To learn this takes awareness, practice, and a knowledge of alternative interpretations. The ICS provides all three.

Trainees should also be informed that the intent is not to find the "right" or "true" interpretation for a given episode, but rather to find the interpretation(s) which is(are) preferred by persons from the other culture or that distinguish one culture from the other. In other words, the aim of the ICS is to help trainees put themselves in the shoes of people from the target culture and to begin to see the world from their perspective. To train people to think more like a "native" is an important but difficult task; because of the way in which it is constructed, the ICS can be particularly helpful in this task.

## Comparison with Other Training Methods

Distinguishing features of the method are its research base (research is used both in the development of the instrument and on evaluations of its effectiveness), its theoretical foundation on attribution theory, and its utilization of psychological principles that have been shown to increase learning, such as active learning, involvement, continuous feedback, and self-pacing.

It is customary to divide learning approaches into cognitive, affective, and behavioral approaches. Usually cognitive methods, such as lectures, impart infor-mation. Behavioral methods, such as role plays, reinforce behaviors which are appropriate in the target culture. Experiential methods, such as simulation games, strive to teach through the experiences the trainee undergoes.

The ICS is usually classified as a cognitive method because it focuses on the acquisition of knowledge or information by the trainee. However, the process by which the information is acquired by the trainee is in a sense experiential: it is acquired by a trial-and-error process which mirrors the experience of entering a new culture, but without the risks of failure and embarrassment.

In addition, the ICS uses the behavioral techniques of feedback and rein-forcement. The material is not only factual, it also covers the behaviors and feel-ings of the persons involved, thus incorporating cognitive, behavioral, and affec-tive content. Cognitive, behavioral, and experiential components, therefore, are brought together in the ICS, both in the process of learning and the content of what is learned. Yet, because of the strong cognitive component, it is more suit-able for use in situations where methods that are primarily experiential or behav-ioral would, perhaps, be less suitable, such as in certain university courses, in some training programs for businesspersons, or even in training non-U.S. popu-lations.

Perhaps more than other methods, the ICS, by simulating problematic inter-cultural encounters, deals with the kinds of situations trainees can expect when they enter a new culture. Thus it helps trainees develop more accurate expectations in cross-cultural interactions.

The ICS is less dependent than other methods on having people from the target culture available to interact with the trainee. It also relies less on trainer expertise in a particular culture. The expertise is provided by the ICS itself, which is developed by experts in the relevant cultures after extensive research.

Although the ICS is simple to use, construction of an ICS is a lengthy, expensive, and complex process requiring, among other things, knowledge of the best approaches to elicit culturally appropriate and valid information, expertise in research methods, extentive data collection, cultural expertise, skills in capturing events and situations in written form, and sensitivity to the nuances of language.

Because of the level of expertise and skill required, and because the technique for its construction is continuously evolving, development of an ICS should not be undertaken without specific training or consultation with people experienced in constructing them. Such training is necessary to develop the skills outlined above and to ensure that the episodes capture cultural differences and reflect cultural complexitites while avoiding stereotypes.

The cost and effort involved in the development of an ICS are the method's major drawbacks. Consequently, existing ICSs should be used whenever possible.

The ICS has been *the* most extensively evaluated cross-cultural training method. Eighteen evaluation studies have shown it to be effective in reaching most of the goals of the method as they have been outlined in this chapter (for reviews of most of the studies, see Albert 1983; see also Cushner 1989, and Pollard 1989). These include:

❖ enabling trainees to make isomorphic attributions,
❖ imparting knowledge of the subjective culture of the target group,
❖ helping trainees develop more accurate expectations in intercultural interactions,
❖ helping trainees interact more effectively with persons from the target culture,
❖ improving knowledge and application of cross-cultural communication concepts,
❖ enhancing the intercultural adjustment of sojourners,
❖ reducing the rate of premature returns from overseas sojourns,
❖ increasing trainees' intercultural sensitivity,
❖ improving the task performance of trainees when they are overseas.

The overall strength and consistency of the findings are impressive (despite a few minor inconsistencies and the fact that not all of the studies documented behavioral changes), especially when considering that the evaluation studies differed greatly with respect to the ICSs used, the target cultures involved, the age and status of the trainees, the length and context of the training, and the approach of the researcher.

In conclusion, the ICS has proven to be a versatile and useful method of cross-cultural training, one that has continued to evolve to meet emerging needs and that has been effectively applied in a variety of situations and with varied populations.

# References

Albert, Rosita D. "The Intercultural Sensitizer or Culture Assimilator: A Cognitive Approach." In *Handbook of Intercultural Training: Issues in Training Methodology,* vol. 2. Edited by Dan Landis and Richard Brislin. Elmsford, NY: Pergamon (1983): 186-217.

————. "Communication and Attributional Differences Between Hispanics and Anglo-Americans." *International and Intercultural Communication Annual* 10 (1986a): 41-59.

————. "Conceptual Framework for the Development and Evaluation of Cross-Cultural Orientation Programs." *International Journal of Intercultural Relations* 10 (1986b): 197-213.

————. *Communicating across Cultures.* Unpublished manuscript, 1991.

Albert, Rosita D., and J. Adamopoulos. "An Attributional Approach to Culture Learning: The Culture Assimilator." *Topics in Culture Learning* 4 (1976): 53-60.

Brislin, Richard W. "A Culture-General Assimilator: Preparation for Various Types of Sojourns." *International Journal of Intercultural Relations* 10 (1986): 215-34.

Brislin, Richard W., Kenneth Cushner, Craig Cherrie, and Mahealani Yong. *Intercultural Interactions: A Practical Guide,* vol. 9. Cross-Cultural Research and Methodology Series. Beverly Hills: Sage, 1986.

Cushner, Kenneth. "Assessing the Impact of a Culture-General Assimilator." *International Journal of Intercultural Relations* 13 (1989): 125-46.

Fiedler, Fred, T. Mitchell, and Harry C. Triandis. "The Culture Assimilator: An Approach to Cross-Cultural Training." *Journal of Applied Psychology* 55 (1971): 95-102.

Pollard, W. R. "Gender Stereotypes and Gender Roles in Cross-Cultural Education." *International Journal of Intercultural Relations* 13 (1989): 57-72.

Triandis, Harry C. *The Analysis of Subjective Culture.* New York: John Wiley, 1972.

# Resources

Locating ICSs is not always easy. Please contact the sources indicated below *directly*—except for the Hispanic and Anglo-American ICSs, the author of this article does not have additional information about locating the ICSs cited. In addition to the chapters by Brislin and Triandis in this section of the *Sourcebook,* the best resources are the following:

❖ A chapter by Albert (1983) in the *Handbook of Intercultural Training* which presents the most extensive description of the ICS to date, supplies a brief description of many of the existing ICSs, summarizes evaluation studies done using them, and provides information on how to obtain most existing ICSs. (Please also note the updated information below regarding whom to contact for ICSs.)

❖ Two articles which appeared in a special issue of *International Journal of Intercultural Relations on Theories and Methods in Cross-Cultural Orientation* no. 10 (1986): 197-234, edited by Judith Martin. One, by Albert, delineated the nine fundamental issues that all training programs should address and how the ICS addresses them, and the other, by Brislin, discussed the culture-general ICS (see citations above).

❖ Original articles by Albert and Adamopoulos (1976) and by Fiedler, Mitchell, and Triandis (1971) on the assimilator (see citations above).

For information on obtaining copies of the PC version of the ICS and various sets of episodes from some existing ICSs in electronic form, as well as for the ICS on interacting with Southerners, please contact Professor Dan Landis, Department of Psychology, University of Mississippi, University, MS 38677.

For information on the culture-general assimilator please see Brislin's chapter in this *Sourcebook.*

For the episodes on U.S. gender roles, please contact Dr. William R. Pollard, Youth for Understanding, 426 Pennsylvania Avenue, Suite 198, Fort Washington, PA 19034.

For information on the status of the Hispanic/Latin American ICS and the Anglo-American ICS, please contact the author at the Department of Speech-Communication, University of Minnesota, 460 Folwell Hall, 9 Pleasant St., S.E., Minneapolis, MN 55455.

For information on an ICS for Navajos, see Michael Saltzman (1990). The construction of an ICS training for non-Navajo personnel, *Journal of American Indian Education,* vol. 30, pp. 25-33, as well as the M.A. thesis by Linda Zimmer-Vadas (1988) entitled "A computer-based cultural assimilator for educators: Welcome to Navajoland," Department of Teacher Development and Curriculum Studies, Kent State University.

For the ICS for Chinese scholars, see Agnes May Chen (1984), "Developing an American culture assimilator for students and scholars from the People's Republic of China, M.A. Thesis, UCLA.

For the assimilator for Australians going to Japan, see Rob Elzinga (1983), *Japan: a culture assimilator.* National Institute of Labour Studies and the Australian/Japan Foundation. ISBN: 0725802170.

For the ICS for Japanese visiting the U.S., see K. Ito (1982), "A culture assimilator for Japanese visiting the U.S.A." Program of overseas university cooperation. University of Illinois, Champaign-Urbana, Illinois.

# The Culture-General Assimilator

## Richard W. Brislin

### History

The idea for a culture-general assimilator emerged during the development of two writing and editing projects. The projects were the writing of *Cross-Cultural Encounters: Face-to-Face Interaction* (Brislin 1981) and the editing of the *Handbook of Intercultural Training* (3 volumes, Landis and Brislin, eds. 1983). In researching these books, it was necessary to explore a wide range of materials in the collections of large libraries, since much of the literature is organized according to who is involved in intercultural encounters—businesspeople, foreign students, diplomats, technical assistance advisors, residents of newly desegregated neighborhoods—rather than the generic characteristics of those encounters. Yet, as disparate as the sources on this subject matter were, I began to see a pattern. After going through hundreds of books and journal articles, I realized that the authors were talking about very similar concepts. No matter what their exact role, people engaged in extensive intercultural contact have to adjust their thinking and behavior; they are faced with challenges to their preexisting knowledge and prejudices; they find certain behaviors offensive when judged according to their own systems; and they cannot accomplish tasks in familiar ways. These common issues arise wherever extensive interaction takes place—with American businesspeople in Japan, with African foreign students in Pakistan, or with Palestinian Arabs in Israel. Because of the existence of culture-specific assimilators (Albert, Triandis, this volume) and the research studies that have demonstrated their usefulness, I felt that a culture-general assimilator could be developed to illustrate these commonalities.

One of the distinct benefits of the assimilator approach is that it captures how people really think about their intercultural interactions. People think in terms of the "war stories" that describe events in which they participated or which they observed: stories that show the mistakes they made, their inability to get tasks accomplished, their misunderstandings with people in the host culture. Memories of specific people and their behavior are evoked by these stories, and the impact of the behavior or event is so great that people want to share the stories with others.

Each critical incident within a culture assimilator captures an experience people are likely to have when they move across cultural boundaries. Culture-specific assimilators do this for people from a particular background moving to a designated culture, for instance, members of the American middle class moving to urban Thailand. The culture-general assimilator, on the other hand, includes incidents likely to happen anywhere, whether across national boundaries or within a complex culture (such as Anglo-Hispanic interactions within the United States) and to anyone, whatever his or her background or status.

Culture assimilators do not stop with the presentation of incidents. Rather, trainees are asked to identify underlying reasons for misunderstandings, difficulties, and the stresses and strains experienced by sojourners, which have been the focus of research by psychologists, communication specialists, anthropologists, and others. Consequently, developers of training materials can draw upon these analyses. Especially fruitful research on the underlying reasons for interpersonal difficulties has been done on:

❖ differing attributions about the causes of behavior,

❖ differences in status that affect encounters but that are missed by one of the parties in the interaction,

❖ stresses brought on *not* by events themselves but by the difference between expectations and the events.

These concepts and many others have been incorporated into the Culture-General Assimilator (published as *Intercultural Interactions: A Practical Guide,* Brislin et al. 1986). Recent work has integrated critical incidents into a text (Brislin 1993) and into a collection of modules suitable for various cross-cultural training programs (Brislin and Yoshida 1994).

We decided to call the method an "assimilator" rather than a "sensitizer" because, when the materials were published, the former term was better known than the latter, and we did not want to lose the advantages that familiarity can bring to the introduction of new training materials. The choice between "assimilator" and "sensitizer" was difficult, however, and we recognize arguments in favor of the latter (Albert, this volume).

## Description

The best way to introduce this set of materials is to examine one of the one hundred incidents in the collection, together with the alternative explanations of the incident. In formal training programs, participants read and discuss the incident, either as part of a plenary session led by the trainer or as members of small groups.

*Example:* Who's in charge?

The president of Janice Tani's firm asked her, as chief executive of the marketing division, and her staff (three male MBAs) to set up and close an important contract with a Japanese firm. He thought his choice especially good as Janice (a Japanese American from California) knew the industry well and could also speak Japanese.

As she and her staff were being introduced, Janice noticed a quizzical look on Mr. Yamamoto's face and heard him repeat "chief executive" to his assistant in an unsure manner. After Janice had presented the merits of the strategy in Japanese, referring to notes provided by the staff, she asked Mr. Yamamoto what he thought. He responded by saying that he needed to discuss some things further with the head of her department. Janice explained that was why she was there. Smiling, Mr. Yamamoto replied that she had done an especially good job of explaining, but that he wanted to talk things over with the person in charge. Beginning to be frustrated, Janice stated that she had authority for her company. Mr. Yamamoto glanced at his assistant, still smiling, and arranged to meet with Janice at another time.

Why did Mr. Yamamoto keep asking Janice about the executive in charge?

1. He did not really believe that she was actually telling the truth about who she was.
2. He had never heard the term "executive" before and did not understand the meaning of "chief executive."
3. He had never personally dealt with a woman in Janice's position, and her language fluency caused him to think of her in another capacity.
4. He really did not like her presentation and did not want to deal with her firm.
5. He was attracted to her and wanted to meet with her alone.

Trainees then choose among the alternatives. More than one alternative can contribute to an understanding of the incident. One of the implicit assumptions behind the development of these materials is that intercultural contact is not a collection of encounters with single perfect explanations. Often several issues are involved, and these can be captured in alternative choices. Trainees must consider all the explanations and should not be encouraged to try to focus too quickly on the "one correct explanation." In considering all the alternatives, trainees learn to analyze reasons for incorrect or inappropriate behaviors—an important intercultural skill.

For this incident, most trainees selected alternative three as their first or second choice. Alternative four also provides a good basis for discussion, with many trainees pointing out that the behavior in the incident could be an indirect way of indicating disapproval and that Americans have difficulty reading indirect behavior. For alternative three, trainees read and discussed the following:

This is a good response. Generally, in Asia, although women are found in all strata in the working world, very few (especially in Japan) are in positions where they have a great deal of authority over men. There are more cases where they would be working quite closely with someone with that authority but not possess the actual authority themselves. The fact that Janice was speaking Japanese where many of her assistants were not also added to the confusion over her role.

## Themes

The general theme, then, behind the specifics of this incident is "role and role differences." This distinction between the specifics of incidents and underlying themes is crucial to understanding the Culture-General Assimilator. The one hundred incidents included in *Intercultural Interactions* give life to, and generate trainee interest in, a set of eighteen themes common to extensive intercultural contact. Understanding these themes helps prepare trainees for the specific intercultural experiences they will have during their specific assignments. Trainees are not likely to remember everything in the training package, but they can develop a command of the themes and see their usefulness in analyzing intercultural experiences.

The eighteen themes, each of which is presented in four or more of the one hundred incidents, are grouped under general headings as follows:

A. *Experiences That Engage Emotions*: A major reason that intercultural experiences have so much impact and are so memorable is that they engage people's emotions in a way for which they are unprepared.

  1. *Anxiety.* Concern about whether or not one's behavior is appropriate and the resulting feelings and symptoms of stress.

  2. *Disconfirmed Expectations.* Becoming upset because the situation differs from that which they expected.

  3. *Belonging.* Wanting to feel accepted by others but encountering difficulties because as sojourners they have the status of outsiders.

  4. *Ambiguity.* Difficulty in formulating appropriate behaviors in another culture because of the ambiguity of the stimuli one receives.

  5. *Confrontation with One's Own Prejudices.* Responding negatively to those who are different because of one's own prejudices is a deep-seated part of one's socialization.

B. *Knowledge Areas*: Difficulties and misunderstanding in commonly discussed topics that people learn as "the facts" in their own culture.

  6. *Work.* Differences exist between attitudes toward work and the proper relationship of task effort and social interaction within the workplace.

  7. *Time and Space.* Concepts of time as well as proper spatial orientation for interpersonal encounters vary greatly.

  8. *Language.* Attitudes toward language use and the difficulties of learning the spoken language versus the "reading" language can cause problems.

  9. *Roles.* Large differences exist between role expectations from culture to culture: for example, what does a boss do? Are limits placed on women because they are women?

  10. *Value of Group versus Individual Allegiances.* Whether one is concerned with loyalty to a group (culture, family, and so on) or forms alliances with individuals one by one varies widely from culture to culture and is part of people's sense of their personal identity.

11. *Rituals and Superstitions.* One culture's "intelligent practices" are another culture's rituals and superstitions.

12. *Hierarchies: Class and Status.* The relative importance of class distinctions and the markers of high versus low status differ from culture to culture.

13. *Values.* Understanding values, which are internalized views of the world, is critical in cross-cultural adjustment.

C. *Bases of Cultural Differences*: The underlying, often invisible factors in the organization and communication of information.

14. *Categorization.* People in different cultures place the *same* elements (perceptions, thoughts, pieces of information, behaviors) into *different* categories, and it is the use of the resulting categories that can cause misunderstandings.

15. *Differentiation.* Increasing differentiation of information within a given knowledge area causes confusion or misunderstanding and sometimes causes people who treat the information with less differentiation to be judged as ignorant.

16. *In-group–Out-group Distinction.* People who are not members of the group must recognize that there are some in-group behaviors in which they can never participate.

17. *Learning Styles.* The style in which people learn best differs from culture to culture.

18. *Attribution.* People observe the behavior of others and judge it or attribute to it reasons for its occurrence according to their own values, beliefs, and expectations.

# Procedures

### Small-Group Discussions

In actual programs, colleagues and I have used the materials in various ways. One effective approach is to break the trainees into small groups. Each group reads and discusses three incidents that are concerned with the same theme. The designation of which incidents are associated with which theme can be found in Brislin et al. (1986, 52). Groups develop a consensus solution or solutions to each incident and also identify an underlying theme. Then, a spokesperson for each small group reports back to the entire group. The report consists of a review of one, two, or three of the incidents, depending upon the time available, and a discussion of the theme. You can subsequently expand upon the incident(s) and themes, as appropriate for the specific purposes of the training program (for example, educational applications for foreign students, economic aspects for businesspeople).

## Role Plays

The incidents can also be used as the basic outlines for role plays. Small groups of trainees choose an incident, assign different people to play each part, decide upon the basic elements of the dialogue, and then play out the incident for the whole group. For instance, if the "who's in charge" incident was role-played, one person would play Janice, another would play Mr. Yamamoto, and several others could play Janice's associates. Key elements in the dialogue could include Mr. Yamamoto saying, "You speak Japanese so well. I'm sure your superior is very proud of you." Janice could then follow with, "He has told me he appreciates my skills in Japanese as well as in the long-range planning of marketing strategies." As part of their planning, groups usually agree on the final line or action that will end the role play.

A good question for trainers to use, following the role play, is: "What did you learn above and beyond what you would have learned by simply reading the incident?" My strong advice is that people involved in a role play should stick to what is agreed upon in the planning meeting prior to its presentation. Surprises in a role play often bring up painful memories for one or more of the players, causing an interruption in the training session to resolve the mental anguish that a person is experiencing. Other guidelines for conducting role plays in training can be found in the chapters by McCaffery, Pettit and Frelick, and Fletcher (this volume).

## Special Uses

One interesting use of the materials is that they can guide culture-specific resource people (people socialized in that culture, returned sojourners, and the like) in being more effective in culture-specific training programs. Unless these people know something about cross-cultural training, they often present a disconnected and rambling account of their personal stories. Using the Culture-General Assimilator can help them focus their presentations. If they are familiar with the eighteen themes, they can give examples of how each is useful in analyzing experiences in the specific culture. They might modify or give special interpretations of some of the incidents, whether they focus on the specific culture or not. For instance, in a training program for people going to Japan, the incident about Janice would fit well; while in a program focused on some other culture, it could be used to stimulate thoughts about what women can and cannot easily do in *that* country.

Another use is in the training of trainers. Here people can be assigned to write their own culture-specific incidents using the one hundred as models. In long professional-development workshops where the materials are introduced to trainers for their own later use, I always have a session on writing new incidents for their own day-to-day work. People have written good incidents about health-delivery services to the elderly when the professional and patient are from different cultural backgrounds, issues faced by sign language interpreters for the deaf, problems faced by adolescents trying to make friends in a new school, and so forth. Trainers can also write incidents to communicate difficult and sensitive points about intercultural interaction in a relatively nonthreatening manner since the points are integrated into interesting, often compelling, critical incidents (examples in Brislin and Yoshida 1994).

My feeling about cross-cultural training is that it should include material about both the benefits (such as internalized understanding of cultural relativity, decreased authoritarianism) and the difficulties of extensive interactions. I have long had the concern that too much cross-cultural training deals only with pleasant, nonthreatening, and sentimental-romantic aspects of intercultural contact. The real difficulties of adjustment stress, prejudice and discrimination, failure to accomplish tasks, coping with seemingly hopeless bureaucracies, and interactions with genuinely abrasive people go underdiscussed. Trainers who agree with this premise can choose incidents from the one hundred, or write their own, that deal candidly and honestly with such difficulties. In the one hundred, for instance, there are incidents that deal with psychosomatic illness, the breakup of long-term relationships, depression, exclusion from interpersonal relationships, drug abuse, feelings of paranoia, and so forth.

Given that the eighteen themes are drawn from the research literature in the behavioral and social sciences, the Culture-General Assimilator can (and has) been used as a text in college and university-level courses in both intercultural communication and cross-cultural psychology. The incidents capture students' attention and interest, and professors can expand upon the ideas in their own presentations. They can also add to the course a touch of reality for students who have not had much, or any, intercultural experience of their own.

## Considerations and Contexts for Use

### Why Are the Incidents Culture-Specific?

There may be a seeming contradiction for a culture-general assimilator to be based on one hundred incidents, each of which takes place in a specific culture. One explanation is pragmatic. In testing the materials prior to publication, users wanted to know where the incidents took place because this is one clue in developing a solution. In the example presented previously, users did *not* want to read about Janice's interactions in an unspecified Asian country.

Another reason stems from research on how people best learn concepts. According to Glaser (1984), people learn by taking part in specific experiences and then generalizing from them. It is hard to teach a generalization directly without specific examples. The one hundred specific critical incidents provide the basis for developing a more conceptual knowledge base (the eighteen themes). People can later apply these to widely varying situations including assignments in countries other than those used in the assimilator or when involved in interactions with members of other cultural groups within their own country.

### For Whom Does the Assimilator Work Best?

When trainees bring an intellectual interest to their upcoming intercultural experiences, they enjoy working with the materials and the materials seem to be

effective. "Intellectual" does not correspond to the amount of education participants have. Culture-general assimilator materials adapted for adolescents worked
well with high school students preparing for junior year abroad programs sponsored by AFS International/Intercultural Programs (Cushner 1989). Trained exchange students showed cognitive gain, better adjustment, and improved interpersonal problem solving.

If trainees accept one or more of the following suggestions, then use of the
materials has been successful.

❖ A culture-general preparation can guide culture-specific preparation.

❖ The themes provide a framework for upcoming specific experiences.

❖ Variations of the incidents take place all over the world.

❖ Going through the incidents and themes will encourage the development of
an internalized set of standards for successful adjustment to upcoming specific experiences.

Other training groups with whom the materials have been used successfully
are: Peace Corps, staff at International Houses (several countries), overseas
businesspeople, workers in refugee resettlement camps, cross-cultural counselors, sign language interpreters for the deaf, health-care workers, administrators
and teachers at schools with a multicultural student body, and foreign students
beginning their studies abroad.

The materials are not as successful if trainees are looking for very specific
information they can use in their work the day after training. For example, I used
the materials with Caucasian alcohol rehabilitation counselors who worked in
rural villages in Alaska among Eskimos and other Native Americans. They wanted
materials, approaches, and content they could use in their counseling sessions
scheduled the day they returned to their jobs. The materials are not as successful
with a group seeking such specific information.

## A Final Thought

One consequence of an interdependent world is that people in any one country
have to learn to think in intercultural terms. There are far too few opportunities
for such learning. Even when people have extensive cross-cultural interaction
within their own country or on an overseas assignment, there are infrequent opportunities for them to explore and to integrate what they have learned. In my
opinion, one of the country's most wasted resources is the international and intercultural experiences of its citizens, for instance, Peace Corps (or its equivalent)
returnees, students on college campuses who have had a year abroad, and
businesspeople reintegrating themselves into their home offices after an overseas
assignment. The Culture-General Assimilator allows returnees to interpret their
experiences within a conceptual framework. It is especially useful for them, since
many of the incidents will remind them of experiences they had. Then, they can
begin to look at their intercultural encounters not as a random set of occurrences
but as a rich set of personal experiences that can become useful resources in
whatever career paths they undertake.

# References

Brislin, Richard. *Cross-Cultural Encounters: Face-to-face Interaction*. Elmsford, NY: Pergamon, 1981.

———. *Understanding Culture's Influence on Behavior*. Fort Worth, TX: Harcourt Brace Jovanovich, 1993.

Brislin, Richard, Kenneth Cushner, Craig Cherrie, and Mahealani Yong. *Intercultural Interactions: A Practical Guide*. Newbury Park, CA: Sage, 1986.

Brislin, Richard, and T. Yoshida, eds. *Improving Intercultural Interactions: Modules for Cross-Cultural Training Programs*. Thousand Oaks, CA: Sage, 1994.

Cushner, Kenneth. "Assessing the Impact of the Culture-General Assimilator." *International Journal of Intercultural Relations* 13 (1989): 125-46.

Glaser, R. "Education and Thinking: The Role of Knowledge." *American Psychologist* 39 (1984): 93-104.

Landis, Dan, and Richard Brislin, eds. *Handbook of Intercultural Training*, vol. 3. Elmsford, NY: Pergamon, 1983.

# Resources

Course outlines for both intercultural communication and cross-cultural psychology offerings that use the Culture-General Assimilator (together with other suggested books appropriate for college course work) are available. These can be obtained from Dr. Richard Brislin, East-West Center, ET, 1777 East-West Road, Honolulu, HI 96848.

# Culture-Specific Assimilators

## Harry C. Triandis

## History

The idea of a culture assimilator or intercultural sensitizer (Albert 1983) emerged in 1963 at the home of Larry Stolurow. Around the table were Fred Fiedler, Charlie Osgood, and this author. We had just received a contract from the Office of Naval Research to work on intercultural communication, interaction, leadership, and training. We were puzzled over such matters as:

1. How does one find out what is important about cultural differences that should be known to a person going to another culture?
2. How does one communicate what is important?
3. How does one evaluate whether or not the information that is communicated makes a difference?

Our host, Stolurow, urged us to put the information into computers and have people respond to questions posed by the computer. All those around the table agreed that this was a good idea. The remaining question was how to implement it.

Over the years we answered the above questions. Answers to the first one produced the analysis of subjective culture (Triandis 1972); answers to the second resulted in the culture assimilator (Fiedler, Mitchell, and Triandis 1971), and answers to the third question produced some methods for evaluating the training (Triandis 1977).

## Description

The original idea was to develop a computer program, but in producing the first examples of the method it seemed preferable to use a known and more easily manageable medium—the printed word. Now that the method has been tested in print and it works, we expect to see others adapting it to computer technology.

In the future the interactive video disc or CD-ROM is likely to provide the ideal vehicle for culture assimilators.

An assimilator has three basic parts:

❖ an *incident,* involving two or more people from two cultures who interact in culturally characteristic ways;

❖ four or five *attributions,* explanations or interpretations of why people in the incident acted the way they did;

❖ *feedback,* given after each attribution to provide cultural information that will help the trainee see the incident the way people from the other cultures are likely to see it.

Let us consider a specific example. The incident below was developed by Clay et al. (1973) on the basis of interviews carried out in the early 1970s. It may not be as correct now as it was when it was developed, but that illustrates the point that culture assimilators have to be changed as cultures change. This assimilator was designed to train black hard-core unemployed to interact successfully with the white establishment.

## The Incident

John, a twenty-year-old black man, and Jim, a nineteen-year-old white man, were looking for work. They both had recently been laid off by a cookie factory where they had worked together for about two years.

As part of the dismissal procedures, the men were referred to prospective employers. Each man had been scheduled for a job interview with a new company on the following Monday.

Jim, the white man, arrived at the interview wearing a standard shirt and tie and appearing very neat and clean. John, the black man, also arrived at the interview very neat and clean, wearing an expensive blue and green knit sweater. John had often received compliments from his black friends about this sweater. Consequently, he thought that it was the correct thing to wear.

When John talked to the interviewer, he was told that there were no jobs open with that company. However, he later found out that Jim had gotten a job.

## Attributions

Why did Jim, the white man, receive the job while John was told that there were no openings? (Page numbers cited are from original publication.)

a. Because Jim was white and the job interviewer was prejudiced. (Please turn to page 101-3.)

b. The interviewer thought that if John could afford such expensive clothes he did not need the work. (Please go to page 101-4.)

c. Jim, the white man, was wearing the standard shirt and tie, while John, the black man, was not. (Please go to page 101-5.)

d. When a black and a white apply for the same job, the white usually gets it. (Please go to page 101-6.)

The trainee sees the episode, the question that follows the episode, and the four or five attributions; then he or she selects an attribution and turns to a page where feedback is provided. The feedback page starts with a repetition of the attribution. For example: You selected (a): Because Jim was white and the job interviewer was prejudiced.

**Feedback**

1. This is quite possible, but there isn't any reason for that belief in *this* story. What other reasons could the interviewer have had? Please go back to page 101-1 and reread the story.

2. No. This is not the best answer. In fact, chances are the employer did not notice how expensive John's clothes were. You are on the right track, though. Try another answer.

3. Yes. By wearing the standard shirt and tie, Jim gave himself an added "advantage" over John. Job interviewers are more likely to hire a man wearing a shirt and tie rather than one with a sweater, no matter how expensive. This is stupid, but that's the way it is. Some interviewers may feel that people who dress conservatively will also have other habits that will make them better employees. Remember: the last thing an interviewer wants is complaints from a foreman that one of the people selected for employment has caused trouble. (Please go now to page 102-1.)

4. No. There is nothing in the story to indicate that there was only one job. Also, something else is different between the two men besides race. What is it? Try another answer.

> Notice: There is an attempt in this case to empathize with the trainee, by indicating that the world is not a fair place. But reality is also injected. The assimilator is not going to "improve" any culture; it just reflects that culture as it is.

An ideal assimilator consists of 100 to 200 episodes with attributions and feedback. By working through an assimilator, a trainee learns a great deal about the current state of a specific culture. It is important to remember, when you are using an assimilator, that you are not training people to select "right" answers and avoid "wrong" ones. The basic aim is to reach the point where the trainee makes attributions that are isomorphic to the attributions made by people from the other culture. That means, if an American is learning about Japan, the American would assign causes to the behavior of the Japanese that are more or less like the causes that the Japanese assign to their own behavior. In the Jim and John example, the trainee is supposed to suppress the emphasis on how *expensive* things are and pay more attention to how *conventional* things are.

## How Are Assimilators Constructed?

You need to know how assimilators are constructed before you can use them efficiently. Also, you may want to construct an assimilator yourself. It is somewhat complicated, but manageable by a person who understands empirical research—or who can consult with a trainer or researcher experienced in developing assimilators. The best description of how to construct assimilators can be found in Albert (1983). In this section I provide an *approximate* description to help you conceptualize this activity. Do not construct an assimilator before reading Albert (1983) and the chapter by Albert in the present volume.

There are two principal ways to proceed in constructing assimilators (Triandis 1984), empirically or theoretically. Each way has its advantages.

*Empirically.* First identify a sample of bicultural experts. For example, if you were to prepare an assimilator for Americans going to Japan, you would identify a sample of Americans who have lived in Japan for at least a year. Then, interview these experts and ask questions like: "Can you think of an incident that changed the way you perceived American-Japanese relations?" or "What did you find most difficult to understand when you first arrived in Japan? Tell me a story that illustrates this difficulty."

*Theoretically.* One can study anthropological accounts or cross-cultural studies that analyze the relevant cultures. Discussions about differences between societies, such as differences between collectivism and individualism (Triandis 1990), provide many ideas for the construction of assimilator episodes.

For example, one of the differences between those who live in what sociologists call collectivist societies and those who live in individualist societies is that collectivists do not make friends as easily as individualists, but once they have made friends they enter into more intimate relationships than do individualists. An incident can be constructed that makes this point:

> Mr. Iwao arrives in the United States from Japan and is invited by some American students to a party. Mr. Iwao is impressed and delighted by the friendliness of the Americans, who tell him to drop in and see them again. He does go to see them, but is surprised that the hosts are somewhat embarrassed and clearly did not mean for him to drop in.

Basically, any cultural difference can be illustrated with episodes. Some of the differences might be linguistic, such as the meaning of "first floor," which differs between the United States and Europe, and "lift," which is an elevator in England. Other differences can be quite elaborate, involving deep cultural orientations.

We have already noted that as technologies develop, the assimilator may be put onto an interactive video disc or CD-ROM format. This would allow trainees to react to staged situations in which, let us say, Japanese and Americans have interacted. One might show all kinds of inappropriate or offensive behaviors (for example, placing one's legs on a table) and the reactions to them.

The interactive technology would also enable the trainee to do things that change the behavior of the actors in the video. For example, the trainee might push a computer key and lower the actor's foot to the ground. The trainee's actions can receive feedback, such as green colors for correct and red colors for wrong moves. This kind of technology is now available for sales training, but is very expensive (approximately half a million dollars for ten hours of training). An advantage, however, is that these discs can be copied and thousands of people can be trained simultaneously. The basic idea of the assimilator can be used flexibly with modern technology.

### Validation of the Items

An important advantage of the assimilator is that the items can be validated empirically while the assimilator is being constructed. This is quite different from some cross-cultural training methods where the trainer teaches elements of the culture that intuitively make sense to the trainer, but which in fact may not be important or even valid.

To validate assimilator items, present the episodes and attributions you developed, based on information from the experts or the theorists, to two sample groups. Suppose you are developing an assimilator for Americans to learn about Japan; you might use fifty Japanese and fifty Americans. Each person selects one attribution for each incident. Then for each incident you, the assimilator constructor, can tally the frequency with which a particular attribution was chosen by each culture group.

For example, for a given episode you may have:

**Frequencies**

| Attribution | American | Japanese |
|:---:|:---:|:---:|
| a | 11 | 13 |
| b | 15 | 5 |
| c | 12 | 32 |
| d | 12 | 0 |

Compute a chi-square to find out if the two distributions are statistically different. (Directions for computing a chi-square can be found in any basic statistics textbook.) In this case it is obvious that the Japanese pick attribution *c* while Americans are picking all four attributions about equally. So, the Japanese prefer answer *c*. If the chi-square is not significant, this means that the item is not good and should be discarded. You usually start with twice as many incidents and their attributions as the final number of incidents that appear in the finished assimilator. You may well need 300 draft incidents to get 150 validated incidents. This means that the making of assimilators can be expensive. A lot of work occurs before the training begins.

## Procedures for Using the Method

One way to use assimilators is simply to give the book or disc to trainees and let them work their way through it on their own time. The advantage of doing it this way is that people who are very busy can have the assimilator available and use it during moments of free time. The disadvantage is that people who are *very* busy may not get to it at all!

To liven things up you can have trainees read the incidents, role-play the situations, and discuss the answers. This has the advantage of motivating trainees but the disadvantage of taking a lot of time. Each incident could well take fifteen minutes and, at four incidents per hour with some breaks, a group may not be able to do more than twenty-five incidents per day, so that a 150-incident assimilator (that can usually be worked through by an individual in about six hours) would take six days.

You might look for a compromise that incorporates both of these ways of using the assimilators. You might, for instance, role-play twenty-five incidents, and ask the trainees to work through the remaining incidents on their own. As far as we know, the more incidents a trainee studies, the better. It is like learning a language: eight years of German are twice as good as four.

If you decide to use role playing, have a trainer from the target culture present to increase the face validity of the training.

## Contexts for Use

Assimilators have been used to train students going abroad, American advisors to foreign military organizations, and managers of multinational corporations. Evaluations have shown that *when the trainees are motivated,* assimilator training improves their sense of well-being and effectiveness in the other culture. But the problem of motivation is a big one. Many people think they know all about what to do in the other culture and that they do not need to learn anything before they go there.

This is illustrated by a study (O'Brien, Fiedler, and Hewitt 1971) of a group of students going to Honduras for the summer as volunteers to give vaccinations to villagers. Some of the students had been to Honduras the summer before. Half the total group, randomly selected, were given assimilator training and half were not. Upon their return, a content analysis of their diaries was done to assess how well the students adapted to the local situation and to see if the assimilator-trained students had done better. The research team concluded that assimilator-trained students had not adjusted better than the untrained—until they split the sample into those who had been to Honduras the previous summer and those who had not. It was then found that the students who had been to Honduras before *and* who had been trained with the assimilator were significantly better adjusted during this their second stay in the country than those who had been assimilator-trained but had *not* been to Honduras before.

Motivation provides the explanation for the research results. The students who had been to Honduras the summer before knew that there were things they did not understand about Honduras and were eager to learn. The ones who had never been to Honduras thought they knew all about what to do there and therefore devalued and failed to benefit from the assimilator.

It is fair to conclude, then, that the ideal trainee is one who is eager to learn and willing to spend the time necessary to work through the assimilator and attend to its lessons. And the best time to train is when the trainee is most ready. That may well be on the plane or just after the trainee has arrived, or slightly later, after the trainee has had some negative experiences and feels confused and depressed. Culture shock should motivate people to learn. The success reported by Pollard (1989) with training eight to twelve weeks after arrival in the host culture suggests that, when it is an option, waiting is effective. What is clear is that the portability and self-instructional format of the assimilator are distinct virtues compared to other training methods that demand special contexts or facilities.

## Problems to Be Avoided

**Boredom.** Boredom can be a problem; some people are bored when reading books, especially serious books. Experiential games, simulations, and the like are more engaging. The question is: How much do people learn in a given period of time with each method? Certainly some trainees will prefer the efficiency of the assimilator (in six to eight hours one learns a great deal more than in most other kinds of activities), but others may want the training to be more stimulating. Mixing the assimilator-training and role playing is one way to hold back the boredom.

**Possible stereotyping.** Does assimilator-training solidify stereotypes? It is possible, if the assimilator is constructed to give only black-and-white answers. However, "good" assimilators qualify their interpretations and provide a sense of the probabilities (for example, most Japanese would do that, though some would do the opposite). In any case, all human thinking involves manipulation of categories—and stereotypes are categories. Therefore, stereotyping is unavoidable. As trainers we want to turn stereotypes into sociotypes—valid ideas about the attributes or behaviors of a group of people. By using validated information, the assimilator does that. Furthermore, as Albert's (1983) review shows, the method works. It seems likely that it works because it converts stereotypes into sociotypes.

## References

Albert, Rosita D. "The Intercultural Sensitizer or Cultural Assimilator: A Cognitive Approach." In *Handbook of Intercultural Training,* vol. 2. Edited by Dan Landis and Richard W. Brislin. New York: Pergamon (1983): 186-217.

Clay, G., et al. *Culture Assimilator for Interaction with White People.* Champaign, IL: University of Illinois, Department of Psychology, 1973.

Fiedler, Fred E., T. Mitchell, and Harry C. Triandis. "The Culture Assimilator: An Approach to Cross-Cultural Training." *Journal of Applied Psychology* 55 (1971): 95-102.

O'Brien, G., Fred E. Fiedler, and T. Hewitt. "The Effects of Programmed Culture Training Upon the Performance of Volunteer Medical Teams in Central America." *Human Relations* 24 (1971): 304-15.

Pollard, William R. "Gender Stereotypes and Gender Roles in Cross-Cultural Education: The Culture Assimilator." *International Journal of Intercultural Relations* 13 (1989): 57-72.

Triandis, Harry C. *The Analysis of Subjective Culture.* New York: Wiley, 1972.

————. "Theoretical Framework for the Evaluation of Cross-Cultural Training Effectiveness." *International Journal of Intercultural Relations* 1 (1977): 19-45.

————. "Theoretical Framework for the More Efficient Construction of Culture Assimilators." *International Journal of Intercultural Relations* 8 (1984): 301-30.

————. "Cross-Cultural Studies of Individualism and Collectivism." *The Nebraska Symposium on Motivation,* 1989. Lincoln, NE: University of Nebraska Press, 1990.

## Resources

Albert (1983) provides an extensive list of the available assimilators and where they can be purchased. As noted above, trainers will want, in some cases, to make their own assimilators. This allows for much greater specificity—for example, you can produce assimilators that take the gender, social class, or rural-urban background of the trainees into account. Using computers, when the opportunity is available, to provide assimilator training, you can have each trainee work through only those incidents likely to be maximally beneficial, given the trainee's previous knowledge and background.

# Using the Case Study as a Training Tool

## Lee Lacy and Janie Trowbridge

Everyone talks about the effectiveness of case studies as a training strategy. But in fact, few trainers use them to prepare individuals for cross-cultural experiences. We have heard trainers say: "Most cross-cultural training is of short duration, and we don't usually have time to develop and/or deliver case studies."

## Description of the Method

A case study is an account—usually written—of a realistic situation, including sufficient detail to make it possible for the participants in a training program to analyze the problems involved and to determine possible solutions (Nadler 1984, 95).

In practice, distinguishing a short case study from a critical incident or the text of a role play is sometimes difficult. A longer case study will usually contain several incidents, several characters, and details about the context of the situation. A case study usually takes place over a period of time and concludes with a problem for the reader to resolve. In terms of length and complexity, a case study is to a critical incident what a simulation game is to a role play.

The use of case studies in training is sometimes called the "case method technique." Case studies are most often associated with an instructor-led format. However, cases can be created for self-paced instruction and for computer-based programs.

The components of a typical case study are the case itself, which may include separate descriptions of the perspectives of the different characters, followed by a set of questions. These questions are usually discussed in small or large groups with the instructor in the role of facilitator. Cases may also include supporting documents, such as readings, memoranda, organizational procedures, reports, even films or videos. For example, Janet M. Bennett provides many quotations from a variety of sources at the end of the Salman Rushdie case (this volume).

# History of the Case Study Method

The case study method has its modern roots in the use of court records, in cases presented to Harvard Law School classes as early as the late nineteenth century, and in the use of real-life business problems in Harvard Business School classes beginning in the early 1900s.

The use of case studies in cross-cultural training—that is, in preparing the learner for interaction with cultures other than his or her own—is also connected with anthropological research. Anthropologists in the field have a long tradition of collecting life histories from members of a culture as one way of learning what is normal and appropriate behavior there. In an article published in 1960, anthropologist Edward Hall describes a case in which a business deal sours because of cultural differences in timing and the use of space (Leeds-Hurwitz 1990, 278).

Today case studies comparable to Hall's are used successfully with learners from many different types of business, government, and academic institutions, including foreign service personnel and family members, Peace Corps volunteers, corporate employees, and university staff, faculty, and students. They provide participants with concrete examples of problems caused by cultural differences in communication and other behavior patterns.

# Considerations for Using Case Studies

In deciding whether or not to use the case study method in cross-cultural training, it is useful to consider the factors discussed below.

## Program Goals and Objectives

Case studies are used primarily to develop and refine cognitive skills, such as analysis and decision making. Consider using case studies if your cross-cultural training goals and objectives are:

❖ identifying and solving problems which have their roots at least in part in cross-cultural differences,

❖ developing alternative approaches and strategies,

❖ making decisions which take into account different cultural perspectives and their consequences for these decisions.

Case studies are thus designed as a method for developing ways of approaching complex or stressful situations which can be practiced in the safety of the classroom.

> [The method] will facilitate maximum understanding of those situations, of the people in them, and of the several outcomes that might result when one or another of the people emphasizes certain values rather than others. Furthermore, the case studies afford the student an opportunity to practice this method of tackling problems before he is personally involved in situations that he may find confusing, frightening, or overwhelming (Ross 1979, 142).

In addition case studies may be used to develop:

❖ Awareness and appreciation of cultural differences and of the *complexity* of the types of situations participants are likely to encounter in cross-cultural settings overseas and in one's own country;

❖ Skills in group dynamics, such as consensus building, managing discussions, influencing others to accept a certain point of view, and dealing with cross-cultural interaction if the group is multicultural;

❖ Information-collecting skills called forth in exploring the human and material resources available to support the case study.

The two case studies in this section, "A Pregnancy at St. Theresa's" and "Salman Rushdie and *The Satanic Verses*," are excellent examples of cross-cultural case studies which can foster the development of many of these skills.

If the program goal is to change participants' behaviors and attitudes, you will be more likely to achieve it by using the case method in tandem with more interactive methods. For example, some trainers present and discuss a case study and then have the participants act it out as a role play.

## Administrative Constraints

**Time.** Development of a case study which meets the needs of a particular audience in a training program is very time-consuming. A long case study, such as the Salman Rushdie case featured in this book, can take from 40 to 60 hours to research and develop. The time needed, of course, depends on how elaborate the case study is to be and how much information has to be collected for its construction. Often colleagues or individuals who are involved in activities similar to those of the target audience are asked to critique drafts of the case, often resulting in suggestions that make rewriting and modification necessary.

The delivery of a relatively short case study, including reading and processing time, can take from an hour to a half day.

**Number of participants.** The method is most effectively used when there is a minimum of 15 to 20 participants and a maximum of 40 to 60 participants. Experienced trainers are likely to handle the larger number more easily than inexperienced trainers.

**Physical facilities.** Ideally the classroom arrangement should be suitable for small-group work, that is, chairs and tables should be movable and the room large enough to accommodate the groups.

## Nature of the Trainees and the Organization

If the participants view the trainer as the expert, they may be frustrated when she/he does not provide the "right" answer. They may also be hesitant to express their own ideas. This is particularly true in organizations which use traditional, nonexperiential approaches to training. An advantage of the case study method is that it is one of the safest experiential-learning methods. The participant does not have to perform in front of the whole group but does have the opportunity to speak in the small groups.

The problem-solving approach of the case method also has the advantage of drawing on the knowledge and experience of the group. However, this may not be appropriate when the members of the group have limited cross-cultural experience.

The predominant learning styles and educational experience of the participants should be considered. Trainees who have not had experience with the case study approach require additional time to become familiar with it.

### Trainer Preferences

Lastly, consider your preferences. Do you have enough experience to develop a case for a particular learning situation when an appropriate case does not already exist? Are you comfortable with the case method? Some trainers are reluctant to facilitate a group discussion, which can have unexpected outcomes.

## Developing or Selecting Case Studies

Once you decide to use the case study method, consider whether to develop one for the training program or to select one which is already available. The main considerations are the time and the resources available to you and the needs of the trainees and their organization. As mentioned above, developing a good case study which meets the needs of the trainees is very time-consuming. On the other hand, finding a suitable off-the-shelf case may be difficult.

Another option for longer-term training programs is to have the students develop case studies based on their own experiences. Ideally, in cross-cultural training, these cases should be written in small groups whose members represent different cultures to ensure that the case problem is fairly presented from more than one cultural perspective. The process of working together on this task also provides participants with an excellent opportunity to develop cross-cultural skills and insights.

The checklist in the Appendix summarizes factors to consider in selecting or developing a case study which meets the needs of a particular training situation. Two other considerations are:

❖ *Should you select or develop a case which is specific to a particular culture or one which portrays an unnamed or artificial culture?* The advantage of developing a culture-specific case is that it gives it more realism, and participants who are preparing for or already living and working within a particular culture will relate to it better. On the other hand, if a certain culture is named, there is the danger that inexperienced participants will overgeneralize about the nationals of that culture on the basis of the case study and may expect these behaviors in similar real-life situations. The danger of stereotyping is ever present. There is also the drawback that participants familiar with the specific culture will question the validity of the case based on their own personal experiences.

❖ *Should you select or develop a case which is specific to a particular function or organization?* In general, participants will find it easier to get involved in and thus will learn more from the case study method if they can relate to the experiences of the case's characters and if the situation is fairly representative of the types of situations they are likely to encounter.

If the case is drawn from the trainees' organization, it should be realistic in every detail—up to a point. The identities of the people and the situations should be appropriately protected. Trainees could be distracted from learning if they recognize the situation on which the case is based.

There is no single answer to these questions. Each training situation has its own demands which usually suggest the best solutions.

Look for case studies with a cross-cultural dimension in Lane and DiStefano (1988) and Robert T. Moran, David O. Braaten, and John E. Walsh, Jr., eds. (1994).

If you are developing a case yourself, sources include interviews, organizational methods and procedures, written reports, newsletters and periodicals, manuals, and training courses on the same or similar topics. An excellent resource on the development of instructor-led and self-paced case studies is American Telephone & Telegraph's Trainer's Library, vol. 3 (1987).

## The Case Study in the Program Design

Case studies can be used in the beginning, the middle, or the end of the program. The main considerations are: (1) the purpose of the case study in your course design and the learning objectives it supports, (2) the level of the course participants in relation to the sophistication of the material presented, and (3) the other learning strategies you are planning to use.

### Purpose of the Case Study

In terms of your design, the purpose of your case study may be to develop participants' skill and knowledge areas, which are mentioned in the section "Considerations for Using Case Studies," or to evaluate the skills and knowledge acquired in the course, or both.

If you are emphasizing the development of deductive reasoning skills, such as the application of cross-cultural concepts to intercultural problems, the case study should be positioned toward the beginning of the program after the presentation of the conceptual material.

If you are focusing on the development of inductive reasoning skills, such as problem solving and decision making, in which the students are primarily responsible for discovering or developing cross-cultural insights and principles, then you will want to place the case study toward the middle or end of the program, after participants have been exposed to the necessary material.

If you are using the case study as a tool for evaluating participants' synthesis and application of skills and knowledge acquired during the program or to allow them to evaluate their own learning, then, obviously, the case study will be placed at the end. You should exercise caution, though, in using case studies as an evaluation tool, since it is difficult to measure objectively such things as cross-cultural problem-solving skills or the development of cultural awareness. At best, the trainer can gauge the depth of an individual's or a group's insights and understanding of behaviors in a cross-cultural setting.

### Juxtaposition with Other Methods

Case studies are usually more demanding and involve the trainee in a higher degree of activity than does the lecture format. For this reason, consider scheduling less taxing activities before and after the case study. Some trainers use the case study toward the beginning of the program as a way of capturing the interest of the participants.

On the other hand, case studies are less demanding and less active than other experiential-training strategies, such as role plays and simulation games. If you are concerned about your trainees' level of comfort with participating in interactive-learning exercises, you may want to place a case study in your design just before a role play or simulation game, since the case study is less risky.

## Delivery of the Case Study

The processing of the case study is as crucial to the learning as the case study itself and is often neglected or implemented ineffectively. If the purpose of the case study method is to develop an approach to problem solving, then you should make sure that the trainees reflect on and analyze not only the content of the case but also, and more importantly, the method by which they arrived at their proposed solutions to the case problem.

Once participants are clear about the goals of the session, they typically read the case study and are then divided into small groups to work on the discussion questions. The large group is reconvened, the small groups report on their responses to the questions, and you, as facilitator, guide the large-group discussion and help trainees draw their own conclusions.

### Delivery Steps of a Case Study Session

**Step 1.** In the first step there are several options: The case can be read individually or in small groups, or to save time it can be distributed prior to the session. You may distribute the entire case to all groups or pass out parts of it to different groups. For example, each group could be assigned the perspective of a different protagonist.

**Step 2.** The small-group task should be clearly spelled out to the participants. Members of the group should be selected to record the group responses and to report to the large group.

**Step 3.** Following the small-group reports, lead the large group through the experiential-learning cycle; that is, require the participants to reflect on their experience, to draw conclusions about their learning from the content and the process of answering the questions in their small groups, and to consider applications to their own cross-cultural experiences.

Your role in this process is:

❖ to serve as the timekeeper responsible for moving the group through all steps of the learning cycle;

❖ to facilitate the clarification of points by the participants themselves;

❖ to ensure that the opinions and ideas of all the participants are expressed, examined, and recorded;

❖ to keep the participants focused on the task so that the discussion does not degenerate into a bull session;

❖ to identify and handle harmful stereotyping and other distracting behavior.

An effective variation on this process is the sequential or progressive case study. Information comprising a case is passed out in segments over the duration of a training program. The participants process each piece of information and make recommendations based on it. Later in the program, they receive additional information which may require them to reconsider previous decisions.

## The Case for Cases

In summary, a well-developed case study which is effectively delivered has the following advantages in cross-cultural training:

❖ It reflects the actual complexities of cross-cultural interaction and illustrates that such situations are rarely as simple as they seem. It encourages participants to question the notion that there is one right way or one correct answer.

❖ It helps participants learn to weigh carefully the many factors which affect cross-cultural interaction and to avoid snap judgments which may have negative consequences for the trainee once on the job or in the field.

❖ It encourages students to learn from each other and to appreciate different opinions and is thus particularly effective in a group representing different cultures.

Since it is time-consuming to develop case studies, and since cross-cultural training programs are usually short, the field needs to have a clearinghouse of tested cross-cultural case studies. These cases would represent the types of situations frequently encountered by the wide variety of groups involved in cross-cultural interaction. Although such a clearinghouse does not yet exist, there are several places listed in the Resources section to turn to if you want to know more about case studies.

Authors' Note: The authors gratefully acknowledge the helpful suggestions of their colleagues at the Foreign Service Institute and in the cross-cultural training field, including many of the authors in this book.

# References

Leeds-Hurwitz, Wendy. "Notes in the History of Intercultural Communication: The Foreign Service Institute and the Mandate for Intercultural Training." *Quarterly Journal of Speech* 76 (1990): 262-81.

Nadler, Leonard, ed. *The Handbook of Human Resource Development.* New York: John Wiley, 1984, 1995.

Ross, Robert. "The Case Study Method." In *Intercultural Sourcebook: Cross-Cultural Training Methodologies,* edited by David S. Hoopes and Paul Ventura. Yarmouth, ME: Intercultural Press, 1979.

# Resources

In addition to the previously referenced sources for case studies, the following are recommended:

American Telephone & Telegraph and Addison-Wesley Training Systems. *Techniques of Instructional Development,* vol. 3 of The Trainer's Library. Reading, MA.: Addison-Wesley, 1987.

Asante, Molefi, Eileen Newmark, and Cecil A. Blake. *Handbook of Intercultural Communication.* Beverly Hills, CA: Sage, 1979.

Eitinger, Julius. *The Winning Trainer.* Houston: Gulf, 1984.

Kohls, L. Robert, and John Knight. *Developing Intercultural Awareness: A Cross-Cultural Training Handbook.* Yarmouth, ME: Intercultural Press, 1994.

Lane, Henry W., and Joseph J. DiStefano. *International Management Behavior: From Policy to Practice.* Scarborough, ON: Nelson Canada, 1988.

Moran, Robert T., David O. Braaten, and John E. Walsh, eds. *International Business Case Studies for the Multicultural Marketplace.* Houston: Gulf, 1994.

Pfeiffer, J. William, and Arlette C. Ballew. *Using Case Studies, Simulations, and Games in Human Resource Development.* San Diego: University Associates, 1988.

Watson, Charles E. *Management Development Through Training.* Reading, MA: Addison-Wesley, 1987.

**Appendix**

## Checklist for Developing or Selecting Case Studies for Cross-Cultural Training

_____ 1. Is the case based on real cross-cultural situations or conflicts which the participant is likely to encounter?

_____ 2. Is the case relevant to the trainee's function or role in a cross-cultural situation?

_____ 3. Does the case describe events rather than analyze them?

_____ 4. Does the case involve conflict around cultural values, perceptions, and/or interpretations?

_____ 5. Are the different cultural perspectives of the case's protagonists portrayed so that the reader may be able to understand the logic behind their behaviors?

_____ 6. Does the case provide sufficient tension or drama to retain the trainee's interest throughout the reading and discussion of the case?

_____ 7. Does the case problem lend itself to multiple solutions?

_____ 8. Does solving the case problem require consideration of two or more different cultural perspectives?

_____ 9. Is enough detail or information provided in the text of the case so that the trainee can analyze and identify possible solutions?

_____ 10. If questions follow the case:

_____ a. Do the questions meet the learning objectives of the session?

_____ b. Are the questions analytical rather than descriptive?

_____ c. Do they require the learner to reflect on what has happened?

_____ d. Do they require the learner to draw conclusions about what she/he has learned from the content of the case and the process of arriving at a solution?

_____ e. Do they require the learner to consider the application of what has been learned to his/her experience?

_____ 11. Has the case been validated by representatives of the cultures, the organizations, and the functions or roles portrayed in the case, as well as by appropriate subject-matter experts?

_____ 12. Do you have a plan for testing, evaluating, and revising the case?

# Intercultural Value Conflicts: A Pregnancy at St. Theresa's

## Joseph J. DiStefano

You are an expatriate working in another country in which goals, mores, and behavior differ sharply from those defined as appropriate by you. To complicate matters, expatriates from still other countries hold positions of authority in the organization for which you work. Their values differ from both yours and those of your hosts. How involved should you become in conflicts among the parties? How much do you assert yourself, even when invited by your hosts to express your opinions? These are some of the issues addressed in "A Pregnancy at St. Theresa's."

## History of the Case

The case study in this chapter evolved from a student report in an MBA course, "Human Problems in International Management," at the School of Business Administration, the University of Western Ontario. Under my supervision, the report was developed into a case which has been slightly edited for the purposes of this volume. For reasons which will be obvious after reading the case, the student involved in the original situation disguised the names of the people, the school, and its location in Ghana. When he wrote the report, he was trying to improve his understanding of both the situation and his own behavior in it.

Several factors should be noted prior to discussing the case:

First, the case describes the situation *as the person involved experienced it*. It is *not* an "armchair" case fabricated from theory or from a synthesis of several real events. Secondly, the events are told from the point of view of the person in the case who has to take action or make a decision. The reader may well have reason to question the perceptions of the central figure in the case. Indeed, there is enough information to suggest that his perceptions differ substantially from both the Ghanaian teachers and from the nuns—whose perceptions also differ from each other.

The point is that users and writers of cases need to take care not to mix their own analyses or perceptions into either the case-teaching or case-writing process. This proscription, however, does not prevent the teacher or trainer from adding personal commentary after the students have completed their analysis. Similarly, case writers can provide guidelines for teaching the case in a separate note. Such guidelines usually contain suggested study questions, an analysis of the case, and recommendations regarding timing, related readings, and the use of visuals and other support materials. Sometimes the teaching note includes what actually happened in the situation, that is, the outcome of the case. (See the Resources section for availability of the note for this case.)

Finally, this case ends at a decision point. Since this is a teaching case rather than a research case, details or analytic frameworks which might be of use for making the decision, solving the problem, or doing research, but which were not part of the main actor's consideration at the time of the events, are not included.

This is one of several differences between teaching and research cases. Research cases typically include analytic commentary and/or are organized according to a conceptual framework consistent with the purpose of such cases. Research cases are meant to examine patterns, to generate or test hypotheses, and are often written from the point of view of an a priori framework. Relevant data are gathered, selected, and organized in a particular format because the researcher needs comparable information for a number of similar situations. In contrast, the purpose of teaching cases is to develop decision-making skills and conceptual abilities in the participants through repeated analysis and discussion. Therefore, these cases include only data available to the principals in the real situation, and the data are selected and organized according to these people's experience. For an elaboration of this distinction between teaching and research cases, see Erskine, Leenders, and Maufette-Leenders (1981) and Yin (1984), respectively.

## Procedures for Use

### Objectives

The critical point in using cases is to decide what your main objectives are. In this case, for example, are you using the case as part of culture-general training or training that focuses on Ghana specifically? Are you mostly concerned with training international volunteers about value differences between them and their hosts, with getting readers to examine their own biases and prejudices, with developing *skills* for responding to tough questions, or with transmitting conceptual *knowledge* (the process versus content distinction)? Of course, one may hold several of these objectives, but being clear about what you are trying to accomplish with a particular case is crucial. Deciding on the priority of your objectives will determine the questions you ask your reader to prepare, the types of readings assigned, the dynamics of the discussion, and so forth.

**Analysis and Plan**

No matter how good the teaching notes prepared by the case author are, to use the case most effectively it is important to do your own analysis. In "A Pregnancy at St. Theresa's," the key points are:

❖ The value differences among the three groups in the situation
   1. Brian, the volunteer
   2. Sister Maria Goretti (the headmistress) and related clergy
   3. the Ghanaian teachers

❖ The different assumptions and habits regarding conflict, conflict resolution, and leadership among the three groups

❖ An analysis of the rights and responsibilities of each of the parties

Another approach to the data in the case is to consider Brian's development in the situation. More specifically, what processes has he gone through, for example:

1. Entry
2. Trust building
3. Information gathering
4. Problem defining
5. Clarifying his own purpose
6. Developing options
7. Evaluating the consequences of each option
8. Deciding on strategy
9. Planning implementation of his choice

There is sufficient data to assess the first five items, but the reader needs to further develop item five and work out items six through nine.

Once you have analyzed and decided how to use the case, you need to fit it into the time allotted. You should also give careful consideration to what activities will precede and follow. For example, if you have just finished conducting the simulation *BaFá BaFá* (Shirts, this volume), you might start with an analysis of the case that ties into the experience with the simulation. If the case is primarily a discussion vehicle, it is advisable to think about the following:

❖ a schedule for the main points you want covered, with time reserved for meeting unexpected developments and for identifying and responding to participants' priorities

❖ questions which will elicit the issues you want discussed and which will facilitate transition between topics

❖ when you will use the chalkboard or newsprint to maximize the impact of the content of the discussion or analysis

❖ the approach to be taken in the closing lecturette

# Considerations

This case has been used successfully in undergraduate and graduate courses in organizational behavior, international and intercultural management, and intercultural communication. In a training context it has been used with middle managers and consultants and to orient and train volunteers and businesspeople going on international assignments (for example, Canadian University Service Overseas, Canadian International Development Agency). It has been used in both culturally homogeneous and culturally heterogeneous groups.

There are, however, two major potential problems in using the case. If you have relatively naive undergraduate students with little or no travel experience or little academic background in anthropology, sociology, or international relations, they are unlikely to see that the indirect way that the Ghanaian staff deal with the clergy may be a culturally preferred mode of managing conflict. Similarly, they may not see Brian's culturally influenced biases in how he views the sisters and his relationship with the Ghanaians. The best way to deal with these problems is to schedule this case after some basic material on culture and ethnocentrism has been presented. It is also important to supplement the assignment with specific readings (see recommendations below).

A second problem lies in the possibility of stereotyping the sisters in the case. Some students might be quick to attribute unconditional blame. However, the objective is to *explain* rather than blame. It is therefore important that a clear picture of the nuns' values, roles, and objectives be developed from *their* point of view, so that students appreciate the psychological integrity and consistency of each of the three perspectives represented in the case. Otherwise the discussion can degenerate into church bashing. Intolerance by participants is no more desirable than the apparent intolerance of the sisters for the traditional values described by Brian.

# Resources

A complete, detailed description of the course for which this case was developed, sample outlines, and teaching notes for the cases in the course are available from the teaching manual *International Management Behaviour: From Policy to Practice* (Lane and DiStefano 1992). A copy of the teaching note for the case presented here is available from the Case & Publications Division, School of Business Administration, University of Western Ontario, London, Ontario N6A 3K7. If you have little experience in leading case discussions, you will profit from reading *Teaching with Cases* (Erskine, Leenders, and Maufette-Leenders 1981). General information about the use of cases for international training is also available in the *Handbook of Intercultural Communication* (Asante, Newmark, and Blake 1979, 421-47).

If you are concerned about your own level of expertise in international or intercultural issues, you will find a wealth of good advice in "A Painless Approach to Integrating 'International' into OB, HRM, and Management Courses" (Mendenhall 1988/1989). This article also contains some excellent general references, the best of which are cited here. The premier textbook involving cross-cultural issues and management is *International Dimensions of Organizational Behavior* (Adler 1992). One of the first empirically based research reports with variables pertinent to the case can be found in "Motivation, Leadership, and Organization: Do American Theories Apply Abroad?" (Hofstede 1980). A number of newer works have also been published which might be of general interest to the reader. These include *Competitive Frontiers: Women Managers in a Global Economy* (Adler and Izraeli, 1994), *Managing Cultural Differences* (Harris and Moran, 1991), and *Riding the Waves of Culture* (Trompenaars, 1993). A series of films/videotapes called "Going International" (Nos. 1-5. Griggs Productions, 411 15th Ave., San Francisco, CA 94118) are also valuable in sensitizing students and teachers to the issues in the case (see References).

Two other readings which are older but of particular value for this specific case are "The Pitfalls of National Consciousness" (Fannon 1966) and "Social Stratification and Economic Processes in Africa" (Fallers 1964). Both of these are reproduced in *Comparative Management: Organizational and Cultural Perspectives* (Davis 1971).

Notwithstanding the resouces and background the teacher brings to the use of this case, the best "resource" is careful preparation of the case in the context of the training program in which it is embedded. Repeated use, with thoughtful reflection on past experience and revisions based on retrospective analysis, should produce good results.

## Case Study

# A Pregnancy at St. Theresa's

**Introduction.** Sitting in the teachers' staff room during a break between classes, Brian Robertson found himself at the receiving end of a pointed question. The Ghanaian teachers were chatting about the apparent dismissal of their colleague, Mary Kpodogah, after she had a baby without the benefit of either a traditional or church marriage. During a pause in the conversation, Ambrose Okraku turned to him and asked, "What would *you* do about the situation?"

Just a week before he had been thinking about it as he looked out the window of St. Theresa's Girls Secondary School and watched the headmistress, Sister Maria Goretti, walking slowly back to the convent. He marveled at the tremendous personal strength with which she had founded and developed the school. This strength and tenacity had kept her trying to mold the young Ghanaian students into what she referred to as "civilized, virtuous women," against apparently overwhelming odds. At the same time, Brian was deeply angered by the almost desperate attempts of the European nuns to segregate the school, the students, and themselves from the rest of Ghanaian society. It was almost as if they feared contamination. Their attempts to maintain their own culture had put the nuns in several uncomfortable situations since Brian had been at the school, and it was leading to increasing friction between the sisters and the Ghanaian staff. The problem of Mary Kpodogah threatened to bring relations to the breaking point.

Mary Kpodogah was one of the school's junior teaching staff. At the end of the previous school year, Mary's swelling girth had communicated her condition to the whole school. About two weeks before the new term was to begin, her child was born. Now, five weeks into the term, and a week after she should have come back from her maternity leave, it was becoming apparent that Mary was not going to be permitted to resume teaching at St. Theresa's.

Brian had been wondering whether he should take any action with either the staff or the sisters over the apparent friction. Now he had no choice. At a minimum he had to answer Ambrose's question. And he didn't have much time to consider his reply.

**Background.** Brian had been at the school for over a year, having come to the town of Ayensi in southern Ghana with the Canadian University Service Overseas (CUSO). He was happy to be where he was—at St. Theresa's, a small Catholic boarding school of about 500 girls run by six English-speaking nuns and a priest, all of whom were from European countries. Since arriving, Brian had formed several close friendships among the fifteen Ghanaian teachers, and these friends had taken great pride in introducing him to their own society. At the same time Brian maintained friendly, though casual, relationships with the nuns and the three other white lay teachers. As time passed, he became quite proud of the school and felt more and more that he should do something to ease the bad feelings between the administrators and the African staff.

Speculation among the Ghanaian teachers had begun during the last term over what the headmistress might do about Mary. At that time most of them hoped that Sister Maria Goretti would permit Mary to return after the birth, but they expected that the headmistress would likely take a much harder line. The opinion seemed to be that she wouldn't go out of her way to help Mary any more than she had to. During the last couple of weeks Brian had noticed a revived interest in the subject.

He had to admit, from what he had seen, that there was considerable justification for the pessimism of the Ghanaian teachers. The nuns were continually checking on the staff to make sure they were on time for class. If they were late, which happened on more than one occasion, the nuns would rebuke them in front of their colleagues. Other examples of less-than-trusting behavior came to mind. The Ghanaian teacher of domestic science gave vivid descriptions of the interrogations she was subjected to when required by the headmistress to account for her purchases. The nun's extreme suspicion of any black male, even staff, seen on the school compound after classes was a stock joke among the teachers.

Brian remembered personal examples which gave credence to the Ghanaian's negative expectations about their relationships with the religious administrators. For example, Sister Maria Goretti had once remarked to him, "I don't think these people will ever be able to run their country. They just have no sense of responsibility." Even Father Standing, the priest in charge of school construction, often spoke disparagingly to Brian about his mason, "who after ten years still cannot put up a straight wall." Brian wondered cynically if the fact that the priest was usually standing over the mason screaming at him had anything to do with the problem.

Brian puzzled over this feeling of resignation among the Europeans that the Ghanaians would never amount to anything. The hopelessness seemed to persist in spite of considerable evidence to the contrary. He thought part of the explanation was the limited success of the church in changing basic values of Africans anywhere on the continent. He also believed that the clergy's pessimism combined with the Africans' rise to political power, which in Ghana inevitably meant the takeover of the educational system, had generated a very defensive posture on the church's part over its remaining means of influencing attitudes—mainly its schools. He thought perhaps that this accounted for the extreme reluctance of the religious orders to let outsiders participate in running the schools.

As he pondered these issues, Brian knew that the problem posed by Mary Kpodogah's dismissal was probably only a part of the general deterioration of relations between the Ghanaian staff and the administration. To check his facts, Brian went to Sister Joseph, the senior chemistry teacher, and asked what Mary's position was. Sister Joseph confirmed Mary's dismissal and explained the sisters' viewpoint, "It wouldn't be setting a good example for young Catholic girls to have a teacher with an illegitimate child. If she were married, it would be different." Sister Joseph concluded, "The regional Catholic school board will likely find Mary a teaching position in a local girls' elementary school." This puzzled Brian even more. He failed to see the logic of such a transfer, given the nuns' view that Mary's presence was a potentially corrupting influence. But he decided against pursuing the matter further at that time.

**Mary's background and reactions.** Mary came from one of Ayensi's most prominent and devout Catholic families. Her father was the head of a government department in a different region of Ghana. Two of Mary's sisters were students at St. Theresa's. From talking to the rest of the staff and from what he had seen when he visited the Kpodogah family to see the baby, it appeared to Brian that the family accepted the situation without any great feelings of shame. In fact, Mrs. Kpodogah seemed ecstatic about her grandchild.

Neither did Mary nor her family appear to be upset about her dismissal from the school. During the previous term, she and Brian hadn't talked about the implications of the pregnancy for Mary's continuing to teach at the school. Now that the nuns had acted, Mary seemed only mildly irritated at what she termed their pettiness. However, Brian had noted that Mary had not come back to the school's compound to see her friends since her dismissal. It was his impression that the job wasn't important to Mary or her family. She could get another teaching position in time, especially with help from her family.

As Brian understood traditional Ghanaian customs, having a child before marriage was a serious offense. At best it would have meant compromising the woman's chance of getting married in the future; at worst it would have led to being banished from the village. But as Ghanaian society became more urban, family control over children became less strict and social values changed to take account of increasing sexual relations among unmarried couples. Now, illegitimate births had less stigma attached to them as long as the father was willing to provide for the mother and child financially. In fact, many men preferred to have their mates pregnant before marriage as proof of the woman's fertility. From hearing the comments of his students, whose candor about sexual matters never failed to amaze him, it seemed to Brian that the objective of many girls was to find boyfriends of high enough status and income to support them. Babies, with or without the benefit of marriage, were considered a natural outcome of the relationship.

Mary's boyfriend was the dispenser at the Ayensi hospital pharmacy. Apparently he was going to be sent to England soon for a pharmacy course. As far as Brian knew, the two were not living together, but their relationship had existed over a period of several years. People in the community seemed to accept, even approve of, the couple's arrangement. Brian wondered what effect Mary's dismissal would have on St. Theresa's reputation in the town.

**Staff and administration relations—should Brian intervene?** The need for improvement in relations between the local staff and the sisters was painfully obvious to Brian. Yet he was hesitant to act personally for several reasons. First, the sisters were extremely jealous of their control over the school and were very set in their ways. As far as Brian could ascertain, Sister Maria Goretti modeled her authoritarian, centralized administration on her own earlier experience in a convent school in Europe. The teachers had to go to her even to get pencils and paper. If she went to Accra for the day, virtually no decisions could be made. When the nuns had tea or a meal, the school stopped. Staff meetings served mainly to discuss, then ratify, suggestions made by the headmistress. Brian had the clear sense that the sisters neither expected nor wanted a long-term concern for the school from the local staff.

A second reason for Brian's hesitation to intervene in the situation was the past behavior of the Ghanaian teachers. On several occasions they had studiously avoided directly opposing the headmistress on controversial issues. During one staff meeting, for example, Sister Maria Goretti had asked the teachers to foster improvement in the students' language skills by speaking only English to them. Brian knew that the local staff felt strongly about maintaining their tribal language and that the issue was a sensitive one. Yet, he noted, instead of voicing their concerns, the Ghanaians had mumbled their agreement. Of course, they had subsequently ignored the request and continued talking in the vernacular to the students as they always had done. Brian couldn't understand why they refused to confront the headmistress over these issues and wondered if Mary Kpodogah's case would be treated in a similar fashion.

So in the absence of action by the Ghanaians on their own behalf, Brian wondered if he should play a part in initiating change. He realized that he was only a visitor who would be leaving the country at the end of the year, and he knew he didn't fully grasp the history of the school, its goals, functions, and the like. He also recognized that as a CUSO volunteer, he had been sent to Ghana to fill a specific teaching need. Considerable pressure had been put on all volunteers during their training to avoid overstepping their roles. They had heard of the problems encountered by U.S. Peace Corps volunteers who had made the error of trying to make significant changes where they operated.

On the other hand, Brian enjoyed excellent relations among the Ghanaians and thought that they viewed him as sympathetic and sensitive to their feelings and views. Moreover, he was on good terms with the headmistress and the other nuns. Because of this, he thought he was in a position to influence them to change the sisters' attitude that the school was theirs, and theirs alone, to run. His personal conviction was that Sister Maria Goretti should try a more participative approach by actively encouraging the Ghanaian staff to run more of the school's affairs.

**What now?** Little did he know how soon he would have to resolve these contradictory views and feelings within himself. During the usual midmorning tea break between classes, Brian found himself sitting with several of the other teachers listening to them talk in their vernacular tongue. He understood enough to know that the subject of their discussion was the situation of Mary Kpodogah. Then, during a pause in the conversation came the fateful question from Ambrose Okraku, who turned to Brian and pressed, "What do *you* think should be done about Mary?!"

# References

Adler, Nancy J. *International Dimensions of Organizational Behavior.* 2d ed. Boston: PWS-Kent, 1992.

Adler, Nancy J., and D. N. Izraeli, eds. *Competitive Frontiers: Women Managers in a Global Economy.* Colchester, VT: Blackwell, 1994.

Asante, Molefi K., Eileen Newmark, and Cecil A. Blake, eds. *Handbook of Intercultural Communication.* Beverly Hills: Sage, 1979.

Davis, S. M. *Comparative Management: Organizational and Cultural Perspectives.* Englewood Cliffs, NJ: Prentice-Hall, 1971.

Erskine, J. A., M. R. Leenders, and L. A. Maufette-Leenders. *Teaching with Cases.* London, ON: Research & Publications Division, School of Business Administration, University of Western Ontario, 1981.

Fallers, L. A. "Social Stratification and Economic Processes in Africa." In *Economic Transition in Africa,* edited by M. J. and M. Harwitz Herskovits, Evanston, IL: Northwestern University Press (1964): 113-30.

Fannon, Franz. "The Pitfalls of National Consciousness." In *The Wretched of the Earth,* edited by Franz Fannon. New York: Grove Press, 1966.

Harris, Philip R., and Robert T. Moran. *Managing Cultural Differences.* Houston: Gulf, 1991.

Hofstede, G. "Motivation, Leadership, and Organization: Do American Theories Apply Abroad?" *Organizational Dynamics,* Summer 1980.

Lane, H., and Joseph J. DiStefano. *International Management Behaviour: From Policy to Practice.* 2d ed. Boston: PWS-Kent, 1992.

Mendenhall, M. "A Painless Approach to Integrating 'International' into OB, HRM, and Management Courses." *Organizational Behavior Teaching Review* 13, no. 3 (1988/89): 23-37.

Shirts, R. Garry. *BaFá BaFá: A Cross-Cultural Simulation.* Del Mar, CA: Simulation Training Systems, (formerly Simile II), 1983.

Trompenaars, Fons. *Riding the Waves of Culture.* London: Economist Books, 1993.

Yin, R. K. *Case Study Research, Design and Methods.* Beverly Hills, CA: Sage, 1984.

# Case Study: Salman Rushdie and *The Satanic Verses*

## Janet M. Bennett

I n general the case-study approach to learning is designed to enhance participants' analytical and decision-making capabilities. Rather than relying on their
own experiences or on conceptual material from the trainer, learners are required to assess and react to a real-life context.

## Background

In this case study the context is the intercultural conflict triggered by the publication of Salman Rushdie's book *The Satanic Verses*. The material in the case study
is extended over time and contains multiple critical incidents. It requires learners
to shift frames of reference among culture groups and, therefore, to practice what
many educators and trainers feel is an essential intercultural skill. There are several reasons why the Rushdie situation is ideal for an intercultural case study.

First, the issue illustrates perspectives from multiple frames of reference:
Rushdie's, the publisher's, Muslims', American writers', politicians', scholars',
and so forth. If such a case were to appear to represent a single frame of reference
or to reflect a bias toward one value system, it would diminish its effectiveness.

Second, the case study demonstrates violation of deep core values in each
culture. *The Satanic Verses* does not merely reflect trivial concerns, but rather
assaults seemingly unquestionable values in each society, particularly the values
of the sacred in Islam and freedom of speech in the West.

Third, the outcomes of decisions about this case are significant to each culture. If learners assess that the outcomes to a case study are meaningless, it becomes less engaging to debate the decisions. That is clearly not the case with *The
Satanic Verses*.

# Procedures

## Step One

You should provide the participants with the material for the case study before any actual large-group discussion. In distributing the case, clarify the goals either in writing or by discussing them with the group. These goals include increasing the learners' ability to:

1. understand their own cultural frame of reference,
2. shift cultural frames of reference,
3. analyze deep, cultural value conflicts,
4. practice decision making in the context of significant value differences,
5. appreciate the ethics and value systems of other cultures and therefore increase their cognitive complexity, empathy, and tolerance of ambiguity.

## Step Two

You may begin by asking participants to read the case study at home, underline the relevant points, and write a paper on their responses to the case.

## Step Three

In a large group, facilitate the discussion of the essential elements requiring consideration in the case. Depending on the instructional context in which the case study is used, you may wish to supplement the written case study with other material to provide further context for an understanding of the cultural dynamics. For instance, for an intercultural communication program, you might include additional material on value contrasts.

Because of the unusually controversial nature of this case study, it is essential to clarify that this conflict has been selected to honor the cultural values involved, not to debase them. By carefully reflecting on all points of view in a nonevaluative climate, the group can go beyond a single frame of reference to achieve a deeper understanding of other cultural points of view.

## Step Four

Divide participants into small groups of five to seven members. They should be asked to role-play an editorial board from a publishing company that is considering whether or not to publish a paperback version of the Rushdie novel. (If the group is familiar with other cultures, you may choose to have them role-play publishers from the different countries grappling with this decision: the United States, Great Britain, France, Egypt, India, Pakistan.)

The task should be carefully defined for the group according to the "Publishing-Team Discussion Guidelines" included at the end of the case study. Each publishing team should work with relevant facts and reach a consensual decision on how to handle the manuscript. They should be prepared to discuss their decision and the reasons for it in the large group.

Case Study

# *The Satanic Verses* by Salman Rushdie

Salman Rushdie, a self-described "hybrid creature," was born in Bombay, India, in 1947 of well-to-do Kashmiri Muslims. As a teenager, he was educated in London at Rugby, followed by Cambridge, where he read history with an emphasis on Islamic subjects. He lived briefly in Pakistan after he graduated in 1968, but quickly returned to London where he married a British woman and had a son. His first novel was a critical and commercial failure. However, his second book, *Midnight's Children,* won Britain's most coveted award for fiction, the Booker Prize in 1981. *Shame,* published in 1983, also was nominated for the Booker Prize. By this time, Rushdie was recognized as one of the most important writers of his generation.

In September 1988, Viking Penguin published Rushdie's novel, *The Satanic Verses,* in the United Kingdom. Controversy immediately surrounded the author, the book, and the publisher. A fictional exploration of the sacred and the profane, the book has variously been described as "stylistically dazzling," "lyrical, scathing, inquisitive, and at times, bewildering," and "full of both insult and wit." Others have felt it distorts history and disfigures the characters of the most holy persons in Islam. Muslim critics charged that Rushdie had knowingly blasphemed the Prophet and profaned the Islamic faith. Riots occurred in Britain, where over two million Muslims live. By October 5, 1988, ten countries had banned the novel, including India, Pakistan, Egypt, Saudi Arabia, South Africa, and Bangladesh.

In January 1989, an angry crowd in Bradford, England, publicly burned a copy of the book. A photograph of the burning received wide circulation internationally. Throughout February riots continued, with six killed in Islamabad, Pakistan; one killed and one hundred injured in Kashmir, India; twelve killed and forty wounded in Bombay; with other demonstrations in New Delhi, Calcutta, Darjeeling, Varanasi, Patna, and Siliguri, India. On February 15, 1989, the Ayatollah Ruhollah Khomeini, Iran's spiritual leader, called for the execution of Rushdie for his blasphemy against Islam, the Prophet, and the Holy Koran. Within two days a bounty of 2.6 million dollars was placed on the author's head, an amount doubled within the week by an Iranian philanthropist.

Sequestered under the protection of Scotland Yard, Rushdie issued a carefully worded statement in an effort to quell the controversy. He wrote: "As author of *The Satanic Verses* I recognize that Moslems in many parts of the world are genuinely distressed by the publication of my novel. I profoundly regret the distress that publication has occasioned to sincere followers of Islam. Living as we do in a world of many faiths, this experience has served to remind us that we must all be conscious of the sensibilities of others."

His apology was brushed aside by the Ayatollah, who responded, "Even if Salman Rushdie repents and becomes the most pious man of his time, it is incumbent on every Moslem to employ everything he's got, his life and wealth, to send him to hell."

By the end of February the controversy had achieved unprecedented proportions. British airlines received bomb threats, as did Viking Penguin, Rushdie's publisher. Sales of the book soared, and a second U.S. printing was under way. Meanwhile, bomb threats caused several booksellers, including B. Dalton, Waldenbooks, and Barnes and Noble, to remove the offending text from their shelves in an effort to protect the well-being of their employees.

Viewing this as an assault on freedom of speech, American writers' groups issued statements in support of Rushdie. Twenty-one writers, including Norman Mailer, Gay Talese, E. L. Doctorow, Susan Sontag, and Robert Stone read excerpts from the book in a public demonstration of solidarity in New York.

Economic and political sanctions were exchanged when twelve members of the European Community pulled their envoys from Iran in response to Khomeini's death sentence. The Netherlands, West Germany, France, and Spain slowed credit to Iran and limited economic ties worth nearly $4 billion. Iran severed relations with Britain. The United States, having no diplomatic relations with Iran, considered further economic sanctions, as did Japan, which threatened to cut by one-third the purchase of Iranian oil.

The foreign ministers of the forty-six-member Organization of Islamic Conference condemned the book, but stopped short of affirming the death sentence and of breaking diplomatic ties.

Meanwhile, the book was scheduled to be translated into twenty languages. A paperback edition was planned, and publishers in France and Germany were debating whether to issue versions of their own. Canada was reviewing the book, before allowing any further imports, to determine whether or not the text violated the national law against hate literature.

In the United States, popular folk singer Cat Stevens, who converted to Islam, announced his support for Khomeini's death sentence and inspired protests throughout the country. One radio announcer smashed a copy of "Morning Has Broken" by Cat Stevens on the air; another swapped 102 copies of *The Satanic Verses* for any Stevens record.

In June, the Ayatollah Ruhollah Khomeini died, although his condemnation of Rushdie was reiterated.

Rushdie and his second wife, American writer Marianne Wiggins, separated in August 1989.

In January of 1990, the Muslims in Great Britain reaffirmed their commitment to pursue Rushdie unless the book were withdrawn. The first week of February, the successor to Khomeini, the Ayatollah Ali Khameni, declared that the religious decree "about the writer of the blasphemous book *The Satanic Verses* is still valid and must be implemented."

The main political opposition group in Iran, the Mujahedeen Khalq, condemned this position, accusing Khameni of trying to divert attention from his political problems in Iran.

Regarding publication of the paperback edition, Rushdie offered several reasons in support of its publication: to keep the book in print for the maximum period of time and avoid having the book suppressed through the back-door route of being "out-of-print," to make the book available for study at colleges, and to maintain the principle that the book is innocent and wrongly accused.

### Perspectives on "The Satanic Verses" Controversy

"Salman Rushdie has touched a sensitive nerve in us all. When scholars try to explain the Islamic response to his book, they should not be accused of advocating Ayatollah Khomeini's position. The academic community in America not only must defend intellectual freedom for Mr. Rushdie, but also must demonstrate the courage and intellectual openness required to examine and understand why Ayatollah Khomeini's actions struck a responsive chord in millions of fellow humans in a globe we all share."

—John O. Voll, professor of history and
chairman of the history department at
the University of New Hampshire, in
*The Chronicle of Higher Education,* March 22, 1989

"Writers who condemn Islamic religion as fanatical are being 'blatantly ethnocentric and ignorant'.... People should not equate the actions of Khomeini with the actions of the rest of the Islamic world."

—Interview with Jon Mandaville, professor of history at
Portland State University, in
*Vanguard,* February 24, 1989

"One point where there is substantial departure between Judeo-Christian and Moslem theology is theocracy, or the merging of religion and state. Though not all countries with Moslem majorities are theocracies, most embrace this sentiment to some degree. Thus when someone insults the prophet Mohammed, he hasn't just insulted a historical figure or a religious philosophy. He has collectively insulted an entire people—everything about them.

"A second point of departure is the intense mental prohibitions Moslems feel against discussion of the personal life of Mohammed.... It is absolutely forbidden to say or do anything that could be disrespectful to the prophet. Many pious Moslems hesitate even to pronounce Mohammed's name, referring to him as 'the holy prophet' and invariably appending 'peace be upon him.'"

—Gregg Easterbrook, a contributing editor to
*Atlantic Monthly, Newsweek,* and
*Washington Monthly,* in
*The Washington Post,* February 21, 1989

"Muslims in Balton [England] had burned *The Satanic Verses* early in December of 1988 and had suffered the humiliation of being totally ignored. The Bradford Muslims called the papers. They hired a British lawyer to advise them. They made a videotape of their book burning and sold the rights to use it. (They still charge what amounts to twenty-seven hundred dollars to anyone who wants to use the footage.)"

—Jane Kramer, "Letter from Europe" in
*The New Yorker,* January 14, 1991

"Mohammed Al-Asi said a 'unanimous' Islamic legal system has recognized the legitimacy of the death penalty in three situations: murder, adultery, and 'when a person deserts his Islamic congregation and community.'

"'Rushdie has renounced Islam and has insulted and lampooned the person of the prophet,' he said. 'Both carry the death penalty.'

"'This is not a matter of schools of thought in Islam,' he added. 'This is not an issue of Imam Khomeini. He had the ability to pronounce a verdict in the Moslem world that other heads of state could not muster the courage to do.'"

—Interview with Mohammed Al-Asi,
Leader of the Islamic Center in Washington, D.C., in
*Oregonian,* March 10, 1989

"To put it simply as possible: I am not a Muslim. It feels bizarre, and wholly inappropriate, to be described as some sort of heretic after having lived my life as a secular, pluralist, eclectic man...where there is no belief, there is no blasphemy."

—Salman Rushdie, in *Newsweek,*
February 12, 1990

"'The book is really very, very offensive,' he said gently, with no bitterness. 'I cannot overstate this. And I cannot expect you—you who are not a Muslim—to feel this...this was something that the author deliberately did. This was not just a slip of the pen.'"

—Interview with Dr. Ali Mugram al-Ghamdi,
Director General of the Islamic Cultural Center,
London Central Mosque, in
*The New York Times Magazine,* January 29, 1989

"People ask, do I believe in censorship? Do I support the death sentence for Salman Rushdie? Would I kill him myself on the Ayatollah's orders? Of course not. I am fiercely opposed to both censorship and murder. But I almost hesitate to issue that denial, because it obscures what I think is the real issue, which is the long-standing essential inability of East and West to understand each other."

—Taghi Modaressi, child psychiatrist,
psychoanalyst, novelist, and Iranian, in
*The Washington Post Book World,* March 12, 1989

"Any attack on you is directed at us all. Censorship in literature is the enemy of literature and death threats, addressed for whatever reason, if they succeed in silencing the author, would mean not only the end of literature but the end of civilization."

—Elie Wiesel, in *The New York Times Book Review,*
March 12, 1989

"We should have told the Ayatollah that one move towards Rushdie and we would bomb Tehran out of existence."

—Terry Dicks, British Conservative party lawmaker,
Associated Press, February 27, 1989

"It is regrettable that a foreign government has been able to hold hostage our most sacred First Amendment principle. Nevertheless, the safety of our employees and patrons must take precedence."

—Leonard Riggio, CEO at B. Dalton Booksellers, Associated Press, February 27, 1989

"Every culture has its sacred objects, and in the United States, the flag is likely to be one. A current example is the furor in Chicago over an art display that includes an American flag placed on the floor where viewers may step on it. War veterans are picketing...politicians are threatening a boycott...a woman has been arrested. The protests should help Americans understand the outrage in the Islamic world over Salman Rushdie's novel...."

—Editorial, *Oregonian*, March 11, 1989

"Condemning it for blasphemy, devout Muslims are proud to say they have never read Salman Rushdie's *The Satanic Verses*. Many of its defenders haven't read the novel, either."

—*Newsweek*, February 27, 1989

"'This Rushdie issue is being used as an instrument of Iranian politics,' says Marvin Zonis, a University of Chicago expert on the Middle East. 'Khomeini likes creative chaos, so now he's abetted the cause of the conservatives.'"

—*Newsweek*, February 27, 1989

"Khomeini was eighty-eight, and failing, and his mullahs were determined to offer him a course with which—at far less risk than with a hostage crisis and for far less money than with an eight-year war—he could revive his flagging authority as a leader and his angry battle against a corrupt West and a corrupted Islam."

—Jane Kramer, "Letter from Europe" in *The New Yorker*, January 14, 1991

"Slowly, slowly, a point of view grew up...which held that I knew exactly what I was doing. I must have known what would happen; therefore I did it on purpose, to profit by the notoriety that would result. Even if I were to concede (and I do not concede it) that what I did in *The Satanic Verses* was the literary equivalent of flaunting oneself shamelessly before the eyes of aroused men, is that really a justification...for rape?"

—Salman Rushdie, in *Newsweek*, February 12, 1990

## Publishing-Team Discussion Guidelines

### The Question:

Should our publishing company print and distribute a paperback version of Salman Rushdie's novel *The Satanic Verses*?

Your team should work with facts relevant to this question and reach a consensual decision (no voting!) on how to handle this manuscript. You should be prepared to discuss your decision with the large group and to share your response to the following issues:

To what extent have you taken into account:

❖ the relationship between theology and the state in Islamic countries?

❖ the sensibilities of Muslims regarding blasphemy?

❖ the degree to which Rushdie knew what he was doing?

❖ the sensibilities of Americans (or people of other countries being role-played) regarding freedom of speech?

❖ the safety of your employees?

❖ the culture of Islamic societies?

❖ the culture of Western societies?

❖ the profit potential of the book?

❖ the deaths which may result from conflicts over this?

## Resources

Asante, Molefi K., Eileen Newmark, and Cecil A. Blake, eds. *Handbook of Intercultural Communication.* Beverly Hills, CA: Sage (1979): 421-46.

Kohls, L. Robert, and Ellen Ax. *Methodologies for Trainers: A Compendium of Learning Strategies.* Washington, DC: Future Life Press (1979): 37-47.

Pfeiffer, William, and Arlette Ballew. *Using Case Studies, Simulations, and Games in Human Resource Development.* San Diego: University Associates, 1988.

Yin, Robert. *Case-study Research: Design and Methods. Applied Social Research Methods* Series, vol. 5. Newbury Park: Sage, 1989.

# Intercultural Training: The Effectiveness Connection

## Robert Hayles

The objective of this chapter is to articulate some of the costs and benefits of doing intercultural training. Costs include time, money, and the use of other resources; benefits range from being "the right thing to do" to productivity gains to economic benefits. Intercultural training is intended to help participants think, feel, and behave more effectively in contexts where there is more than one culture represented. In a sense the effectiveness connection must be made at several levels: the quality of the training, the increased capabilities of the participant, and the benefits derived by the organization or group.

Intercultural training makes use of cognitive activities (lectures, discussion, reading, media presentations), affective involvement (experiential exercises, emotional encounters, values/attitude clarification), and behavioral development (learning languages, norms, gestures, and the like). To be effective, training must address the variations in learning styles that exist among the participants and reach beyond increasing the level of knowledge (head) to engaging feelings (heart) and building behavioral skills (hand).

Training is most effective when it is part of a larger systemic effort, such as organizational development or a transition or formation process that is directed toward creating and sustaining excellence. Effectiveness of intercultural training is highest when all these components are present and consonant with audience needs. The assessment of effectiveness can include the following factors:

❖ Individual participants: actual learning of facts and behavior, growth in self-knowledge, and improvement of individual performance as ranked, rated, counted, and judged by oneself and others.

❖ Group and organizational performance: attrition, productivity, reliability, and profitability.

❖ Quality of training: logistics, style, substance.

Outcomes are clearly affected by many variables in addition to training. This reinforces the necessity of using training as one of several components in an overall effort to improve individual and organizational performance. To initiate our exploration of the effectiveness connection, let us begin by mentioning some of the changes in our world that make intercultural training advisable.

# Demographic and Other Changes

Demographers and labor experts note two kinds of labor shortages: frictional and structural. Frictional shortages occur where the people with the skills needed to perform the tasks exist but they are not located where the task is. In the near future we will be facing more of the other kind of shortage, structural. This is where the people with the skills to perform the desired work do not exist in the numbers and with the education and training that is required. This means that countries like Japan, Germany, Canada, Australia, and the United States will have to attract, educate, and train people who are not Japanese, German, Canadian, Australian, or American to meet local and worldwide needs.

Another major change occurring worldwide is the role of women. Business, education, government, and family will not prosper without the full participation and partnership of both men and women. Many people believe there is a male culture and a female culture. Most people agree that culture directly impacts on gender roles and role expectations and that the way in which men and women communicate is an intercultural issue.

In the vast majority of technologically developed nations, workforce diversity is increasing in at least the following ways: (a) there are greater representations of indigenous people and nondominant ethnic and religious groups within the workforce; (b) the birth rate is increasing in populations with low per capita incomes and less formal education and decreasing in populations with high incomes and more formal education; (c) inflation and economic uncertainty are stimulating people to work longer and thus expanding the age range of workers; (d) new technologies enable people with severe disabilities to engage in productive work; (e) global mobility and immigration are increasing; (f) greater numbers of women are pursuing advanced degrees and seeking employment; and (g) human and civil rights movements are making diversity in the workplace and variations in lifestyles more apparent.

Business, education, and government organizations are becoming more global. Few businesses can function successfully without using products from, trading with, or marketing to customers in different countries. It is difficult to think of any businesses that are not at least discussing international potential. The media provide more and more evidence of this trend. Business magazines and business sections of newspapers and major publications almost always mention more than one country or population.

# Costs of Intercultural Training

Some intercultural learning can occur when people travel and socialize across cultures, but generally these experiences go unexamined and are not often applied to other situations. This learning comes virtually free to organizations and institutions, but these experiences must be explored to discover how they can enhance the capabilities of employees to function with people who are culturally different.

Formal training incurs direct costs for needs assessment, facilities, materials, trainers, preparation, follow-on work, evaluation, travel, staff time and more. Dietary restrictions, translation services, holidays, family matters, child care, and other special concerns that arise in multicultural groups may appear to add even more costs. However, these issues must be taken into account for any business activity as the workforce and the population become more diverse.

Professional development for people who do intercultural training also is costly. Just as this book had to be updated so do the people who do this work. It is necessary for organizations to provide opportunities for their trainers to become more proficient in their field.

# Benefits of Intercultural Training

There has been a general growth of awareness—certainly in the United States—that cultural issues are important and need to be dealt with effectively. Terms like culture shock are becoming common. People are concerned even if they do not know what to do. There has also been some growth in the number of organizations which do intercultural training, as well as growth in the number of people and organizations doing domestic multicultural work in nations like Australia, Canada, the Netherlands, Sweden, the United Kingdom, and the United States. Advancement of the intercultural field and professional expertise is demonstrated by the membership of organizations like the International Society for Intercultural Education, Training, and Research (SIETAR International), which grew from a few hundred members in the early 1970s to over two thousand in the late 1980s. Such increases in future are unlikely to occur unless the value of cross-cultural training is recognized.

### Personal Growth and Social Skills

Empirical documentation of the benefit of cross-cultural experience can be found in the literature on school desegregation. One of the most respected and prolific contributors to this literature was Stuart Cook at the University of Colorado. In his 1979 article, he argued from a strong research basis that children who go to school in integrated settings tend to acquire greater social skill and achieve more personal growth than their counterparts in segregated settings. Furthermore, academic learning did not significantly or measurably decrease in integrated or desegregated settings. On a more personal level, I have experienced more rewarding relationships among people who are culturally different when those individuals have extensive intercultural training, living, and/or working experiences.

## Professional Development

Many of the skills developed during intercultural training are the same skills required for professional success. Doing business globally means navigating and negotiating where cultural differences abound. Roger Fisher and Scott Brown (1988), of the Harvard Negotiation Project, described explicit instances of business and political failures where lack of intercultural expertise was a significant factor. For example, unwittingly scheduling meetings on Yom Kippur (a Jewish holiday) has had a negative impact on many business deals. During the war in Vietnam, a number of misperceptions about how the North Vietnamese viewed the war had a significant impact on American policy. In negotiating with the Soviets, Americans accused their adversary of not caring about the *spirit* of an agreement, while the Soviets felt the Americans were not diligent enough in demonstrating complete and positive *adherence to every letter* of a treaty.

The field of special education also provides a useful analogy. Teachers trained in special education learn to work with students who are different. They develop diagnostic and communication skills enabling them to work successfully with students having learning difficulties. These same skills make them extraordinarily effective with all students. Likewise in the realm of negotiation, a person trained to negotiate in more than one culture is likely to be highly capable in many different industries and settings.

Intercultural skills enable a person to function more effectively within any diverse culture. An example of professional skills that stem from an intercultural base comes from research by Manuel Ramirez III and Alfredo Castenada (1974). Their research clearly demonstrated that individuals who can function in two or more cultures and who can think in two different styles (field-independent and field-sensitive) are faster and more successful in leading problem-resolution sessions in small multicultural groups.

Intercultural skills were essential to the success of an executive administering a complex scientific research and development program with a billion-dollar per year budget (Hayles 1989). There are two keys to much of this individual's success: first, the ability to work with people who are different and, second, the ability to coordinate the efforts of many different people and a variety of organizations. This executive was able to function across many organizational boundaries (for example, the private and public sectors, and the political and military arenas) and deal with the variety of individuals within those institutions (including those who are research-oriented or finance-oriented or deeply religious or from different age groups and ethnic groups) to produce a unified, successful program. All this required extraordinary cross-cultural sensitivity and a high level of intercultural skill.

## Creativity and Innovation

Nancy J. Adler (1986) provides both theoretical and anecdotal evidence showing that leading-edge products are increasingly likely to emerge from partnerships across national and functional boundaries. Intercultural training (formal and/or informal) is the foundation for such success. Adler cites some specific examples of success facilitated by intercultural cooperation in such areas as new-product development, receptivity to new ideas, the fostering of new perspectives, and the establishment of better communication (82). She points out that managers and employees are apt to attribute patterns and changes in behavior to influences other than culture, but when presented with the idea of culture, they can see the potential for positive impact.

Rosabeth Moss Kanter (1983) studied the twenty-year financial performance of companies having progressive human resource systems compared to those with less innovative practices. The progressive firms were "significantly higher in long-term profitablity and financial growth" (19). One characteristic of progressive human resource management is an emphasis on training to work with cultural differences. This innovative training clearly contributes to the long-term picture.

Robert Ziller (1972) reviewed the small-group performance literature and concluded that on complex tasks requiring creativity, innovation, and problem solving, heterogeneous (race, gender, personality) groups significantly outperform homogeneous groups in quality and quantity of output. Therefore, intercultural training that builds an ability to work successfully in bi- and multicultural groups can be seen to increase the chances that the quality and quantity of performance or productivity will be enhanced in the workplace.

Conversations with computer scientists and engineers present during the early days of Silicon Valley's development indicate that cultural diversity was a major factor in this economic and technological boom. Learning to work with culturally different talent facilitated rapid advances in technology and products. John Naisbitt (1984) conducted research to determine why the majority of social inventions occurred in five particular states in the United States. He concluded that "it's difficult to say why, other than to observe that all five are characterized by a rich mix of people. And richness of the mix always results in creativity, experimentation, and change" (xxvii). Training to facilitate the successful performance of culturally diverse groups supports individual and organizational successes in many sectors.

### Cost Savings and Productivity Enhancements

Experts provide quantitative estimates and clear examples of how intercultural training leads to:

- ❖ fewer early returnees from international assignments,
- ❖ lower relocation costs,
- ❖ higher job performance,
- ❖ greater productivity,
- ❖ more happiness in and overall personal, family and professional adjustment to international situations,
- ❖ fewer incidents which cause, at a minimum, embarrassment to a country or organization.

The early return from an international assignment of one employee with a salary of $60,000 per year means a loss for the employer of $240,000.*

## Revenue Enhancement

Organizations that train personnel to be interculturally effective are positioned for loss avoidance and business gains. Avoiding losses that can result from a lack of intercultural sensitivity and skill go hand in hand with enhancing revenue. For example, in academic environments it is common knowledge that students go where they feel valued and welcome. Educational institutions that do not engage in intercultural training to create and maintain diversity-friendly campuses may experience declining enrollments and tuition income. The ones that do intercultural training in a context of overall organizational development will see maintenance and, possibly, growth in enrollments in the near and long term.

Businesses which ignore intercultural issues will find themselves on the banned side of restrictive purchasing ordinances or institutional investment guidelines. These ordinances and guidelines restrict purchases of goods, services, and stock from businesses engaging in practices such as operating in countries with limited human rights, failing to comply with employment equity legislation, and sanctioning biased treatment of women or culturally different populations.

Companies whose advertising is insensitive to cultural diversity have lost market share. Evidence can be found worldwide (Fisher and Brown 1988, 68). For example, a major Canadian clothing retailer was boycotted in response to monocultural advertisements; auto sales were seriously affected by ads that included a poor French translation that touted "corpse by Fisher" rather than "body by Fisher"; and, finally, poor baby food sales in Africa could be directly traced to the baby pictures on the jar labels. Typically, in Africa products are labeled with pictures of the containers' contents instead of likely consumers. This cultural error led to significant repackaging and public relations expense.

Fisher and Brown also examine the costs of culturally insensitive behavior by citing how the actions of key officers in a major construction firm, perceived as insulting to prospective customers in the Middle East, deterred multimillion-dollar contract acquisitions, and how Gillette's failure to exhibit loyalty for and maintain stable relations with its distributors in Japan was equally costly. Stability and loyalty are not as critical to doing business in the United States, but ignoring them in Japan caused Gillette to lose dominance to Schick in the Japanese market. Schick's dominance in the Japanese market can be traced directly to its culturally appropriate, loyal relationship with one distributor.

"Euro Disney's troubles, both cultural and financial, have been widely covered in the European media" (USA Today 6 October 1993). Between financial woes and cultural gaffes, there has been plenty to write about. French journalists

---

* This estimate and other examples of cost savings are provided in L.Robert Kohls (1984); Gary Fontaine (1986); Richard W. Brislin, Norman G. Dinges, and Gary Fontaine (1981); Edward T. Hall (1960); Susan Nelson (1984); James A. Lee (1966); Michael F. Tucker, Vicki E. Baier, and Stephen H. Rhinesmith (1985); Michael F. Tucker (1987); Philip G. Benson, Gail B. Hare, and Michael F. Tucker (1980).

branded Disney a cultural imperialist. Disney's lack of success in Europe was facilitated by not paying attention to cultural differences such as drinking and eating patterns. Disney imported its no-alcohol policy from the United States, prohibiting alcohol in park restaurants in a country where wine is commonly drunk with meals. Further, unlike Americans, who eat at any time, Europeans tend to all eat lunch at the same time, which created long lines. The French disliked the lines for food and rides, since it reminded them of being back in the war. "As far as learning about a foreign culture, we're getting there" admitted Michael Eisner, former Walt Disney Company chairman.

On a more positive note, there are several examples of using cultural knowledge effectively. A major mining project in South America is an example of revenue enhancement that can be traced to intercultural training. This project was contracted to two very different corporations—one, a construction firm, and the other, an extractive/mining firm—with very different corporate cultures. They had to create a smooth-functioning team that included both corporations and the national government. Failure to work effectively across national and organizational cultures would be very costly. Every day of schedule slippage would mean three million U.S. dollars in lost revenues to the host country. A significant investment in intercultural team building facilitated this project's success.

Another success story is a U.S. computer firm which is currently the industry leader in several areas in Asia and the Far East. Paying attention to local cultural factors and using indigenous human resources extensively are major factors in its success. A final example is the growth of Toyota and Honda manufacturing operations in the United States, which has been facilitated by Japanese success in learning to live, negotiate, and manage in American culture.

**Peace**

Even small amounts of intercultural training contain the potential to prevent simple misunderstandings that lead to poor political relationships. It would have been helpful if the American media had reported Nikita Khrushchev's remarks at the United Nations in 1962 from a Soviet perspective. When Khrushchev stated that "we will bury" the Western world, he meant that the Soviet system would simply outlive Western systems, as children often outlive their parents and then bury them. Without this understanding, many Americans considered his language threatening. If we had understood the real intent of his words, we might have seen the end of the cold war much sooner. As it turned out, of course, Khrushchev was wrong.

The continued use by political leaders of institutions like the U.S. Institute of Peace, the Harvard Negotiation Project, and the Centre for Applied Studies in International Negotiation suggests some understanding of the value for intercultural training in our quest for world peace. Other indicators of a widespread belief that intercultural training makes a difference are the continued support for cultural ambassadors and cultural exchange programs, the success of language training businesses, and the daily use of language interpreters.

You also hear more often these days that "intercultural training is the right thing to do!" In the beginning of this chapter, I mentioned the head, heart, and hands of intercultural training. With increasing attention to the head, heart, and hands of our managers, employees, diplomats, families, and political leaders, we may expect to achieve cooperation and effective communication among the rich diversity of people who live in our world.

# References

Adler, Nancy J. *International Dimensions of Organizational Behavior.* Boston: Kent, 1986.

Benson, Philip G., Gail B. Hare, and Michael F. Tucker. *Determination of the Impact of Revised Screening System for Overseas Assignment.* (Report for Task Order EG-13). Washington, DC: Naval Military Personnel Command, 1980.

Brislin, Richard W., Norman G. Dinges, and Gary Fontaine. "The Impact of Cross-Cultural Training on Overseas Adjustment and Performance: An Integrative Review." (Report No. NR 170-924). Washington, DC: Office of Naval Research, 1981.

Cook, S. "Social Science and School Desegregation: Did we Mislead the Supreme Court?" *Personality and Social Psychology Bulletin* 5, no. 4 (1979): 420-37.

Fisher, Roger, and S. Brown. *Getting Together: Building a Relationship that Gets to Yes.* Boston: Houghton Mifflin, 1988.

Fontaine, Gary. *Managing International Assignments: The Strategy for Success.* Englewood Cliffs, NJ: Prentice Hall, 1986.

Hall, Edward T. "The Silent Language in Overseas Business." *Harvard Business Review* (May-June 1960): 2-11.

Hayles, Robert. *Multicultural Workforce: Issues and Opportunities.* Paper presented at the 14th annual conference of the Arizona Affirmative Action Association, Phoenix, AZ, May 1989.

Kanter, Rosabeth Moss. *The Change Masters: Innovation and Entrepreneurship in the American Corporation.* New York: Simon and Schuster, 1983.

Kohls, L. Robert. *Intercultural Training: Don't Leave Home Without It.* Washington, DC: International Society for Intercultural Education, Training and Research, 1984.

Lee, James A. "Cultural Analysis in Overseas Operations." *Harvard Business Review* (March-April 1966): 106-14.

Moore, M. T. Euro Disney's Culture Shock. *USA Today* (6 October 1993).

Naisbitt, John. *Megatrends: Ten New Directions Transforming Our Lives.* New York: Warner, 1984.

Nelson, Susan. "Learning to Work Overseas: Recognizing that the American Way is not the Only Way is a Big Step Toward Success." *Nation's Business* (March 1984): 59-60.

Ramirez, Manuel, and Alfredo Castenada. *Cultural Democracy, Bicognitive Development and Education.* New York: Academic Press, 1974.

Tucker, Michael F. "Predicting Success on Foreign Assignments." *Relocation/Realty Update* 3, no. 24 (June 1987): 7-10.

Tucker, Michael F., Vicki E. Baier, and Stephen H. Rhinesmith. "Before Takeoff: What Your Overseas People Need to Know." *Personnel* (December 1985): 106-14.

Ziller, Robert. "Homogeneity and Heterogeneity of Group Membership." In *Experimental Social Psychology,* edited by C. G. McClintock. New York: Holt, Rinehart and Winston (1972): 385-411.

# About the Authors

**Rosita D. Albert**, raised in São Paulo, Brazil, in an intercultural milieu, studied in the U.S. and France. She has a Ph.D. in social psychology from the University of Michigan, and speaks Spanish, Portuguese, French, and English. Currently an associate professor in the Department of Speech-Communication at the University of Minnesota, she teaches intercultural communication, publishes widely in the field of cross-cultural education and training, and serves as a consultant to business and educational institutions.

**Janet M. Bennett, Ph.D.** is codirector of the Intercultural Communication Institute (ICI) in Portland, Oregon. She directs the ICI/Antioch Masters Intercultural Relations degree program and also maintains an active consulting and training practice. She publishes on the topics of training methodology and constructive cultural marginality.

**Milton J. Bennett, Ph. D.** is codirector of the Intercultural Communication Institute (ICI) in Portland, Oregon. He is the director of graduate studies for the ICI/Antioch Masters Intercultural Relations degree program and also maintains an active consulting and training practice. He publishes on the topics of intercultural theory and developmental approaches to training for intercultural sensitivity.

**Judee M. Blohm** is a cross-cultural educator and trainer. She specializes in instructional design and development of experiential-learning activities for specific groups and purposes. She provides training for adults and young people for various governmental agencies and private organizations and develops skills in others through training-of-trainers workshops. She also writes and edits cross-cultural materials and training manuals.

**Richard W. Brislin** is a research associate at the Institute of Culture and Communication, East-West Center, in Honolulu, Hawaii. Since coming to the East-West Center in 1972, he has directed programs for international educators, cross-cultural researchers, and various specialists involved in formal programs that encourage intercultural interaction. His many books, beginning with *Cross-Cultural Research Methods* (1973, with W. Lonner and R. Thorndike), have enriched the intercultural field. Recent publications include *The Art of Getting Things Done: A Practical Guide to the Use of Power* (1991) and *Intercultural Communication Training* (with Tomoko Yoshida).

**William Dant** has worked in the field of international exchange since 1970. In the U.S., Africa, Europe, and the Middle East, he has held positions in a variety of organizations including the School for International Training, Peace Corps, the Fulbright exchange program, and Youth for Understanding (YFU) International Exchange. He currently is Division Director of the Hubert H. Humphrey Fellowship Program at the Institute for International Education. Bill has a special interest in intensive cross-cultural and language training, especially with multicultural staff and participants.

**Cajetan DeMello** is the original creator of the Contrast-American role envisioned by HumRRO scientists and developed by Dr. Edward C. Stewart. For thirty years, as Mr. Khan in cross-cultural communication training programs, he role-played work-related scenarios to illuminate through contrast behaviors the value systems and cultural predispositions and assumptions of Western societies. He consults in the public and private sectors for cross-cultural training programs on cultural pluralism and ethnic diversity in human resource development and management.

**Joseph J. DiStefano** is professor at the Western Business School, University of Western Ontario, London, Canada. He has lectured, researched, and consulted in eighteen countries for universities, companies, governments, and development agencies. From 1984 to 1988 he directed a major project of management education and development between his school and the Faculty of Economic Management at Qinghua University in Beijing and from 1990 to 1993 was the Royal Bank Professor of International Business.

**Shirley A. Fletcher** is an organization development consultant with twenty-one years of experience. She specializes in organizational culture change through the elimination of institutionalized racism, sexism, heterosexism, and other forms of oppression.

**Graeme Frelick** is a senior consultant and trainer with Training Resources Group, Inc. (TRG), a human resources development company based in Alexandria, Virginia. He designs, conducts, and manages training programs and organizational development efforts for private- and public-sector clients in the United States and in developing countries. Fluent in French, he has conducted numerous overseas training assignments in Africa, Asia, Central America, the Middle East, and the Caribbean.

**Robert Hayles**, vice president of Human Resources and Diversity for the Pillsbury Technology Center of the Grand Metropolitan Food Sector, is responsible for all human resources functions, including valuing diversity. A human resources generalist who has consulted for and led diversity efforts in public, academic, civic, and private-sector organizations, he has a doctorate in social science and has done postgraduate work in business. He has served in leadership positions in organizations such as the Association of Black Psychologists, American Society for Training and Development, and the International Society for Intercultural Education, Training and Research.

**Paul R. Kimmel** has more than twenty-five years' experience in designing, delivering, and evaluating training programs in intercultural awareness and communications. He has worked with many multinational businesses, government agencies—both international and domestic—and academic institutions in providing predeparture, entry, and reentry programs for Americans working abroad, international scholars coming to the U.S., and diplomats. He is currently developing intercultural programs to improve relationships among ethnic groups in conflict.

**Lee Lacy** is director of the Office of Special Services for the U.S. Peace Corps and former director of the Overseas Briefing Center at the Foreign Service Institute. For the last twelve years she has been managing training and information systems and conducting cross-cultural training and organizational development activities for Peace Corps, the Department of State, and other foreign affairs agency personnel.

**Jack Levy** is a professor of multicultural education at George Mason University in Fairfax, Virginia. In addition to preparing educators in intercultural curriculum and instruction, he conducts diversity training sessions for government and private-sector groups.

**James A. McCaffery** is the vice-president of Training Resources Group, Inc. in Alexandria, Virginia and has been designing, delivering, observing, and reflecting on training in multicultural settings for twenty-five years. The chapter he wrote comes from his experience in using different kinds of role plays in many different countries for over a quarter century.

**John Pettit** is a senior consultant and trainer with Training Resources Group, Inc. in Alexandria, Virginia. He specializes in management improvement and is experienced in developing short-term targeted training and organizational development programs. Assignments in Africa, Asia, South America, and the Caribbean require him to use adult-learning methodologies in diverse settings.

**Dianne M. Hofner Saphiere** is the founder and director of Nipporica Associates, an intercultural consulting and training firm specializing in the Japan-United States interface and global business team productivity. Ms. Hofner Saphiere is on the faculty of the Summer Institute for Intercultural Communication and a recipient of the 1994 Junior Interculturalist Award for Achievement from SIETAR International.

**R. Garry Shirts** is founder and president of Simulation Training Systems (formerly Simile II) in San Diego, California. In addition to *BaFá BaFá,* he is the author of several other simulations, including *Star Power, Pumping the Colors,* and *Where Do You Draw the Line?* An educational psychologist and training systems designer, his simulations are used by governments, corporations, and schools in over sixty countries.

**Dorothy A. Sisk** is an internationally known trainer and consultant. She has been speaker and consultant in many countries including Australia, Brazil, Bulgaria, China, France, Mexico, the Philippines, Portugal, and South Africa. She is author or coauthor of several books and articles on leadership, creativity, and talent development.

**Barbara Steinwachs** has been using and designing simulation games for training and organizational planning situations since 1969. She lives and runs in the woods on the steep bluff of Keuka Lake in upstate New York. Although deeply involved in her community, she finds time to devote to the North American Simulation and Game Association and to the International Society for Intercultural Education, Training, and Research.

**Edward C. Stewart** began his career as an experimental psychologist in the field of perception and became a cultural psychologist following an early investigation of cross-cultural differences in communication, thinking, and cooperative behavior. His contrast-culture model of training derives from his research and teaching in various universities in the United States, Japan, and Europe and from living abroad for ten years with his family. Since 1989, he has devoted most of his energies to constructing a framework for cultural analysis which combines the insights of psychology, political science, and economics with time-honored cultural processes.

**Harry C. Triandis** is professor of psychology at the University of Illinois. He was at the 1968 Colorado meeting where the International Society for Intercultural Education, Training, and Research (SIETAR International) was first conceived. In 1987, he received an honorary doctorate from the University of Athens, Greece, for his work in cross-cultural psychology.

**Janie Trowbridge** has a master's degree in human resource development from George Washington University and is fluent in French and Czech. She has lived in Eastern Europe, Asia, and Africa. As a training consultant, she headed the Foreign Service Institute's initiative to improve cross-cultural training, and as an organizational development consultant, she worked with the banking system of the Czech Republic and the Slovak Republic.

**Albert R. Wight,** whose Ph.D. is in organizational/industrial psychology, is a specialist in organization development and training. Since the early 1960s he has been developing and promoting participative/facilitative approaches to management, training, education, corrections, and development. He has been involved with cross-cultural training for the last thirty years and, with Anne Hammons, developed *Peace Corps Guidelines to Cross-Cultural Training*, a seminal work in the field. When he is not consulting, which he has been doing for the World Bank in Pakistan the last seven years, he lives on his ranch in Wyoming.

**Forthcoming** from the Intercultural Press: *Intercultural Sourcebook,* Volume 2. To provide readers with an early glimpse of the contents of the second volume, here is the Table of Contents.